BIOGRAPHY IN THE LIVES OF YOUTH

BIOGRAPHY IN THE LIVES OF YOUTH

CULTURE, SOCIETY, AND INFORMATION

W. Bernard Lukenbill

LIBRARIES UNLIMITED

A Member of the Greenwood Publishing Group

Westport, Connecticut • London

KH

Library of Congress Cataloging-in-Publication Data

Lukenbill, W. Bernard.
   Biography in the lives of youth : culture, society, and information / by W. Bernard Lukenbill.
      p. cm.
   Includes bibliographical references and index.
   ISBN 1–59158–284–9 (pbk. : alk. paper)
   1. Children—Books and reading—Social aspects. 2. Teenagers—Books and reading—Social aspects. 3. Biography—Study and teaching. 4. Biography as a literary form. 5. Moral education. 6. School libraries—Activity programs. 7. Children's libraries—Activity programs. 8. Young adults' libraries—Activity programs. 9. Libraries—Special collections—Biography. I. Title.
Z1037.A1L83   2006
920.007—dc22   2006007466

British Library Cataloguing in Publication Data is available.

Library of Congress Catalog Card Number: 2006007466
ISBN: 1-59158-284-9

First published in 2006

Libraries Unlimited, 88 Post Road West, Westport, CT 06881
A Member of the Greenwood Publishing Group, Inc.
www.lu.com

Printed in the United States of America

The paper used in this book complies with the Permanent Paper Standard issued by the National Information Standards Organization (Z39.48–1984).

10   9   8   7   6   5   4   3   2   1

9|19|06

I dedicate this book affectionately to my only granddaughter,
Mia August Lukenbill, born 9 January 2005.
May she enjoy a long and happy life.

CONTENTS

ILLUSTRATIONS

ACKNOWLEDGMENTS

I appreciate the help and encouragement extended to me by so many people as I wrote this book. My wife, Shirley Lukenbill, read all the pages of the manuscript and offered me her critical judgment and useful suggestions gained from her vast experience in working with youth. My grandson Aaron was always on hand with his smiles to encourage me when I stumbled or grew discouraged. He served to remind me of why the writing of this book was important to me. My illustrator, Richard H. Hendler Jr., accommodated me with his skilled advice as we considered and planned the original art needed for this book. Barbara Immroth graciously allowed me access to some of her family pictures as I searched for authentic images of people and events. The staff of School of Information, University of Texas at Austin, graciously helped me with many tasks involved in the management of this project; and my editor, Sharon Coatney, at Libraries Unlimited kept a keen and perceptive eye on the manuscript as it developed throughout its many revisions. To all of you—Thanks!

INTRODUCTION

PURPOSE OF THE BOOK

Biography surrounds us as it is part of our everyday existence. We cannot escape the good and bad influences that biography brings to us, nor can we escape how biography influences our behaviors and attitudes. Each person has a biographical history that is unique; all families have genealogies that are laced with the collective biographies of individuals. Throughout history biography has been used to celebrate the good as well as the evil that we find in societies and cultures. Ancient societies such as the Egyptian, Caledonian, Greek, and Roman cultures used biography to define their leaders and to state how they saw themselves as a society. Medieval European society continued this tradition, especially through the emphasis it placed on biographies of religious people and others of power such as the saints; church leaders such as bishops, theologians, and popes; and kings and the powerful in society. Modern society uses biography to provide information about culture, to celebrate both achievement and notoriety, and to reinforce desirable social attitudes and behaviors.

This book therefore looks at ways that biography is used and can be used to inform youth about their society and culture through the classroom and library as well as through their individual pursuits. It likewise considers how biography can serve as a tool for improving student learning and improving their ability to use information effectively in modern society.

ISSUES IN BIOGRAPHY

Taken as a whole, biography raises many complex issues. Recognizing this and the importance of biography in the lives of youth, this book considers questions and concerns about how to use biography and biographical theories to inform and support our use of biography in library and school environments.

Biography for the very young is also an important issue and one that certainly needs more investigation; therefore, the book attempts to address some concerns associated with this such as appropriateness of forms and styles (e.g., fictionalized biography); subjects and interests; and cultural and social values presented to younger children.

As just mentioned, biography plays a huge role in how society sees itself. Therefore, discussions here consider biography as a social and cultural message system that imparts vital social messages to youth.

The historical use of biography with youth will also be analyzed as a means of helping us understand how critical evaluative standards for biography have evolved over time and how they are currently applied in the use of biography with modern youth. Closely related to this will be a discussion of the developmental needs of youth and how the use of biography has historically attempted to meet those needs.

Every field and discipline has its biography, and this book will look briefly at how biography is used and developed in selective fields including such areas as literature, political discourse, journalism and reporting, art, and music. Mass media and the advent of electronic information systems have given added strength to the role of biography in modern society. Consequently, the book will discuss the role of biography as commentary on modern society and life, and how it is disseminated through industrial enterprises such as film, print, and the Internet.

It concludes with a look at newer issues or at least some rethinking of some older issues. These include the marketing and publishing of biography, emerging reading interests, the merging of fiction and biography, and the development of new forms of biography that might be influenced by newer forms of presentation such as the graphic novel and newer forms of mass media such as cable television.

1

BIOGRAPHY: ITS PLACE IN LIFE AND LEARNING

INTRODUCTION

Biography in Life

Temple University scholar and *The Nation* contributor Elayne Tobin suggests that in recent decades the interest in biography has become an obsession with Americans, partly influenced by anxieties they face in modern life. Based on her research she concludes that modern biography plays an important role in defining and perhaps even stabilizing the American middle class and its views on life. She believes that when faced with social concerns, economic problems, and other insecurities, the American middle class turns to biography to help them better comprehend and make sense out of their lives.[1] Can the same thing be said of youth and biography?

Defining Biography

The *Oxford English Dictionary* (OED) defines *biography* in two ways: (1) the history of the lives of individual men, as a branch of literature and (2) a written record of the life of an individual. Both of these statements are true, but they do not reveal the complexity of biography in modern life. A brief review of *biography* in *Bartlett's Familiar Quotations* reveals more of its complexities.[2] A reading of the following descriptions by notable persons demonstrates how biography is often interpreted.

- Biography is a very definite region bounded on the north by history, on the south by fiction, on the east by obituary, and on the west by tedium.
  —Philip Guedalla (1889–1944), British author and historian. Quoted in *Observer* (London, March 3, 1929).

- Biography is: a system in which the contradictions of a human life are unified.
  —José Ortega y Gasset (1883–1955), Spanish essayist and philosopher.
  Reprinted in *The Dehumanization of Art and Other Essays* (1968). From
  "In Search of Goethe from Within," *Partisan Review*
  (New Brunswick, Dec. 1949).

- Biography, like big game hunting, is one of the recognized forms of sport, and it is [as] unfair as only sport can be.
  —Philip Guedalla, British author and historian. Quoted by Robin Maugham
  in "The Art of Biography," *MD* March 1980.

THE IMPORTANCE OF BIOGRAPHY IN SOCIAL LIFE AND CULTURE

Perhaps some of these definitions are revealing and assuming, but they do not really convey the importance of biography in modern life and society. Biography plays an important role in transmitting vital cultural information to youth. If used wisely, it can help youth become better persons and contribute more to the improvement of their world. On a personal level, it can contribute to academic achievement, the growth in self-awareness, and the development of useful social and intellectual skills for later in life. We often think of biography as consisting only of important people or of ordinary persons who have done extraordinary things; but biography can be very personal and can be used to help develop an appreciation of family and community, as well as help in the assessment of personal life situations and understanding. As such, biographical analysis using narrative approaches is an important therapeutic approach to counseling. Family biographies, often conveyed through pictures, can also give youth a sense of identity and continuity. Figure 1.1 shows an East Coast upper-middle class family gathered together for a family portrait in the early twentieth century. Biographical narrative symbols here include dress, relationship patterns, suggested prosperity, and social status.

**Figure 1.1
Portrait of an East
Coast Family, Early
Twentieth Century.**
[Private collection].

Queen Victoria
T. Sully

Figure 1.2
Portrait of a Young and Beautiful
Queen Victoria, by Thomas Sully,
Displayed as a Cigarette Card, ca.
1901–1917. [Published by permission.
George Arents Collection, the New York
Public Library, Astor, Lenox and Tilden
Foundations.]

On a similar but much grander scale, using narrative symbols, Figure 1.2 of the young and beautiful Queen Victoria clearly displays her status and royal bearings. This image was published after her death in 1901 and reflects much of what the public appreciated in royalty. This photograph, along with other celebrates of the time, was published as a cigarette card, designed to promote the marketing and selling of cigarettes.

THE TRADITIONAL USES OF BIOGRAPHY
IN HOME, CLASSROOM, AND LIBRARY

Biography has traditionally been used in schools, public libraries, and other arenas where youth are found to entertain, to instruct, to inculcate important social and culture values, and to socialize youth into correct and acceptable social behaviors. In this regard, biography has been used to promote nationalism, patriotism, loyalty to country and tribe, and religious allegiances. English-language biography intended for children and youth from the nineteenth century onward, including today, has in many ways attempted to promote and to serve one or more of these goals. But in moving away from the didacticism that promoted middle-class values of obedience, loyalty, and hard work, biography for youth today is more concerned with helping them understand human experiences, social concerns, and history. At a more personal level, biography today is often used to help youth understand options and consequences of choices in terms of such areas as gender and social roles, relationships, and achievement.

Educators and parents today recognize that although biography has an educational and social role to play, today's youth often see it as a means of entertainment. Modern culture has often been described as obsessed with celebrities, and the United States and, to a lesser extent, other Western countries are now celebrity-based societies. Publishers, teachers, and librarians, recognizing the power of celebrities, have attempted to provide biographical information based on the current interests of youth. Parents likewise seek readable and age-appropriate biography for their children. These interests are varied and often reflect what they see and/or read about in the mass media.

POPULAR CULTURE, MASS MEDIA, AND BIOGRAPHY

Biography has always been available and promoted in the mass media. In the nineteenth century, periodical literature was especially popular and promoted such names and celebrities as Wild Bill Hickok and heroes from American and world history such as George Washington. Radio also contributed to biographical coverage through its various programs that featured interesting events and personalities such as the broadcast of King George VI's coronation in 1937 and the coverage of the Lindberg Baby Tragedy in the mid-1930s. Other radio programs of a biographical nature included *Hollywood Speaks on the Dodge Victory Hour*, which began in 1928 and featured famous screen actors of the time, and the *Eveready Hour* in 1923, which created the first radio superstar, Wendal Hall.[3]

The 1950s and early 1960s are often referred to as "the golden age of television." Artistic creation flourished and artists and producers were not too much influenced by advertisers' needs to create markets. In those days, education along with art and creativity were the driving forces for program development. As a part of this creative spirit, programs hosted by Walter Cronkite, such as *You Are There* (1953–57), *Eyewitness to History* (1961–62), and *Twentieth Century* (1957–67), and Edward R. Murrow's *See It Now* (1951–58) were able to create and present programs of high quality and of historical and biographical integrity.

Successful television programs of this time often centered around the television lives of celebrities such as George Burns and Gracie Allen, Ozzie and Harriet Nelson, and Desi and Lucy Arnaz. These programs were so biographical in structure that the audiences were asked to believe that the television presentations were real biography and extensions of the performers' real family lives. Off-air presentations through publicity and interviews continued to reinforce the pseudo-reality of the television presentations.[4]

News documentaries came into their own in the early 1960s and challenged American sensitivity with accounts of farm labor exploitations and the emerging homosexual subculture. In terms of popularized biography, Edward R. Murrow with his visits to homes of celebrities, including former U.S. presidents, in *Person to Person* (1953–59) helped solidify the role of biography of the rich and famous in American popular culture. Today biography thrives in the world of cable television. Probably the most famous of the biography production outlets is A&E Television (www.aetv.com) and its biographical presentations and services. Programs on A&E and its Biography.Com (www.biography.com) range from the serious and historical to momentary celebrities. Another television network devoted to mass media celebrity biography is E! Entertainment Television (www.eentertainment.com; www.eonline.com).

Cable television's constant need for programming material has also expanded our definition of *celebrities*. Celebrities now range from movie actors, music performers, sports figures, and politicians to criminals and those accused of serious crimes such as murder, treason, and economic exploitation. What effect does this have on youth in terms of how they are influenced and socialized by such presentations?

IMPACT OF BIOGRAPHY ON ATTITUDES AND BEHAVIORS

Biography impacts attitudes and behaviors because it conveys social and personal expectations and rewards for behaviors. Likewise, it justifies and even suggests new behaviors and attitudes worth considering and emulating.

Biography can also help build positive self-esteem in youth as well as enhance existing beliefs of self-worth. For example, biography has been used by bibliotherapists to help improve damaged self-images and to point the way for better options for behaviors. Biography has been used in positive ways to foster allegiance to country, province and state, clan, family, and religion.

BIOGRAPHY IN COLLECTION DEVELOPMENT, INSTRUCTION, AND TEACHER–LIBRARIAN COLLABORATION

Biography has always been important in building useful collections for the school library media center. Biography is popular with youth, and it is a driving force in many instructional areas. Up-to-date biographical reference materials are in constant demand and often put pressure on the financial resources of the school library media center to meet those demands.

Because biography can be so well integrated into instructional programs, it offers an excellent avenue for networking and collaboration with teachers. The school media center specialist can offer his or her guidance in selection of resources and can promote collaboration with teachers on an equal basis while helping to build instructional units or experiences based on biography. Booktalks in classroom settings based on biography is an excellent way for the library media specialist to become a part of classroom instruction. School library media specialists can also use biography in various ways to enhance general cultural literacy among students. School library media specialists can also interact with parents either individually or within formalized parenting programs to help them understand and use biography with their children at home.

As previously stated, biography surrounds us, and it is important to note that it is not just another type of reading material. It is a powerful cultural and social message that must be understood and nurtured so that its power can be directed for the benefit of all youth.

BIOGRAPHY AND YOUTH

Biography is a major foundation in the modern school curriculum. To name only a few areas, it is found in art, history, the sciences, literature, and social sciences. For example, all curricular areas place emphasis on developing critical analysis skills. The study of history is dependent on interpreting people and facts based on sound evidence. Art relies greatly on understanding the work of great artists and how they have influenced artistic expression as well as how art has been used to celebrate the lives of individuals. Biographical art shows the values and symbols of success that society places on people and events. Science and technology pay attention to important inventors and scientists and their roles in establishing their disciplines.

When used wisely, biography also plays an important role in preparing youth for adulthood. It provides social and psychological support, enabling and encouraging youth to achieve to the best of their potential. Biography offers an excellent avenue for the school library media specialist to develop useful collections, to become actively involved in the instruction and learning of students, and to collaborate with teachers.

The following discussion will attempt to relate biography to the general developmental needs of youth and to outline some of the important characteristics of biography, highlighting its instructional purposes and attributes.

Biography and Developmental Needs

Understanding youth's developmental needs and processes is fundamental in the effective use of biographical materials with children and young adults. Over the years many specialists in psychology have developed a variety of developmental tasks that youth need to acquire successfully as they move toward adulthood. Perhaps one of the best known are those suggested by Erik H. Erikson in his *Identity: Youth and Crisis* (Norton, 1968). He outlined the following stages as necessary for healthy maturation for children, birth to young adulthood:

• **Infant**
  Trust vs Mistrust

Needs maximum comfort with minimal uncertainty to trust himself/herself, others, and the environment

- **Toddler**
  Autonomy vs Shame and Doubt
  Works to master physical environment while maintaining self-esteem

- **Preschooler**
  Initiative vs Guilt
  Begins to initiate, not imitate, activities; develops conscience and sexual identity

- **School-Age Child**
  Industry vs Inferiority
  Tries to develop a sense of self-worth by refining skills

- **Adolescent**
  Identity vs Role Confusion
  Tries integrating many roles (child, sibling, student, athlete, worker) into a self-image under role model and peer pressure[5]

Children and Their Developmental Needs

Although special needs of all children are important, this discussion will consider only those developmental needs thought necessary for the typical child and how they relate especially to biography. These include a wide variety of developmental processes including the physical, cognitive, social, and moral.[6] Children are social beings and their socialization begins at birth.

One overwhelming need children have is to develop social skills necessary to survive in modern societies. From birth, children are dependent on others for their survival. Development of survival skills is based on social awareness. Early on, children begin to process information that allows them to acquire and develop social skills. For example, these include focusing their gaze on the mother or other significant caregivers for feeding, smiling at a human face, and crying as a means of obtaining help and comfort and communicating with others.[7] Further social interaction skills include simple game playing, listening to human voice patterns, and learning how humans socialize and communicate in ways that allow for needs to be met. These early skills form a foundation for later relationship building and attachment formation.[8]

Social worker Peter K. Gerlach writes that beyond these, children will need to learn to think critically, objectively, and independently. He rightly contends that children will need to acquire skills that will help them make sense of their world and to make daily decisions about living. They will need to learn to think in abstract ways, to synthesize ideas and information, and to understand how information is patterned and presented. He further states that children will need to develop means of acquiring information.

They will need to learn to evaluate, retain, prioritize, and apply information in appropriate ways. They will need to learn to cope with new concepts and with abstractions.[9]

In addition, children will need to develop ways of handling their emotions, to learn to effectively manage their thoughts, and to react to the many challenges of life in constructive ways. They will need to learn to show empathy to others and to care about people in the world in general. Developmental needs will certainly include the formation of a healthy self-identity as a unique person, separate from their parents and other important people in their lives. Self-identity will foster a need to develop self-trust and self-awareness. Closely related to these is the need to develop the ability to make safe, emotional attachments to appropriate people, ideas, visions, and principles.

The ability to communicate with others includes written and spoken language as well as how to communicate in situations of conflict. Effective social skills form an important part of communication. These include such skills as tact, empathy, intimacy, trust, assertion, cooperation, appropriate obedience, and respectful confrontation. Self-evaluation is also an important part of self-awareness. The ability to assess one's own behaviors and to take action to unlearn unproductive or harmful habits and behaviors can ensure successful living. Taking responsibility is also a necessary developmental skill. This includes taking responsibility for actions and having the ability to accept consequences for personal behaviors and actions. In addition, development of a satisfying philosophy of life and a personal awareness of spirituality are important.

The development of a concern for their health and body, and how to relate that to the challenges of modern life and choices to be made, are necessary. Health concerns include not only eating habits, hygiene, exercise, and sexual development, but also emotional concerns and the ability to handle life's demands such as money management and spending.[10] Chapter 3 considers biography and developmental needs of young children in more detail.

Adolescents and Their Development Needs

In discussing young adults, the University of Florida Institute of Food and Agriculture Services states:

> The major task facing adolescents is to create a stable identity and become complete and productive adults. Over time, adolescents develop a sense of themselves that transcends the many changes in their experiences and roles. They find their role in society through active searching which leads to discoveries about themselves.[11]

Daniel F. Perkins, writing for the institute, notes that puberty helps in opening the world for the adolescent by providing extended opportunities for new experiences and awareness of both themselves and others. Perkins advises that adolescents need room to explore. They need to be given opportunities for explorations that will allow them to form appropriate adult roles.

Developmental tasks are generally defined and even dictated by cultural and social expectations. Perkins outlines eight important developmental tasks for adolescents. A careful reading of these illustrates how biography can play a significant role in helping the adolescent meet these tasks. They include:

- Achieving new and more mature relations with others, both boys and girls, in their age group
- Achieving a masculine or feminine social role
- Accepting one's physique
- Achieving emotional independence from parents and other adults
- Preparing for marriage and family life
- Preparing for an economic career
- Acquiring a set of values and an ethical system as a guide to behavior— developing an ideology
- Desiring and achieving socially responsible behavior[12]

Developmental Considerations for At-Risk Youth

At-risk youth have special developmental needs that often prevent them from attaining normal levels of development. They often have low self-esteem, poor social skills, and inadequate academic skills. In comparison to other youth, they have increased likelihoods of being subjected to environmental risks such as physical and verbal violence at home and school absenteeism. As they grow older they may experience more involvement with drugs and alcoholism, crime, gang memberships, and suicide. Poverty and living on the edge of poverty also contribute to risk factors. Recent immigrant status and the dislocation often associated with immigrants can also become a factor contributing to risk conditions.[13]

DEVELOPMENTAL NEEDS AND SPECIAL SITUATIONS FOR GAY, LESBIAN, AND TRANSGENDER YOUTH

Although the developmental needs discussed previously are important for both children and adolescents, they generally speak about a normalized heterosexual life for youth. Lifestyles vary widely in society, and as policy makers and providers of services, we must also consider other life options such as gay, lesbian, and transgender youth who often fall into the "youth at risk" group. Although gay, lesbian, and transgender issues often surface at puberty, evidence indicates that sexuality and sexual identity begins much earlier than society would like to acknowledge.[14]

The American Academy of Child and Adolescent Psychiatry notes the following issues and problems associated with the social development of gay, lesbian, and transgender youth:

- Feeling different from their peers
- Feeling guilty about their sexual orientation
- Worrying about the response from their families and loved ones
- Being teased and ridiculed by their peers
- Worrying about AIDS, HIV infection, and other sexually transmitted diseases
- Fearing discrimination when joining clubs, playing sports, seeking admission to college
- Finding employment
- Being rejected and harassed by others[15]

In addition, gay, lesbian, and transgender youth often encounter problems of rejection, humiliation, and physical abuse at school, at home, and in their neighborhoods. Sexual issues and responses such as how to judge appropriate sexual behaviors and advances are of special concern to them. Health concerns including knowledge about sexually transmitted diseases, situations that promote suicidal thoughts and attempts, and substance abuse including the use of tobacco are all significant issues that face many gay, lesbian, and transgender youth in all complex societies.

Hearing Us Out: Voices from the Gay and Lesbian Community, by Roger Sutton (Little, Brown, 1994) addresses some of these issues through the use of biographical information about gays, lesbians, and transgender people and the people who love and care about them.

Aside from gay and lesbian issues, evidence also suggest that transgender issues are affecting children as well as adolescents and are being addressed more openly by concerned parents, educators, and therapists.[16] *Social Services with Transgendered Youth*, edited by Gerald P. Mallon, is among the first books to address situations faced by transgender youth and their families. The articles in the book address issues of violence and verbal abuse faced by these children in their own families, schools, and communities. Problems of identity formation and social isolation and difficulties in forming social and dating relationships in later years are also considered. Age-appropriate sexual responses are likewise discussed. The need for better education for parents and other social agents and caregivers is also considered.

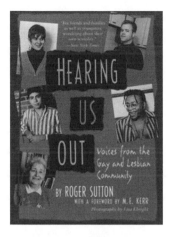

Figure 1.3
Hearing Us Out: Voices from the Gay and Lesbian Community, **by Roger Sutton. Biography as positive identity information.** Published with permission of Little, Brown and Company.

Figure 1.4
Social Services with Transgendered Youth, **edited by Gerald P. Mallon. Discusses the problems of transgendered youth and their families.** Published with permission of Harrington Park Press.

Advice on how to avoid therapeutic (and we might add educational) approaches designed to ensure gender conformity and stereotypical behaviors is strongly stated.[17, 18]

Because transgender issues are marginalized in most societies, little biography material has been written and published for children and young adults. Occasionally, documentary films are produced on the topic and made available through various television and film outlets.[19]

BIOGRAPHY AS SOCIAL AFFIRMATION AND CONFORMITY

From the above discussion, it is easy to see that biography can play an important role in the healthy development of youth, as well as playing a major role in defining the social and cultural aspects of modern society. Not only do we form our self-concepts from our own unique personalities, but we are conditioned in terms of forming a sense of self by the social context in which we live. Biography is a major element in this social context that will influence our views of ourselves as well as of others.

Historically biography has been a means of social control and social affirmation. The ancient Egyptian kings used it well through their monuments and tombs to reinforce their status as gods and absolute rulers, and to ensure their hold on their subjects.

Western culture places emphasis on the separate individual with the ability to link to social groups and individuals of their own choosing. But within the broad definition of individualism, most people need to be associated with groups that extend beyond self. This generally includes family, friends, religious groups, communes, volunteer groups, and occupational and work groups. Biography is simply another social means of solidifying the attributes of these groups. For children and young adults, biography serves as an important cultural guide, offering guidance and examples. In this sense, biography has been used to promote cultural identity; to stimulate emotional commitment to ideas, groups, and values; and to provide a vehicle for role modeling. It likewise offers guidance in terms of broadly accepted cultural and behavioral patterns.

APPROACHES TO THE WRITING OF BIOGRAPHY

Biography has been influenced by a number of approaches or theoretical constructs. It is useful for us to understand some of these so that we as school library media specialists, librarians, and teachers can make useful choices and know how we can use biography more effectively with youth. Broadly speaking, the concepts to be discussed here include:

Literary Approaches to Biography

Biography and History

The Political Biography

Psychology and Biography: Identity, Emulation, and Stimulation

Biography: Perceptions, Values, Beliefs

Biography: Reader Responses

Biography: Curriculum and Instruction

Biography as Therapy

Biography: Society and Mass Culture

Biography and Reference

Literary Approaches to Biography

According to critic Terry Eagleton, literature as we generally understand it today—in terms of its relationship to creative and imaginative expression such as poetry, fiction, and drama—did not emerge until the middle of the nineteenth century. Of course antecedents of it were well established before that period. He contends that literature before that time was largely factual, consisting of political, social, religious, and even biographical discourse. Nevertheless, as literature as a creative and imitative process became more accepted, it too took on a political context. More radical authors such as Blake and Shelley, and most of the major writers of the Romantic period, saw no conflict between literature and social commentary. Although social commentary was a part of the new creative literature, according to Eagleton, by the time of the Romantic period in English literature (eighteenth century), literature as imagination had separated itself from the realities of emerging capitalism. Writers deliberately celebrated the sovereignty of the imagination.[20]

This separation was not entirely at the hands of the writer but was a result of the increasing capitalization of English society and the feeling that literature had no real value in the realities of day-to-day society. It had lost its voice as a political, religious, and moral authority. Although literature had a right to observe society and to make comments, literature was art and must conform to the rules of aesthetics and beauty. Literature must be studied and analyzed to its very core, based on emerging standards of art and aesthetics. Because literature represented the finest example of humanity expressed through beauty, literature throughout the nineteenth and part of the twentieth centuries was offered as a form of social control and as a model of the ideal human society. Lower classes and workers could benefit from exposure to the finest in literature. Social conflict, class differences, the excesses of capitalism, and labor–management conflicts could be avoided through adherence to beauty and truth as expressed in fine literature. Matthew Arnold observed this about education and schools:

> State-established schools, by linking the middle class to the "best culture of their nation" will confer on them a "greatness and a noble spirit, which the tone of these classes is not of itself at present adequate to impart."[21]

This ideology was also emulated by public librarians as they sought to bring books and literacy to children in American and English society. *The Horn Book* magazine is an excellent example of this ideology as applied to youth literature. From its earliest days, this magazine exemplified and supported the aesthetic values found in literature for youth.[22] Along with the editors of *The Horn Book* magazine, adherents to this idea believed that high artistic standards would offer resistance to a vulgar culture dominated by romances, dime novels, working class–inspired melodramas, commercial advertising, and

**Figure 1.5
First issue, *The Horn Book*
magazine, October 1924. The
cover featured the famous
"Three Jovial Huntsmen,"
created by Randolph
Caldecott.** Reprinted by
permission of The Horn Book,
Inc., Boston, MA,
www.hbook.com.

The Horn Book Magazine,
Volume 1, Number 1

abasing mass media. Some argued that labor alienation, and the rise and influence of labor unions, could also be lessened through fine literature.

Biography written according to literary standards emerged from this ideology, becoming an important part of the movement that valued literature for its art and its Hellenistic and cultivating qualities. The writing of biography then assumed its place in art subject to all the standards of aesthetic literary expression and form. As with all fine literature, literary biography was judged according to such central values as richness of thought and language, complexity of analysis and use of symbolism, maturity of judgment, discrimination of values, and serious approaches to moral questions and considerations.[23]

Critic AmyLyn Daldry contends that the intellectual unrest of the 1960s forced new attention on biography as literature. She holds that feminist theories in particular helped foster a more critical approach to the writing of biography by questioning the traditional ways biographies were written, especially in their ignoring of women as subjects.[24] Evidence for this is found in such diverse fields as science and religion. For example, in Jewish and Christian religious studies the traditional interpretations of women's roles are now being reexamined in terms of newer theories about the influence of culture on gender roles and expectations within religious contexts. The attention given to biography of women and minorities since the 1960s also reflects this in terms of biographies for youth. Newbery Medal–winning author Virginia Hamilton provides an example of this with her book *Her Stories: African American Folktales, Fairytales, and True Tales* (Blue Sky Press, 1995).

Biography and History

History and biography are intertwined so much that we cannot separate them easily. Biography is essential to understanding and analyzing history.

Historical biography has much in common with literary biography in that it demands a high level of artistry and attention to aesthetics in its execution. In addition, today we would demand that modern biographers who wish to write about persons rely upon reliable sources and interpret the facts in objective and analytical ways.

Political writer Steve Weinberg notes that ancient biographers such as Plutarch (46–120), Aelfric (ca. 1000), and Giorgia Vasari (1500s) tended to see biography as groups of persons who performed certain social and political roles within the context of their environments. They were hardly critical of their subjects and certainly did not rely upon psychology or even environmental influences that might have influenced their subjects. Plutarch was interested in ethics and centered his interpretations on understanding the characters of significant Greeks and Romans, and the moral implications of their actions. He wrote easily and relied heavily upon anecdotes and generally accepted commentaries of his time to make his points. His work became popular in England in the 1500s, and it served as a major source for Shakespeare's dramas *Coriolanus*, *Julius Caesar*, *Anthony and Cleopatra*, and *Timon of Athens*.

Aelfric was an Anglo-Saxon prose writer who wrote about theology. He is best remembered today for his *Lives of the Saints*. Although this work is currently in print, no suitable translations for youth are yet available. Vasaro was an Italian architect, writer, and painter. He is appreciated today by scholars for his *Lives of the Artists* (10 vol., translated into English 1912–14). Vasari provided an enlightening discussion of his contemporaries, and his work serves as a fundamental source for our current knowledge of Renaissance artists.[25] Unfortunately, no modern translations of any of these works suitable for youth appear to be in print.

Other important historical biographies that have influenced biography writing today include James Boswell's biography of Samuel Johnson (1791), Thomas Carlyle's *Sartor Resartus* (1833–34), Ernest Renan's *Life of Jesus* (1863), Henry Adams' *The Education of Henry Adams* (1918), and Lytton Strachey's biographies of important Victorians.[26]

Histories or biographies as literary forms have often been accused of being dull and uninteresting to the general reader. The emergence of narrative biography writing in recent years may have addressed some of these complaints in positive ways. David McCullough, Walter Isaacson, and Joseph J. Ellis are examples of this kind of new writing. They have emerged as fine storytellers who apply historical details to create interesting and up-close historical personalities.[27]

Likewise, our understanding and acceptance of how biographical information should be presented has been influenced by mass communications. The rise of the docudrama and more penetrating interview methods are especially noteworthy. Cable television has also contributed to the popularity of biography through such outlets as the Biography Channel (www.biography.com). More will be discussed about these later in this chapter.

Presenting historical biography to young children can be challenging. Charlotte S. Huck and her colleagues state that in attempting to reach children, authors have used several writing techniques. These range from "strict authenticity to liberal fictionalization."[28] They contend that the trend today is authenticity. Nevertheless, some argue that fictionalized biography has a place in biography writing for youth. In fictionalized biography close attention to authenticity and adherence to the historical record ensures that the history of a person's life is accurately presented; but dramatization of selected events, if used with genuine understanding of the historical period and personalities, can increase interest. For example, conversation invented by the author but based on documented evidence is one such dramatization technique.

Mary Lyons used this technique in *Letters from a Slave Girl* about the life of Harriet Jacobs (Scribner's, 1992), and F. N. Monjo used fictionalized biography in writing about Mozart in *Letters to Horseface: Young Mozart's Travels in Italy* (Puffin, 1975, 1991).[29]

Jean Fritz, an outstanding writer of biography and history for children, also used a fictionalized approach to her own autobiography, *Homesick: My Own Story* (Putnam, 1982). Based on Library of Congress cataloging procedures widely used by school library media centers and public libraries today, this book is generally cataloged as fiction, but Fritz insists that only a small part of it is fiction. She has also successfully created interesting and appealing authentic biographies for children without the use of fiction. These include *And Then What Happened, Paul Revere?*, *Will You Sign Here, John Hancock?*, and *You Want Women to Vote, Lizzie Stanton?*[30] Russell Freedman is an author that uses a more formal but readable and engaging approach to biography for youth based on the authentic record.[31]

The Political Biography

In recent decades, the political biography has arisen. Based on investigative journalism, this type of biography seems to have become a dominant form for adults today, and some young adults have discovered it as well. Political journalist Steven Weinberg draws a close relationship between Lytton Strachey, who believed that it was the biographer's task not to be complimentary, but to present the facts of a life, and Robert Caro, the biographer of President Johnson who was clear in his assertion about motives and the influence of power.[32] But unlike Strachey, Caro came from a career in journalism and investigative reporting.

Influences of Biography

Jean Strouse, according to Weinberg, contends that biography has replaced the novel in providing readers with questions of character, motivation, morality, social pressure, and internal conflict.[33] Weinberg notes that biography influences how readers view human nature and how they may come to view particular individuals. From a political point of view, we can easily see this in the numbers of biographies and their various points of view expressed concerning political personalities of the late twentieth and early twentieth-first centuries, such as Bill Clinton and his wife, Hillary Rodham Clinton, and George W. Bush and his wife, Laura Bush. Such examples show that a skilled biographer often holds the reputations of others in his or her hands.

Discourse Theory

Discourse theory has a role to play in how we understand the place of political biography. Discourse theory is a political science concept that argues "that meaning is constructed within relational structures that are shaped and reshaped by political struggles." Discourse theory holds that through dialogue and exchange of ideas and information, conflicts can be overcome and one-sided understandings of structures, agencies, power, and authority can be reduced. Political biographies become a part of this discourse as they present varying points of view that must be considered and evaluated by objective observers.[34]

Psychology and Biography: Identity, Emulation, and Stimulation

Identity and Emulation

Most authorities agree that we select biography for several reasons, and among them is our need to identify with someone of worth or of interest to us. We like to read about people whom we admire and whom we want to emulate. Our culture and society often provide strong messages as to what is valued and what will be rewarded through emulation. We see this all around us, especially in mass culture and the attention given to celebrities. Aside from this, our society provides us with a number of identification models including family, friends, groups at work, and school groups. We are rewarded (or punished) by our associations and memberships in social groups. Whatever the case, we seek rewards and an increase in self-esteem through the collective biographies of social groups to which we belong and with which we identify.

Biography is a part of the identification process in that identities and self-concepts are built through acquiring many forms of information. Identities include what we are told about ourselves and others in our homes and schools, what we need to know about others in terms of our life space, and what we observe in mass culture. Psychology author Nicky Hayes states that as early as 1902, authorities suggested that we build our self-concept and identity from what we need internally as well as how we feel other people see us.[35] Psychologist Robert White says that we build our concepts of self through self-dramatization. That is, we take information from very important sources and select and synthesize that into our self-concepts and feelings of self-esteem. White cites E. Goffman's ideas of how we present ourselves to others in social situations. In social groups, we use "the act of impression management" and each member presents himself or herself to others using a biographical self-concept in ways that will enhance status. For example, travel, education, memberships, residences, dress, and ownership of material goods are just a few examples of biographical information that people present to others in social situations. White maintains that this is effective in social situations, but in terms of personality development, self-dramatization—or how we invent and present ourselves—is even more powerful in determining who we are as persons.[36]

Whatever the theoretical approach, reading biographies and the life-dramas and experiences of others, especially those who have achieved status in our society or who have met great challenges, is an important means of self-identity and self-esteem that we can integrate into our personal lives. The late President Ronald Reagan said this about the influence that biography had on him and how it stimulated his social, personal, and political development:

> I realized that my reading left an abiding belief in the triumph of good over evil. . . . These were heroes who lived by standards of morality and fair play.[37]

Social Constructionist Theory

Social constructionist theory can likewise add to our understanding of the psychological influences of biography. This concept holds that because values are time- and place-centered, no absolute values exist. Each person and each culture must construct its own values based on needs and environmental influences of the time. This constructionist process can be influenced by previous values, but they are only one of many influences that can be considered in formulating new concepts of self and society. *We Shall Not Be Moved: The Women's Factory Strike of 1909*, by Joan Dash (Scholastic, 1996) shows us through biographical evidence how women who worked in the garment factories of New York City in the early twentieth century reconstructed their concept of themselves and their rights in society based on emerging new values and circumstances in their environment that encouraged and empowered them to demand changes in how they were treated as women and workers.

Biography: Perceptions, Values, Beliefs

When using biographical materials with youth, it is important to consider how individuals respond to what they read. As we know, every person is influenced by different experiences, and we do not all perceive or react to the same information in the same way. Research tells us that we are likely to respond positively to information based on our perception of reality and the information that continues to reinforce those perceptions.

Marketing research can help us understand perception and how youth selects and responds to biographical information.[38] Market research, based on perception theory, has demonstrated that we select very carefully what we will attend to and retain. From this research we learn that we are more likely to remember and react only to information that reinforces our needs and seems important to us. As individuals we interpret information that comes to us selectively. We select information that reinforces our needs and values, and we are likely to better retain information that matches our needs and existing values.

Marketing research also adheres to motivation theory. Motivation is that inner drive that all people have to fulfill needs. These needs range from the utilitarian to the hedonistic, and the need for pleasure and fun. Attitudes play a role in how we select and use biographical information. Marketing research can be applied here too. Attitude is a combination of our beliefs. Attitudes will influence how we will act and how we will integrate beliefs into our values.[39] Values found in biography are powerful enforcers of attitudes.

One's beliefs and value systems can also play a role in the selection of biographical materials. Belief is the way a person views certain subjects. On one hand, this will apply to the types of biographical subjects individuals are more likely to select for reading. Belief systems will also influence the presentation of the biography by the author. Authors will reveal their belief systems through how they give evidence as to how a biography was constructed, its points of view and biases, how it was researched and documented, and for whom it was intended. The design of format and the selection of graphics can also reveal an author's beliefs about his or her subject.[40]

Beliefs and values influence how one reads for reinforcement of a positive attitude about a subject or how one reads to gather negative information helpful in reinforcing already existing negative opinions. Political and mass culture celebrities are examples of how biographies are written and how they are selected for reading based on personal perceptions of admiration or disdain for the subject, and complimenting or conflicting beliefs, values, and attitudes.

Biography: Reader Responses

Reading expert Louise Rosenblatt outlined two important points as to how readers respond to what they read. The first she calls the phenomenological view. This view holds that the reader and the text are in a dialogue with each other. The text exists, but it must have a reader to center it. The reality of the text cannot be understood until it interacts with the reader. The other view is the political or ideological view. This view contends that texts are results of political, social, and other ideological assumptions. The reader comes to the text also with existing political, social, and ideological views, and these aspects from the reader's background will condition and direct the reading and application of what is read. From what we know about human behavior based on social research, the political-ideological view seems the most useful to use as we attempt to understand how youth responds to biography.[41] The phenomenological view has merit as well. For example, if one comes to a biographical text knowing nothing about the subject or the culture in which the life was lived, the information is inert until the reader responds to its information symbols through dialogic interaction of reader with the text.

Reader-interest research reinforces some of these marketing and reader-response concepts. Research indicates that modern youth like to read about contemporary personalities, including sports figures, entertainers, and even popular political figures. They also like to read about people who are perhaps less well known, but who do exciting and interesting things. They also like to read about people who have faced life head-on and who have overcome great obstacles and handicaps. This tells us that the reading of biography is based on perceptions, values, attitudes, beliefs, and actions, and the need for positive self-identity. Youth generally read what will reinforce psychological and social needs for approval and acceptance. They read to give them a sense of direction, and they read for survival information based on how others have managed their lives.

Providing youth with biographical materials is much like marketing a product. Marketing provides a product that is wanted and needed. Marketing creates an awareness of the product and informs and educates the potential buyer or user about how it will satisfy needs. As in marketing, school library media specialists and youth librarians must select and promote a variety of materials that address the fundamental needs of youth and that will help them succeed in a complex world.

Biography: Curriculum and Instruction

Curriculum and instruction are parts of culture and society, and as such they will reflect the values and expectations of a given society. Both curriculum and instruction approaches and concepts are based on political as well as educational considerations.

Educators Judy Reinhartz and Don M. Beach tell us that the first modern use of the concept of curriculum was in the 1920s and it was used to define a process rather than a product or result of instruction. According to this definition, curriculum was all the experiences, both organized and unorganized, that contributed to the learning of students.[42] A more specific definition soon followed that considered curriculum to be all those experiences that take place in a school under the guidance of the school and its teachers.[43] Planning and process were then and are today the dominant factors in curriculum development. Well-known theorist Bruner defined curriculum in this way:

> A curriculum reflects not only the nature of knowledge itself, but also the nature of the knower and the knowledge-getting process . . . where the line between subject matter and methods grows necessarily indistinct.[44]

Instruction is one of the outcomes of planning in that it outlines in detail how the goals and objectives of the curriculum will be executed and presented to learners through various experiences. Typically instruction involves analysis of learners and their needs, consideration of mandated instructional objectives, setting of goals and rationales, selection of content and instructional applications, selection of materials and resources, assessment of learning outcomes, and evaluation and restructuring as necessary in the instructional processes.

The use of biographical materials falls easily into these definitions. Biographical materials and their applications both as content and materials for instruction can be applied to all aspects of the instructional process. Later chapters will discuss some specific applications of biography in curriculum and instruction.

Biography as Therapy

Most literate societies have always considered books and reading as powerful influences on behaviors and values. Examples of the use of reading range from religion to politics. Official censorship by governments of reading and books as well as censorship of individual members and writers of groups and organizations are well known, if not legendary, and reinforce the perceived power that reading has in society and culture. Aside from this, psychology has also considered bibliotherapy as a powerful influence on behaviors. In 1978 Rhea Joyce Rubin defined *bibliotherapy* as "a program of activities based on the interactive processes of media and the people who experience it. Print or nonprint material, either imaginative or information, is experienced and discussed with the aid of a facilitator."[45] Rubin states that there are three basic types of bibliotherapy:

1. Institutional: Takes place in institutions such as hospitals and prisons, and uses information and other insight-oriented literature or media.

2. Clinical: Conducted by clinically trained librarians or psychologists with groups of clients having emotional or behavior problems. The goal is to encourage insight or behavior changes using appropriate materials.

3. Developmental: Used with the average population and designed to promote and maintain good mental health and to encourage self-awareness; both fiction and nonfiction materials are used.[46]

Generally, institutional and clinical bibliotherapy are conducted by a clinically trained psychology expert who often works closely with a librarian, with the actual application of the therapy remaining under the control of clinical psychologists. As previously stated, developmental bibliotherapy is designed to facilitate normal personal and social development.

Developmental bibliotherapy may also be used to help correct inappropriate behaviors that are developmentally based. For example, a school library media specialist that understands youth developmental needs may use books and media to address needs of groups as well as individuals. Perhaps a fourth grade class is demonstrating undemocratic behaviors and harmful social groups are forming. A teacher or school library media specialists may use developmental bibliotherapy to help correct such situations. On the other hand, librarians might work closely with a shy student to help him or her feel more comfortable with peer groups. One of the hallmarks of these two types of bibliotherapy is that they involve discussion, reflection, and personal catharsis.

Developmental bibliotherapy differs from reading guidance in that it is designed to bring about behavior changes whereas reading guidance is intended to help youth find materials to read based on their own needs and wants.[47] The school library media center specialist can apply his or her knowledge of biographical materials to both of these approaches to therapy.

Problems addressed in the bibliotherapeutic process include improving problem-solving skills; helping youth better understand other people such as the elderly; addressing racism and sexism; improving personal and social development; and helping youth deal with the loss of parents through death, divorce, or separation. The study of bibliotherapeutic interventions has been conducted largely through dissertation and thesis research, and there are strong indications that the technique does have influence on improvement of self-concept and self-esteem. This research seems to indicate that the expertise and skills of the facilitators, extensiveness, and reinforcement of bibliotherapeutic interventions play important roles in fostering positive impact on self-esteem and self-concepts of children and adolescents.[48, 49, 50, 51]

Biography: Society and Mass Culture

It can be argued that biography is the glue that binds society and culture together. There are many ways to define *society* as well as *culture*, and every discipline has its own perspective on these two terms. Without going into excessive detail, this discussion will borrow from several fields for its frame of reference. Society comes from the "Latin word that means companion, and in its broadest sense, it means the whole or web of relationships among a people, their culture, and their environment."[52] Anthropologists consider *culture* to be:

[A] system of shared beliefs, values, customs, behaviours and artifacts that the members of society use to cope with their world and with one another, and that are transmitted from generation to generation through learning.[53]

More specifically, *society* means an extended group of people, all of whom share a distinctive cultural and economic organization.[54]

Biographical material developed within a society and a culture carries important social and cultural norms, expectations, and messages. As mentioned earlier, biography has always been used in societies around the world and throughout history to reinforce the values and expectations of the given culture. Depending on the time frame, Western culture has celebrated important religious leaders, artists, saints, inventors, scientists, statesmen, and others in a formal sense through books, decrees, and honors given to selected members of society. Each society and culture expects its youth to know and appreciate selected persons who exemplify the values of the society.

Culture embraces both high culture and popular or mass culture. Matthew Arnold's idea of high culture embraced the concept of knowing the best that the human mind has produced and that is valued by the standards of the intellectual, political, and socially elite.[55] For example, in the United States, opera, symphonic music, and yachting are considered high culture. Generally high culture is determined by the most powerful classes in society.

Simply said, popular culture is the culture of the people and in modern societies it is the interplay of industries—publishing, film, and television, etc.—that disseminate cultural materials and how people accept and use those products. Items that have broad appeal within a society or culture tend to reflect what is immediate, exciting, and momentarily valued.

This helps explain why youth tend to accept biographical materials that are reflected in mass culture and disseminated by the mass media more than items associated with higher levels of culture. Mass culture today is celebrity driven. Film, television, popular music personalities, and sports figures dominate. Concern is voiced by some that this celebrity-focused culture is harmful to youth because of the values that it endorses. Special correspondent for *Vanity Fair* Maureen Orth in her book *The Importance of Being Famous: Behind the Scenes of the Celebrity-Industrial Complex* (Henry Holt, 2004) provides information about celebrities from entertainment, politics, and the news media and about a "celebrity" industry that creates and maintains fame, often compromising personal integrities and values.[56] This aspect of biography will be discussed more in chapter 6.

The school library media center can and must meet the need for both popular and "high-culture" biographical materials by acquiring the better materials and by educating youth to be discerning and critical about how they accept biographical information from both high and mass cultures.

Biography and Reference

Biography plays an important role in reference and information services and programs offered by any school library media center. In fact, it is often said that answers to biographical questions are among the most frequently requested in libraries. Fortunately, biographical materials are found in a variety of sources including encyclopedias, periodicals and newspapers, almanacs and yearbooks, directories, and manuscript and archive collections.

Over the years, a great many outstanding resources have developed to support the need for biographic reference materials. These include sources that provide retrospective information such as the great *Dictionary of National Biography* and the *Dictionary of American Biography*. More recently the *Dictionary of Literary Biography* and the *Dictionary of Scientific Biography* have joined the list. New biographical information continues to be served well by *Current Biography* and *Who's Who* and *Who's Who in America*. Electronic information utilities such as Gale Research (http://isbndb.com/d/publisher/ gale_research.html), EBSCO Information Services (http://www.ebsco.com/ home), Fact on File (www.factsonfile.com), and Grolier® (http://auth.grolier. com/cgi-bin/authV2?bffs = N) have also aided in accessing the wealth of biographical materials available.

The needs for more popularly written materials that meet the needs and interests of students have been addressed by such publications as Omnigraphics' "Biography Today" series (www.omnigraphics.com) and the various publications coming from this publisher. Mass media coverage of biography is available through such publications as *People* magazine as well as television outlets such as the Biography Channel and commercial television programs such as *Entertainment Tonight*.

Problems generally associated with biographical reference materials include the traditional omission of women and minorities and the patriarchal approach taken to women subjects, and the style and the approaches in the interpretation of lives.

Providing access to local biographical information is an issue that must be addressed. Local biographical information is found in local newspapers and magazines, and in published histories and directories such as city and county directories. Directories of local professional, civic, cultural, and social organizations also provide this type of information. The Internet can also offer access to local biographical items. Collecting and organizing local biographical information for access is labor-intensive. Sometimes indexing of local materials is required. Often special filing systems must be maintained such as vertical or information files.

These services are costly in terms of time and work requirements. Nevertheless, these special collections, processes, and services add riches to the collection and help meet the overall goals and mission of the library media center's information program.

CONCLUSION

Biography is associated with all aspects of human life and experiences. Biography affects our personal and group psychology, it helps shape our personal and cultural values, and it can serve as a means of observing and mentoring the directions and foci that our society and culture take in this complex world. Biography is also an excellent means of introducing youth to their cultural heritage. Not only does biography provide a means of meeting information needs, but it can act as a vehicle for social change. Biography can help foster in youth awareness of their world and how to help change it for the better.

Biography continues to play a major role in classroom instruction and curriculum development as it can be applied in all areas of study. Among others, it serves and provides access and support for literature, science, and the social studies, and vocational awareness. It is especially useful for school library media specialists as it offers ample opportunities to help develop information literacy skills in students as well as helping them develop more astute critical cultural analysis techniques.

Similarly, when applied correctly, biography offers personal support and modeling information. Fortunately, school library media center programs over the years have recognized this, and we now have a wealth of biographical materials, resources, and ideas to help us in our goals of assisting youth as they move toward adulthood.

NOTES

1. Elayne L. Tobin, "Fearing for Our Lives: Biography and Middlebrow Culture in Late Twentieth-Century America" (dissertation, University of Pittsburgh, 2001), abstracted in *Dissertation Abstracts International* 62-A (May 2002): 3089.

2. *Bartlett's Familiar Quotations,* 10th ed. (Boston: Little, Brown, 1919), http://www.bartleby.com/100/387.29.html (accessed June 10, 2004).

3. "Old Time Radio Moments of the Century," http://members.aol.com/jeff1070/mcleod.html (accessed July 14, 2004).

4. Tinky Weisblat, "Will the Real George and Gracie and Ozzie and Harriet and Desi and Lucy Please Stand Up? The Functions of Popular Biography in 1950s Television" (dissertation, University of Texas at Austin, 1991), abstracted in *Dissertation Abstracts International,* 52-A (Oct. 1991): 1402.

5. "Erikson's Development Stages," Patient Teaching, Loose Leaf Library Springhouse Corporation (1990), http://honolulu.hawaii.edu/intranet/committees/FacDevCom/guidebk/teachtip/erikson.htm (accessed July 13, 2004).

6. Nicky Hayes, *Teach Yourself: Psychology* (New York: Contemporary Books, 1994), 169.

7. Hayes, 11.

8. Hayes, 13.

9. Peter K. Gerlach, "Kids' Normal Developmental Needs: 25 Roots of Healthy Adult Independence," http://sfhelp.org/10/dvl-needs.htm (accessed Nov. 2, 2005).

10. Gerlach.

11. Daniel Perkins, "Adolescence: Developmental Tasks," Fact Sheet FCS 2118, a series of the Department of Family, Youth and Community Sciences, Florida Cooperative Extension Service, Institute of Food and Agricultural Sciences, University of Florida. Jan. 2001, http://edis.ifas.ufl.edu/BODY_HE820 (accessed June 4, 2004).

12. Perkins.

13. Municipal Research and Services Center of Washington, "Youth & Youth-at-Risk Programs," http://www.mrsc.org/subjects/humanservices/youth.aspx (accessed Dec. 30, 2004).

14. "Child Sexuality," in *Wikipedia, The Free Encyclopedia,* http://en.wikipedia.org/wiki/Child_sexuality (accessed Dec. 30, 2004).

15. American Academy of Child and Adolescent Psychiatry, "Puberty 101: Gay and Lesbian Teens," http://www.puberty101.com/aacap_gayteens.shtml (accessed June 10, 2004).

16. "About Our Transgendered Children and Their Families," PFLAG-TALK/TGS-PLLAG Vitural Library, http://www.critpath.org/pflag-talk/tgKIDfaq.html (accessed Dec. 30, 2004).

17. Gerald P. Mallon, ed., *Social Services with Transgendered Youth* (New York: Harrington Park Press, 1999).

18. Farzana Doctor, "Review of *Social Services with Transgendered Youth*" (New York: Harrington Park Press, 1999), http://www.tpronline.org/articles.cfm?articleID=338 (accessed Oct. 29, 2005).

19. Marjorie K. Mitchell Multimedia Center, Northwestern University, "Sexual Orientation Studies Documentaries (Gay, Lesbian, Bisexual, and Transgender)," http://www.library.northwestern.edu/media/docs/sexual_orientation.pdf (accessed Dec. 30, 2004).

20. Terry Eagleton, *Literary Theory: An Introduction* (Minneapolis: University of Minnesota Press, 1996), 1–46.

21. Eagleton, citing Matthew Arnold, "The Popular Education of France in Democratic Education," 21.

22. Joan Blodgett Peterson Olson, "An Interpretive History of the *Horn Book* Magazine, 1924–1973" (dissertation, Stanford University, 1976), abstracted in *Dissertation Abstracts International,* 37-A (Nov. 1976): 2875.

23. Eagleton, 29.

24. AmyLyn Daldry, "The Artistically Accurate: A Study of Biographical Theory and a Short Biography of Dr. Eleanor Mendell Worsley" (master's thesis, Northwestern State University, 1996), http://www.nsula.edu/scholars/Thesis/Thesisabstracts/HSTtheses/Daldry.html (accessed Nov. 2, 2005).

25. Steve Weinberg, *Telling the Untold Story: How Investigative Reporters Are Changing the Craft of Biography* (Columbia: University of Missouri Press, 1992), 8.

26. "Biography," in *Columbia Encyclopedia,* 6th ed. (New York: Columbia University Press, 2001–2004), http://www.bartleby.com/65 (accessed July 15, 2004).

27. David Rosenbaum, "In Times of Trouble, the Founding Fathers Sell Well," *New York Times,* July 4, 2004.

28. Charlotte S. Huck and others, *Children's Literature in the Elementary School,* 6th ed. (Madison, Wis.: Brown & Benchmark, 1997), 552.

29. Huck, 552–53.

30. Huck, 553.

31. Huck, 555.

32. Weinberg, 12.

33. Weinberg.

34. "Introduction to Discourse Theory," Dr. Jacob Torfling, Roskilde University, http://www.essex.ac.uk/methods/Courses2005/1U05.htm (accessed Nov. 2, 2005).

35. Hayes, 15.

36. Robert W. White, *The Enterprise of Living: A View of Personal Growth,* 2nd ed. (New York: Holt, Rinehart and Winston, 1976), 426–28.

37. Lou Cannon, *Reagan* (New York: Putnam, 1982), 19, citing Jerry Griswold, "Young Reagan's Reading," *New York Times Book Review,* Aug. 30, 1981, from a letter from Reagan to O. Dallas Baillio, Director of the Mobile Public Library, 1977.

38. Gilbert A. Churchill and J. Paul Peter, *Marketing: Creating Value for Customers* (Burr Ridge, Ill.: Irwin, 1995), 240–46.

39. Churchill and Peter.

40. Churchill and Peter.

41. Louise M. Rosenblatt, *Literature as Exploration,* 5th ed. (New York: Modern Language Association of America, 1995).

42. Judy Reinhartz and Don M. Beach, *Teaching and Learning in the Elementary School: Focus on Curriculum* (Upper Saddle River, N.J.: Merrill, 1997), 19, citing J. Wiles and J. Bondi, *Curriculum Development: A Guide to Practice,* 2nd ed. (Upper Saddle River, N.J.: Merrill/Prentice Hall, 1984) and their *Curriculum Development: A Guide to Practice,* 4th ed. (Upper Saddle River, N.J.: Merrill/Prenctice Hall, 1993).

43. Reinhartz and Beach, 20.

44. Reinhartz and Beach, 20, citing J. Bruner, *Toward a Theory of Instruction* (Cambridge, Mass.: Harvard University Press, 1966), 72.

45. Rhea Joyce Rubin, *Using Bibliotherapy: A Guide to Theory and Practice* (Phoenix, Ariz.: Oryx Press, 1978), 2.

46. Rhea Joyce Rubin, "Uses of Bibliotherapy," *Library Trends* 28 (Fall 1979): 243–45.

47. W. Bernard Lukenbill, *AIDS and HIV Programs and Services for Libraries* (Englewood, Colo.: Libraries Unlimited, 1994), 206, citing Joyce G. Saricks and Nancy Brown, *Readers' Advisory Services in the Public Library* (Chicago: American Library Association, 1989), 3–9, 24–72.

48. Suzanne Kay Haag, "A Study of the Effectiveness of a Bibliotherapy Program for Changing Self-Concept at a Fourth-Grade Level" (master's thesis, Northeast Missouri State University, 1990), abstracted *in Masters Abstract International,* 28 (Winter, 1990): 494.

49. Dewayne Arden Green, "A Study of the Impact of Bibliotherapy on the Self-Concept of Mexican-American Children Ten and Eleven Years of Age" (dissertation, University of Northern Colorado, 1988), abstracted in *Dissertations Abstracts International,* 50-A (Nov. 1989): 1252.

50. Lena Marie Nuccio, "The Effects of Bibliotherapy on the Self-Esteem and Teacher-Related Classroom Behavior on Third-Grade Children of Divorce" (dissertation, University of Southern Mississippi, 1997), abstracted in *Dissertation Abstracts International* 59-A (Aug. 1998): 409.

51. Lisa Michele Tilley, "Reading Experiences and the Making of Self: A Case Study Investigating the Construction of Subjectivity by Adolescent Girls" (dissertation, University of Georgia, 2000), abstracted in *Dissertation Abstracts International* 61-A (Feb. 2001): 3092.

52. "Glossary: Living with the Future in Mind," http://www.state.nj.us/dep/dsr/sustainable-state/glossary.htm (accessed Nov. 2, 2004).

53. "Module I: Introduction, I. The Culture Concept," http://www.umanitoba.ca/faculties/arats/anthropology/courses/122/module1/culture.html (accessed July 10, 2004).

54. "Meaning of Society," http://www.hyperdictionary.com/dictionary/society (accessed July 10, 2004).

55. Eagleton, 21, 22–23, 170.

56. Maureen Orth, *The Importance of Being Famous: Behind the Scenes of the Celebrity Industrial Complex* (New York: Henry Holt, 2004).

2

BIOGRAPHY IN THE LIBRARY MEDIA CENTER

INTRODUCTION

Biography is important in school curricula and in public library programming and services for children and young adults. Therefore, this chapter will consider the forces that shape modern life and how biography can be used in instructional ways in the classroom, the school library media center, and the public library. It will offer examples of how biography can be applied in practice in both schools and public libraries to enhance the learning and development processes of youth.

CLASSROOM AND PUBLIC LIBRARY

Objectives of the Modern Curriculum and Instruction

"Curriculum and instruction" is a cultural statement, reflecting values endorsed by nations, states, provinces, and groups. Within school environments, it is a form of government speech, and it is designed not only to educate the young, but also to ensure that national and regional values are inculcated in emerging citizens. In this sense, it is a form of national, state, and provincial policy.

National Objectives

Although countries of the world have common attributes that are incorporated into their individual curricula, national aspirations differ, and these differences are reflected in national curricula. The International Association for the Advancement of Curriculum Studies (IAACS) recognizes these differences in its mission statement by saying that it "supports a worldwide—but not uniform—field of curriculum studies." It recognizes that curriculum must respect national boundaries and that it is "informed by government policies, priorities, and national situations," and will remain national in character for the foreseeable future. Although the organization does not support a global curriculum and international standards, it does recognize the dangers of narrow nationalism.[1]

ROLE OF NATIONAL, STATE, PROVINCIAL, AND
LOCAL CURRICULUM AND INSTRUCTIONAL MANDATES

English-speaking countries that follow a federalist type of government, such as the United States, Canada, and Australia, tend to delegate a large part of education to their states, provinces, territories, and local governments. The degree of freedom given to these governmental units varies within the various federalist systems.

The United States

In the United States, the Constitution is basically silent on the role of the federal government in education. Over the years, this has been interpreted to mean that the responsibility for education falls largely to each individual state. Over the years, states have codified this responsibility into numerous state laws. For the most part, each state has given the overall responsibility to state agencies that, under legislative mandates and authority, set standards and delegate much of the design and implementation of curriculum and instruction to local educational authorities. A major criticism of this arrangement is that it has not produced a standard curriculum that can ensure a uniformly educated student population.

Nevertheless, the American federal government has always had a profound interest in education and has sought to influence education in line with its perceived constitutional mandates. In 1876 the Congress created a non–cabinet level, but independent, Department of Education, headed by a commissioner. It had little enforcement power and acted largely as an information agency. Because of congressional opposition to its scholarly and research orientation under Commissioner Henry Barnard, the department's budget was reduced, and after June 30, 1869, it lost its independent status and became the Office of Education within the Department of the Interior, where it remained until 1939.[2] The modern-day Department of Education was created by the Department of Education Organization Act (20 U.S.C. 3411).

Today the Department of Education is the national educational arm of the federal government. It is a cabinet-level department that reports directly to the president. It develops and disseminates policy, creates various programs and services, and coordinates most of federal assistance to educational programs within the government. Overall, "its mission is to ensure equal access to education and to promote educational excellence throughout the nation."[3]

Increasingly over the years, the American federal government has moved more forcefully into influencing educational policies and directions at state levels through civil rights legislation, various types of federal financial support for programs and services, and mandated government educational laws. The government is now seeking to ensure a more uniform level of school performance through its "No Child Left Behind" legislation. The purpose as stated in law is to "close the achievement gap with accountability, flexibility, and choice, so that no child is left behind." The law requires that all states that wish to receive federal support under this act submit a comprehensive state-level plan to ensure standards, academic achievement, and accountability.[4] Its directive reads:

> All states and schools will have challenging and clear standards of achievement and accountability for all children, and effective strategies for reaching those standards.[5]

Based on such federal mandates, states have responded with curriculum standards.[6]

Beyond that, the Department of Education has listed a number of subject and curriculum areas in which it has an interest. These include art, mathematics, vocational training, foreign language study, reading, writing, science, English as a Second Language, civics, and social sciences. Among others, it is also concerned with meeting the needs of Hispanics, Native Americans, at-risk students, the culturally and economically disadvantaged, the gifted and talented, migrant children, and the handicapped. Because the department delegates the actual formation of curriculum to state and local agencies, it relies heavily upon the broad-based American educational community, including professional organizations, to development specific curricula and instructional programs.

Canada

Under the Canadian Constitution—the British North American Act, 1867—Canada also follows a federalist system. Under this act and constitution, education and its implementation are largely given to the parliaments of the provinces and territories. This authority includes development of curricula and instruction. Canadian curricula for grades K–12 are outlined in some detail at Canada Online's "Canadian Documents and Policy for Canadian Elementary and Secondary Education, by Province and Territory in Canada."[7] Supportive curriculum guides and resources are available at the Canada Online site as well.[8]

Australia

Australia has a federalist government, and in some respects it operates much like the United States and Canada. The national government delegates education to the states and territories. Each state and territory has responsibility for its own educational system. But unlike the United States, there is a considerable degree of uniformity among states and territories. This is probably due to the Australian Qualifications Framework (AQF). This is a national system of "learning pathways that covers 12 different qualifications all linked to universities, vocational education and training and school education." This system allows students to move easily from school to school and from level to level throughout the country's states and territories.[9]

The Australian Ministry of Education, like the U.S. Department of Education, is charged with encouraging and promoting education in the country. The ministry states its goals as:

- Students achieve high-quality foundation skills and learning outcomes from schools
- Individuals achieve relevant skills and learning outcomes from post-school education and training for work and life
- Social development and economic growth are advanced through a strong science, research, and innovation capacity
- International engagement in science, education and training[10]

A major directive that the ministry is now following is the National Goals for Schooling. The National Goals for Education (The Adelaide Declaration on National Goals for Schooling in the Twenty-First Century) is a declaration prepared by important educational agencies in Australia in 1999. It outlined the need for national reporting on educational outcomes. To facilitate this report, the agreement identified these core areas:

- Literacy
- Numeracy
- Student participation, retention, and completion
- Vocational education and training in schools
- Science
- Information technology
- Civics and citizenship education
- Enterprise education[11]

The United Kingdom

The United Kingdom is not a federalist government, and its educational system is centralized. In 1988 the central government imposed a compulsory curriculum on all schools in the United Kingdom (except Scotland). Previously, the Education Law of 1944 gave this responsibility to local authorities and the schools themselves. The national curriculum was an effort

to raise standards. It is not only a curriculum, but it presents the United
Kingdom's national educational policy.[12]

Throughout their careers, students are assessed and are expected to pass
national examinations. The British Council explains the educational and examination system in this way:

> Education in the UK is compulsory between ages five and sixteen.
> Schooling is divided into 4 key stages. Post-16 education takes students for-
> ward to preparation for pre-university study. Most students in the UK leave
> school at the age of eighteen, having sat for 'A' (Advanced) level exams.
>
> * * *
>
> Children are assessed at different stages in their school careers. Different
> types of tests are used. Some of these tests are appropriate only for schools
> which are in the UK, because they measure things which derive from the
> national Curriculum. Other exams, such as the General Certificate of
> Secondary Education (G.C.S.E) are taken by many students [from abroad]
> who are preparing for undergraduate study at university.[13]

The National Curriculum is designed to

> [set] out a clear, full and statutory entitlement to learning for all pupils. It
> determines the content of what will be taught, and sets attainment targets
> for learning. It also determines how performance will be assessed and
> reported. An effective National Curriculum, therefore, gives teachers,
> pupils, parents, employers and their wider community a clear and shared
> understanding of the skills and knowledge that young people will gain at
> school. It allows schools to meet the individual learning needs of pupils and
> to develop a distinctive character and ethos rooted in their local communi-
> ties. And it provides a framework within which all partners in education can
> support young people on the road to further learning.[14]

Subject contents include art and design; citizenship; design and technology;
English; history; information and communication technology (ICT); mathematics; modern foreign languages (MFL); music; personal, social, and health education (PSHE); physical education; religious education; and science. To help
with this curriculum, specific teaching guides and resources are provided.[15]

The European Union

The European Union (EU) includes many countries with different educational traditions. Information concerning education and curriculum in the various countries belonging to the EU is available at the union's website
(www.european-agency.org/contacts/ministry_main.html). For the most part,

this site offers links to the various countries' educational ministries. The information provided is generally in the country's native language.

VALUES, CULTURE, AND BIOGRAPHY FOR YOUTH

Values and Cultural Influences

When we consider the use of biography with children and adolescents in instructional settings, values and culture must be considered. Values permeate biography. Some values found in biography we may well support while others we might reject as unsuitable for the young. Values are not easily agreed to in multicultural societies as much as in the United States, Canada, and Western Europe.

Values are a collection of ideologies that inform people about correct actions. Values offer structure and order to lives, and they are a part of social arrangements and interactions. Values enforce beliefs and goals, and they give support for actions and the institutions that can enforce or endorse values.

In recent years, political and social movements in the United States have increased demands for so-called traditional family values, more recognition of religion in public life, and more positive support of religion by government. Gertrude Himmelfarb contends that modern American culture is decaying as a result of social movements of the 1960s. She holds that cultural patterns previous to the 1960s were better in terms of ensuring the stability of society. She writes that these values included respect for strong traditional families, a belief in an absolute standard of truth and morality, and respect for religion and authority.[16]

Focus on the Family is an American group that strongly supports initiatives to return the country to what it considers to be positive family and religious values. They state as one of their principles:

> God has ordained three basic institutions—the church, the family and the government—for the benefit of all humankind. The family exists to propagate the race and to provide a safe and secure haven in which to nurture, teach and love the younger generation. The church exists to minister to individuals and families by sharing the love of God and the message of repentance and salvation through the blood of Jesus Christ. The government exists to maintain cultural equilibrium and to provide a framework for social order.[17]

Some have suggested that in the viewpoint of this group, government and government policies and directives must play key roles in its initiatives to maintain its ideas of social order.

American public schools have generally considered core values to be those embraced by character education, human relationships, and civic education.

The Character Education Partnership (CEP), located in Washington, D.C., outlines eleven principles of character education. Within these principles they include caring, honesty, fairness, responsibility, and respect for self and others. Schools can incorporate these in the life of the school as well as into the formal curriculum. In doing this, the school can model good behavior, promote the study and discussion of these principles, and use them in human relationship education. Above all, schools must hold all members of the school community accountable for their core values and behaviors. CEP says:

> Good character involves understanding, caring about, and acting upon core ethical values. A holistic approach to character development therefore seeks to develop the cognitive, emotional, and behavioral aspects of moral life. Students grow to understand core values by studying and discussing them, observing behavioral models, and resolving problems involving the values. Students learn to care about core values by developing empathy skills, forming caring relationships, helping to create community, hearing illustrative and inspirational stories, and reflecting on life experiences. And they learn to act upon core values by developing pro-social behaviors (e.g., communicating feelings, active listening, helping skills) and by repeatedly practicing these behaviors, especially in the context of relationships.[18]

Although the U.S. government has an interest in character and values education, it has not developed specific guidelines for such education, but relies on state and local governments to develop and integrate such curricula into their school programs. Nevertheless, in an effort to promote character education, it has funded several curriculum initiatives through its Partnership in Character Education Projects.

This program funded Utah's Community Partnership for Character Education project.[19] The Utah Office for Education states this about the project:

> Character education helps children and youth to understand, care about, and act on core ethical and citizenship values! Quality character education helps schools create a safe, caring and inclusive learning environment for every student and supports academic development. It fosters qualities that will help students be successful as citizens, in the workplace, and with the academic curriculum. It lays the foundation to help students be successful in all of the goals we have for our public schools. It is the common denominator that will help schools reach all of their goals! CHARACTER EDUCATION IS NOT ONE MORE THING ON YOUR PLATE! IT IS THE PLATE!!! [emphasis is the department's][20]

The Utah study cites from Thomas Lickona's book, *Educating for Character: How Our Schools Can Teach Respect and Responsibility* (Bantam, 1991), noting that educating for character involved three moral elements: moral knowing, moral feeling, and moral behavior. In addition, the study identified thirty-six elements of character and asked schools to consider their importance. These included acceptance, caring, common sense, perseverance, problem solving, respect, responsibility, service, tolerance, and trustworthiness. The characteristics most often selected by the schools as important were caring, respect, responsibility, and trustworthiness.

Civic education is another important value supported by American schools. Generally these involve American beliefs and American constitutional principles. The Ann Arbor Public Schools identified the following as fundamental beliefs and constitutional principles that it should teach.

Fundamental Beliefs: Life, Liberty, Pursuit of Happiness, Common Good, Justice, Equality, Diversity, Truth, and Popular Sovereignty

Constitutional Principles: The Rule of Law, Separation of Powers, Representative Government, Checks and Balances, Individual Rights, Freedom of Religion, Federalism, and Civilian Control of the Military

In Great Britain values for the curriculum are stated through the "Statement of Values" developed by the National Forum for Values in Education and Community. The forum recognizes that people have different ways of considering values. Some people see values in religious terms while others are more comfortable placing values within secular frameworks. The forum advises that the set of values it presents is compatible with both points of view.

Basically the values fall into these major categories:

• **The self.** We value ourselves as unique human beings capable of spiritual, moral, intellectual, and physical growth and development.

• **Relationships.** We value others for themselves, not only for what they have or what they can do for us. We value relationships as fundamental to the development and fulfillment of ourselves and others, and to the good of the community.

• **Society.** We value truth, freedom, justice, human rights, the rule of law, and collective effort for the common good. In particular, we value families as sources of love and support for all their members and as the basis of a society in which people care for others.

• **Environment.** We value the environment, both natural and shaped by humanity, as the basis of life and a source of wonder and inspiration.

Taken as a whole, the forum suggests that schools should interpret these values based on views held within the wider community. The forum further notes that there is agreement within British society on these values, and schools and teachers can expect that they will receive the support and encouragement needed to teach these values.[21]

Cultural Literacy

A debate or discussion about cultural literacy is being waged today in the United States within educational and social circles. In simple terms, one argument holds that cultural literacy is gaining an understanding and appreciation of other peoples' cultures and celebrating diversity. The other argument takes the approach that cultural literacy is academic and is based on knowledge of the world and events that have shaped the world—from literature to human conflicts. The latter approach is championed by Eric D. Hirsch Jr. and his colleagues in their book, *Cultural Literacy: What Every American Needs to Know* (Houghton Mifflin, 1987). They continued to promote the idea of cultural literacy through a later edition, *The New Dictionary of Cultural Literacy* (Houghton Mifflin, 2002).

The complaints raised against Hirsch's ideas of cultural literacy is that they are based on a traditional, academic way of seeing the world and they do not consider the wide range of cultures that make up the world. Hirsch feels that by placing too much emphasis on cultural differences and diversity, our culture and social order becomes too fragmented. Others, such as Alice Walker, take an opposing view. In her essay "Whose Culture Is It Anyway?" Walker maintains that to understand cultural traditions, we cannot only look at what great minds and even great social movements have produced, but we must understand that genius and creativity have often been suppressed, and we need to look not only for what was recognized as genius in the past, but for the genius that was suppressed, and through this suppression, realize that knowledge was advanced in creative and anonymous ways.[22]

Literacy and Educational Goals

Within the last few decades educators have been expanding the meaning of *literacy.* Originally the word implied the ability to read and write in a language. Today the word has expanded to include numerous types of expected educational goals and skills. Regardless of what these might be, biography can play a role in helping to attain them.

For example, in their publication *21st Century Skills: Literacy in the Digital Age,* the North Central Regional Educational Laboratory outlined a number of literacies that it feels will affect present and future schools. These include:[23]

- **Basic literacy skills:** Can read, write, listen, speak; has numerical as well as information and technological skills
- **Scientific literacy:** Understands scientific concepts and processes
- **Economic literacy:** Has ability to make informed decisions based on evaluation of cost, benefits, and awareness of limitations of resources
- **Technological literacy:** Understands the nature of technological systems and is comfortable with their use

- **Visual literacy:** Appreciates and understands visual design, techniques of media and its emotional, psychological, and cognitive impacts; understands abstractions and symbolic images found in media

- **Information literacy:** Can ascertain what information is known and available and what is needed to solve problems; can identify, evaluate, and prioritize sources

- **Multicultural literacy:** Understands the value of diversity and knows how beliefs, values, and other forms of sensibilities affect thinking and responses to them; appreciates both similarity and differences found in society, culture, and life

- **Global literacy:** Understands the interconnectedness of all countries based on history and social and cultural characteristics, politics, technology, and linguistics; is able to analyze major social and cultural movements and trends, and to understand the relationships of governmental policies to global health

This report goes on to suggest the following important student behaviors that are needed for success:[24]

- **Inventive thinking:** Adaptability and managing complexity; self-direction; curiosity; creativity, risk taking, higher-order thinking, and sound reasoning

- **Effective communication:** Teaming and collaboration, interpersonal skills, personal responsibility, and interactive communication

- **High productivity:** prioritizing, planning, and managing for results; effective use of real-world tools; ability to produce relevant, high-quality products

Collection development in both school library media centers and public libraries can serve to meet these expectations. In terms of literacy, society as a whole expects schools and libraries to provide a wide range of cultural and social information and experiences. This expectation should help bridge the gap between these two important issues regarding cultural literacy. Library collections can provide both information and the contexts in which information and cultural diversity, pluralism, and information can be presented. Likewise, biographical materials in school library media collections can serve the school-based needs of students in that they offer abundant examples of persons and groups of people who present qualities worthy of emulation. Biographical materials can also help develop critical skills by offering wide examples of how people meet various challenges of life and solve problems.

INFORMATION LITERACY, CRITICAL THINKING, AND BIOGRAPHY

Information literacy has been highly promoted by the American Library Association, the American Association of School Librarians (AASL), and the

Association for Educational Communications and Technology (AECT) for a number of years. The concept is promoted by these organizations as well as by education and youth development groups. Information literacy as it relates to youth development was discussed in chapter 1, and its relationship to art is presented in chapter 8. AASL and AECT describe the information literate student as one who:

- Accesses information efficiently and effectively
- Evaluates information critically and competently
- Uses information accurately and creatively

The information literate student is an independent learner who pursues information related to personal interests, appreciates literature and other creative expressions of creativity, strives for excellence in information seeking and knowledge generation. The information literate student is one who is socially responsible, contributes to society, recognizes the importance of information in a democratic society, practices ethical behavior in regard to information and information technology, and participates effectively in groups to pursue and generate information.[25]

Over the last decade a number of approaches have been developed to help school library media specialists as well as teachers to help students meet these information literacy standards. Perhaps the best known of these is the Big6 model developed by Mike Eisenberg and Bob Berkowitz. The model has six major components:

1) Task definition
2) Information-seeking strategies
3) Location and access to information
4) Use of information
5) Synthesis
6) Evaluation and judgment

The process is explained fully on the Big6 website (http://big6.com).[26]

Critical thinking skills are an integrated part of information literacy. Diane Halpern in her book *Thought and Knowledge: An Introduction to Critical Thinking* (1996) defines *critical thinking* as

the use of those cognitive skills or strategies that increase the probability of a desirable outcome. It is used to describe thinking that is purposeful, reasoned and goal directed—the kind of thinking involved in solving problems, formulating inferences, calculating likelihoods, and making decisions when the thinker is using skills that are thoughtful and effective for the particular context and type of thinking task. Critical thinking also involves evaluating the thinking process—the reasoning that went into the conclusion we've arrived at the kinds of factors considered in making a decision. Critical thinking is sometimes called directed thinking because it focuses on a desired outcome.[27]

Biography is a natural alley to critical thinking and information literacy skills. When used correctly, each serves to advance students' learning, to enhance their critical awareness of the world and the heightening of their perceptions about the human experience.

EXAMPLES OF BIOGRAPHY IN INSTRUCTION

Biography has always been popular with teachers as an instructional resource and technique, and its helpful association with critical thinking and information literacy can hardly be debated. Following are examples of teaching units and strategies that teachers and educators in several English-speaking countries have developed that well illustrate this unique relationship between biography, critical thinking, information literacy, and learning. Internet sites that provide instructional suggestions and resources often related to biography include:

- Apple Learning Interchange, Teaching and Learning, Lesson Ideas, http://ali.apple.com/ali_sites/ali/li.php
- BBC LessonPlans "Schools Starship Teachers," www.bbc.co.uk/schools/ starship/teachers/lessonplans.shtml
- British Library—The World's Knowledge, Services: Learning, www.bl.uk/ services/learning/teachers.html
- Columbia Education Center (CEC) "CEC Lesson Plans," www. col-ed.org/ index.html
- Educator's Reference Desk[SM], www.eduref.org/Virtual/Lessons/ Social_Studies/ History/HIS0009.html
- Canada School Net, www.schoolnet.ca/home/e/; www.csun.edu/ ~hcedu013/GEM
- Gateway to Educational Materials, http://circle.adventist.org/browse/ resource.phtml?leaf = 1849
- College of Saint Benedict/St. John's University, "Educational Resources and Lesson Plans," www.cloudnet.com/%7Eedrbsass/edres.htm
- Library of Congress, The Learning Page, Lesson Plans, http://memory. loc.gov/learn/lessons/index.html
- Marty Levin's Lessons Plans and Resources for Social Sciences Teachers, www.csun.edu/~hcedu013/

- Microsoft Education, www.microsoft.com/Education/LessonPlans.aspx
- Pro Teacher Lesson Plan Collection, www.proteacher.com/ 020002.shtml
- Smithsonian Education Lesson Plans, www.smithsonianeducation.org/ educators/lesson_plans/lesson_plans.html
- Weekend Australian, Lesson Plans, www.theaustralian.news.com.au/ sectionindexb/0,6024,lessons%5E%5ETEXT,00.html

The following are examples of actual lesson plans widely available on the Internet from various sources:

Women in American History: An Educator's Reference Desk Lesson Plan. Submitted by: Kristine A. McIntosh Email: krismc@flash.net. School/ University/Affiliation: Southwest High School, Ft. Worth Tx; Date: April 6, 2000; grade levels: 8, 9, 10, 11; Subject(s):Social Studies/US History; Social Studies/Women's History; Duration: Five Class Periods. Lesson Plan AELP-USH0047. (www.eduref.org/Virtual/Lessons/Social_Studies/US_History/ USH0046.html).

Description: Study of many talented women in American history and the early struggle for women to receive the right to vote. Students read and discuss primary documents, research, and present their findings in written form, orally and artistically. Among others, women biographies to be studied include Elizabeth Cady Stanton, and Maria Tallchief. Suggested resources include Great American Women (www.greatamericanwomen.com) and National Women's Hall of Fame (www.greatwomen.org/home.php).

Portraiture and Technology: An Educator's Reference Desk Lesson Plan. Submitted by June McLeavey and Jimi Emery Email: bartlett@ncia.net, School/University/Affiliation: Josiah Bartlett School, Date: August 27, 1998. Grade Level(s): 6, 7, 8, 9. Subject(s): Arts/History Duration: Six 45-minute sessions (technology equipment dependent), Lesson Plan #: AELP-ARH0010. Available at www.eduref.org/Virtual/Lessons/Arts/Art_History/ ARH0010.html.

Description: Students investigate the importance of portraiture in art history with the help of technology. Students research and study portraits, symbolism used by artists, the life of selected artists, and create their own portrait images using scanner technology. Suggested resources include: Art History Theme Page (www.cln.org/themes/art_history.html), ArtSeek—Internet Art Resources (www.artseek.com/ArtSites/Sites.html) and Museums Index at World Wide Arts Resources (wwar.com/museums.html).

The Two-and-a-Half-Billion-Year-Old Man: A Webquest for Paul Erdös: An Educator's Reference Desk Lesson Plan. Submitted by: Bekir Gur. Email: bekir@cc.usu.edu. School/University/Affiliation: Utah State University / Instructional Technology. Date: April 30, 2003. Grade Level: 9, 10, 11, 12, Adult/Continuing Education. Subject(s): Mathematics/History,

Computer Science. Duration: 1 hour. Lesson Plan #: AELP-MAH0200. Available at http://www.eduref.org/Virtual/Lessons/Mathematics/History/ MAH0200.html.

Description: Based on a Webquest, this unit is designed to help students learn basic biographical information about Paul Erdös, one of the great mathematicians of the twentieth century.

Aristotle: Canada School Net Lesson Plan. Contributors: John J. O'Connor and Edmund F. Robertson Contact Information at joc@st-andrews.ac.uk, School of Mathematics and Statistics, University of St. Andrews, Scotland, Target Audience: Jurisdiction Canada, Province: All of Canada, International. Feb 28, 2001. Grade Range grades 7–13 (approx age 12–17), post-secondary (approx age 18+). Available at www.groups.dcs.stand.ac.uk/~history/ Mathematicians/Aristotle.html.

Description: This is a website that offers a biography of Aristotle as well as information about his contributions in the field of mathematics. Site includes pictures, text, links, and detailed information about the life and influence of Aristotle.

Mary Seacole: ICTeachers Resources (United Kingdom)
Area: History. (General, Ancient Civilisations, Anglo Saxons, Vikings and Normans, Tudors and Stuartism Hanoverians and Victorians, 20th Century). Available at www.icteachers.co.uk/resources/resources_history .htm#20th%20Century.

Description: Provides background information on Mary Seacole and other black people who lived in Britain and contributed to British history. No instructional or teaching approaches are provided.

Beethoven's Ninth Symphony: An Educator's Reference Desk Lesson Plan. Submitted by: Susan Haugland. Email: shaugland@beethoven.com School/University/Affiliation: Byron CUSD #226. Date: December 13, 2000. Grade Level: 7, 8, 9, 10, 11, 12. Subject(s): Arts/Music. Lesson Plan #: AELP-MUS0. Available at www.eduref.org/Virtual/Lessons/Arts/Music/ MUS0204.html.

Description: Provides ideas to accompany the book, *Three Weeks in Vienna*; students are encouraged to study about Ludwig van Beethoven and the premiere of his Ninth Symphony as well as his personality. Useful Internet Resource: "Three Weeks in Vienna—A Singer's Account of the Premiere of Beethoven's Ninth Symphony" containing online versions of the worksheets used for this lesson (www.Beethoven9th.com).

Numerous guides to library-focused lesson plans with biographical contexts are likewise available from many publishing companies including the American Library Association (www.ala.org/ala/ourassociation/publishing/ publishing1.htm); Greenwood Publishing Group (www.greenwood.com) and its member Libraries Unlimited (http://lu.com/); Linworth Publishing, Inc.

(www.linworth.com); Neal-Schuman (www.neal-schuman.com); and Scarecrow Press (part of the Rowman & Littlefield Publishing Group, Inc.) (www.scarecrowpress.com).

BIOGRAPHY IN THE CLASSROOM AND SCHOOL LIBRARY MEDIA CENTER

Collaboration of Library Media Center Specialists and Teachers

The AASL, in their important publication *Information Power: Building Partnerships for Learning* (1998), lists collaboration along with leadership and technology as one of the major elements that can contribute to student learning and achievement. Essentially collaboration is an equal partnership and relationship between school library media specialists and teachers where the librarian develops mechanisms (policies and practices) that make resources and facilities available to teachers. In addition, collaboration allows school library media specialists to become directly involved in the learning process by planning and presenting alongside teachers in the use of materials, resources, and teaching strategies. Ideally collaboration allows media specialists to be an integral part of the teaching and learning process within the school.[28] The popularity and familiarity of teachers with biographical materials and resources often provide avenues for school media specialists to initiate collaboration programs with teachers.

Field Research

A recent field study of library media specialists–teacher collaboration found that most teachers in the study felt that they benefited personally from a collaborative experience with their building library media specialists and that their students benefited from exposure to new resources and information approaches offered by the library media specialist. What seemed to be of most benefit to teachers was exposure to new resources—both print and technological—and the expertise that the library media specialist offered their students. Teachers noted that having a library media specialist assume some of the planning and presentations of instruction gave them more time for other important matters.

In this study focus groups that were involved in the study indicated that library media specialists offered information expertise, thus affecting their effectiveness as teachers. Data from the study seemed to indicate that learning about resources and having help from the library media specialist made them better teachers. Teachers saw how students benefited by new information literacy experiences, and they too appeared to have received both social and personal rewards from the collaboration experience. Teachers in the study felt that their building school library media specialists were very capable of collaborating with them, having expertise in resources as well as understanding the teaching process. From this study it appears that collaboration can be enhanced by library media specialists bringing ideas, concepts, and directions to teachers for consideration. Teachers also felt that a clearly stated policy regarding collaboration with librarians would be beneficial to them as they plan their units of study. Teachers realized that library media specialists are busy and that choices and selection of collaboration projects must be made. Routines for collaboration need to be established. Teachers, especially high school teachers, recognized and well understood this.[29]

Historically librarians have worked well with teachers in offering biographical materials to certain areas—literature study, history and other areas of the social sciences, music, and art. In terms of offering ideas and concepts regarding biography to teachers within a collaboration process, school library media specialists might look at areas that are not usually attentive to biographical materials. Based on an examination of curriculum guides and lesson plans available to teachers through Internet sources, certain areas seem particularly open to biographical resources. These include physical education, many of the areas of science and technology, mathematics, vocational and professional studies, and the critical study of popular culture as it relates to mass psychology and sociology.

Collaboration extends beyond the school. Networking and cooperating with the public libraries and other social agencies in the community offer excellent opportunities for mutually beneficial collaboration projects.

BIOGRAPHY IN PUBLIC LIBRARIES: ISSUES AND GOOD PRACTICES

As an educational institution in society, youth services in public libraries have long recognized their responsibilities to the public. We have abundant evidence of this from the late nineteenth and early twentieth centuries. Because school libraries were not well developed in those years, public libraries assumed much of the responsibility for seeing that students in schools, and youth in general, had access to books and cultural and educational enrichment through story hour, reference services, and curriculum materials support.[30] As school libraries became more numerous and better supported, public library services to youth tended to focus more on the needs of children and young adults outside school. In fact, library authority and critic Mary Kay Chelton stated that the public library had a different kind of educational role to play in the lives of youth than did schools.[31] On the other hand, sociologist Lawrence J. White wrote that if the public library was to survive well into the future, it must assume a more forceful role as an active educational agency in society. He especially felt that this educational role should be directed at children and young adults.[32]

Although the public library is not driven by the school curriculum, it does respond to its needs in terms of reference services, collection development, and Internet needs. In recent years the public library has acknowledged the needs expressed by home schooling and charter school developments.

Recent publications from the American Library Association have outlined how public libraries are an important part of the learning community and how they need to provide services that enhance learning and social awareness. Specifically these include promoting and providing:

- Literacy opportunities
- Independent learning opportunities for children and young adults
- Homework assistance and term paper clinics
- Support and help for youth in developing a strong sense of social responsibility
- Services to parents and families
- Services to infants and toddlers
- Reading advisement
- Information and technology literacy education
- Community awareness and participation
- Collaboration with other government and social agencies
- Outreach services as appropriate to the mission and goals of the library

These publications support the collaborative roles that school library media centers and public libraries must play in meeting their mutual goals and objectives.[33, 34]

Biography can play an essential part in helping to meet these goals and objectives. Obviously, collection development is important in that biography must be well represented in all collections. Biographical materials must meet interests, serve development needs, help with the development of social responsibility, advance literacy, and promote critical thinking.

Many programs and delivery formats can use biography. Biography falls easily into the traditional programs such as booktalks and story hours. Biography can be used in a variety of special programs such as family and parenting services, literacy, information technology instruction, programs and services for at-risk youth, vocational and career services, and recreation programs. Biography can also be used to help promote critical thinking and encourage a more discerning view of mass culture and mass social movements.

Sports biography is a good genre to use as a model to illustrate how biography as a whole can be used in a variety of public library programs. For most people sports have elements that offer entertainment as well as information.

Biography can also be used to provide information about personal values and relationships that are found in modern sports. Similarly, biography can be used to alert youth to what is needed to succeed in today's competitive and demanding world of sports. For older youth, sports biographies can also be used to help develop critical thinking skills relating to the power of sports in culture and society. Because many sports biographies are published as series, youth can be encouraged to develop a critical eye as to how these biographies are crafted, commercialized, and promoted by publishers. Reading clubs, book discussion groups, and viewing experiences can be used to promote this sort of dialogue. Sports biography lends itself to attractive displays, public promotion, and activities such as games and personal appearances of sports figures.[35]

Sports programs emphasizing biographies of interest to males and females can be developed whereby not only are books featured, but actually athletes from the local community can share their experiences in programs. Collectors of sports biographical memorabilia can be identified and invited to participate in programs.[36]

As mentioned, the biographical model or format can be configured to accommodate a variety of situations such as history, travel, science, technology, invention, civic leaders, artists, performers, people in various professions and vocations, and ordinary people who have met and experienced unusual challenges and adventures.

CONCLUSION

In recent decades, the nature of the school curriculum has concerned parents, students, politicians, and others. We see this reflected in numerous statements and directives coming from professional and academic associations and academies. We see this in debates about values and cultural elements to be incorporated into curriculum. We certainly see this in the attention that many, if not all, governments give to the proper construction of curriculum, to how students are taught, to how student achieve, and to requirements for accountability of all who are involved in teaching and learning.

Not only are we as members of society concerned about academic skills, but we have identified and debated various values and literacies to be passed on to youth through formal curriculum, ranging from scientific and technological literacy to cultural literacy.

These literacy movements have impacted both school library media centers and public libraries. Curriculum needs drive the programs, services, and collections of the school library media center, and the educational role of the public library is likewise affected by curriculum directives.

Biography is rich in revealing the diversity of human experiences. Because of this, it has a home in most, if not all, educational concerns of the twenty-first century.

NOTES

1. International Association for the Advancement of Curriculum Studies, "Mission," http://iaacs.levinux.org/mod.php?mod=userpage&page_id=2 (accessed Jan. 5, 2005).

2. "Office of Education Library—Early Years," http://www.ed.gov/NLE/histearly.html (accessed Jan. 5, 2005).

3. U.S. Government Manual, "Department of Education," http://frwebgate1. access.gpo.gov/cgi-bin/waisgate.cgi?WAISdocID=950038315251+1+2+0& WAISaction=retrieve (accessed Jan. 5, 2005).

4. U.S. Department of Education, "Elementary & Secondary Education Part A— Improving Basic Programs Operated by Local Education Agencies," http://www.ed.gov/ policy/elsec/leg/esea02/pg2.html (accessed Jan. 5, 2005).

5. Education World, "National and State Standards," http://www.education-world.com/ standards (accessed Jan. 14, 2005).

6. Education World.

7. Canada Online, "Canadian Documents and Policy for Canadian Elementary and Secondary Education, by Province and Territory in Canada," http://canadaonline. about.com/cs/curricbyprovince/index.htm (accessed Dec. 6, 2005).

8. Canada Online, "Lesson Plan K-8 for Canadian Teachers," http://canadaonline. about.com/od/lessonplansk8/ (accessed Dec. 6, 2005).

9. Australian Government, Office of Education, Science, and Training, "Australian Qualifications Framework," http://aei.dest.gov.au/AEI/QualificationsRecognition/ CountryEducationProfiles/CEP_Aus_EdSys.htm, and http://studyinaustralia.gov.au/ Sia/en/WhyAustralia/AQF.htm (accessed Jan. 12, 2005).

10. Australian Government, "Our 2002 Corporate Plan. Our Goals," http://www. dest.gov.au/portfolio_department/dest_information/corporate_plans_policies/dest_2002_ corporate_plan.htm#Our_goals (accessed Nov. 2, 2005).

11. Australian Government, "National Goals for Schooling in the Twenty-first Century," http://www.dest.gov.au/sectors/school_education/policy_initiatives_reviews/ national_goals_for_schooling_in_the_twenty_first_century.htm (accessed Nov. 2, 2005).

12. "About the National Curriculum. What Is the National Curriculum of England?" http://www.nc.uk.net/nc_resources/html/about_NC.shtml (accessed Nov. 2, 2005).

13. "School Exams," http://www.britishcouncil.org/saudiarabia-education-school_ examinations.htm (accessed Jan. 12, 2005).

14. National Curriculum Online, "About the National Curriculum," http://www.nc.uk.net/ nc_resources/html/about_NC.shtml (accessed Jan. 5, 2005); http://www.nc.uk.net/ webdav/servlet/XRM?Page/@id=6007 (accessed Nov. 2, 2005).

15. National Curriculum Online.

16. W. Bernard Lukenbill, *Collection Development for a New Century in the School Library Media Center* (Westport, Conn.: Greenwood Press, 2002), 35, citing Gertrude Himmelfarb, *One Nation, Two Cultures* (New York: Alfred A. Knopf, 1999).

17. Focus on the Family, "Our Guiding Principles," http://www.family.org/welcome/ aboutfof/a0000078.cfm (accessed Jan. 12, 2005).

18. Character Education Partnership, "Eleven Principles of Effective Character Education. Principle 2. Defines Character," http://www.character.org/site/c.gwKUJhNYJrF/ b.993779/k.1637/Principle_2.htm (accessed Nov. 2, 2005).

19. Utah State Office of Education, "Character Education. Utah's Project in Character Education," http://www.usoe.k12.ut.us/curr/char_ed/fed_proj/utah.html (accessed Jan. 12, 2005).

20. Utah State Office of Education, "Character Education," http://www.usoe.k12.ut.us/ curr/char_ed/default.htm (accessed Jan. 13, 2005).

21. National Curriculum Online, "Statement of Values by the National Forum for Values in Education and Community," http://www.nc.uk.net/nc_resources/html/values.shtml (accessed Jan. 14, 2005).

22. "The Cultural Debate in the U.S.: Whose Culture Is This, Anyway?" http://www.wsu.edu:8001/vcwsu/commons/topics/culture/culture-definitions/whose-text.html (accessed Dec. 15, 2005).

23. North Central Regional Educational Laboratory, *21st Century Skills: Literacy in the Digital Age* (Eugene, Ore.: The Laboratory, 2003), http://www.ncrel.org/engauge/skills/skills.htm and http://www.ncrel.org/engauge/skills/skills21 (accessed Jan. 15, 2005).

24. North Central Regional Educational Laboratory.

25. American Association of School Librarians and Association for Educational Communications and Technology, *Information Power: Building Partnerships for Learning* (Chicago: American Library Association, 1998), 8–9.

26. W. Bernard Lukenbill, *Community Resources in the School Library Media Center: Concepts and Methods* (Westport, Conn.: Libraries Unlimited, 2004), 109–10.

27. Longview Community College, "Critical Thinking across the Curriculum Project— Critical Thinking Definitions," citing Diane Halpern, *Thought and Knowledge: An Introduction to Critical Thinking,* 3rd ed. (Mahwah, N.J.: Lawrence Erlbaum Associates, 1996), http://www.kcmetro.cc.mo.us/longview/ctac/definitions.htm (accessed Jan. 18, 2005).

28. American Association of School Librarians, *Information Power,* 47–57, 90.

29. Barbara Immroth and Bernard Lukenbill, "Promoting Information Literacy & Teacher–Librarian Collaboration through Social Marketing Strategies," Professional Development Grant. Final Narrative Report, Institute for Library and Information Literacy Education (ILILE), Kent State University, 2004.

30. Laura. M. Janzow, comp., *The Library without the Wall: Reprints of Papers and Addresses* (New York: H. W. Wilson, 1927), 311–12, 339.

31. Mary Kay Chelton, "The Educational and Recreational Services of the Public Library for Young Adults," *Library Quarterly* 48 (Oct. 1978): 496.

32. Lawrence J. White, *The Public Library in the 1980s: The Problems of Choice* (Lexington, Mass.: Lexington Books, 1983).

33. Virginia A. Walter, *Children & Libraries: Getting It Right* (Chicago: American Library Association, 2001).

34. Young Adult Library Services Association, *New Directions for Library Service to Young Adults,* with Patrick Jones, edited by Linda Waddle (Chicago: American Library Association, 2002).

35. Michael Sullivan, *Connecting Boys with Books: What Libraries Can Do* (Chicago: American Library Association, 2003), 29–34.

36. Sullivan, 34–35.

3

BIOGRAPHY FOR THE VERY YOUNG

INTRODUCTION

Biography plays an important role in the lives of young children. This chapter looks at how biography can best be used with young children, preschool to fourth grade (ages eight or nine). It first considers autobiography as self-expression in the young, then it considers developmental needs that biography might help address. From there, the chapter moves into a discussion of some major issues we face when attempting to provide good biography for very young children. Included here are: learning how to select and evaluate biography, social behavior issues that biography might influence, major values found in biography, problems in creating good biography for the very young, selection of biographical materials, issues with publishers who provide biographical materials, the history and role of mass media in offering biography to the young, and quality television and radio biography for children. This chapter also includes issues related to how to present biography to young children, including reader's advisory services, bibliotherapy, storytelling and story hour, creative dramatics, theater, and booktalks.

AUTOBIOGRAPHICAL EXPRESSION IN YOUNG CHILDREN

Educators and psychologists are now showing interest in learning how young children use autobiographical concepts about their own lives that might prove helpful for them in mastering a number of developmental tasks. These include development of language and memory skills, which supports the ability to acquire knowledge and to recall it, thus leading to self improvement.[1] Autobiographic concepts likewise lay the foundation for the acceptance and use of biography as a literary form in later years.[2]

Autobiography in very young children is the oral exchange between the child and those that are closely associated with him or her. Parents, relatives, caregivers, and other children are all parties to these exchanges as they help construct the child's autobiography. In fact, toddlers talk about and share experiences with others. Talking about past experiences often begins at sixteen months of age.

Autobiographies of the very young are shared reminiscences with a select and limited community of family and friends. They help inform memory and help the young child place events into a coherent pattern so that they can be remembered and information recalled. Autobiographical sharing helps the young child understand effective talk in their families and cultural groups. Furthermore, autobiographical expression is important to a child's development as it helps form and enhances intimacy, collaboration, and the sharing of common experiences.[3]

As youth grow older and enter school, their autobiographical expressions change. As it moves from an oral expression to the written, it tends to conform to rules and the expectations of formal writing. In some ways, this is at the expense of directness and expressiveness, and the linkage between motivation and form. Consequently, the inventive use of language and style is lost or lessened and the overall autobiographical expression becomes more correct and conventional. As youth move into secondary education, their autobiographies seem to lose their sense of flare and the use of style, form, and language that in earlier years so deeply described their personal lives. For older children, many of the ways in which they previously expressed their unique personages is lost except in "the narratives of a talented few."[4]

Nevertheless, autobiographical expression as used by young children helps prepare them to enjoy biography in later years. Autobiography used by the very young incorporates literary devices that are easily transferred into a better appreciation of formal biography, such as helping them understand the elements of story. Based on these literary elements, by the time children are asked to construct a formal autobiography in school, they can reconstruct their own lives.[5] From there, they are also ready to appreciate learning about the lives of others.

DEVELOPMENTAL NEEDS

Chapter 1 discussed briefly some important developmental needs of children. Information on the developmental needs is abundant, and there is no need to go into excessive detail here.

Lilian Katz outlines some basic needs that all children have, regardless of their social background. These include the need to develop trust, security, and a feeling of being competent. They need to acquire knowledge and skills; they need to develop reasoning and problem-solving abilities. They certainly need to be creative and to develop physically. Socially, they must learn to share experiences and to associate with other children and adults. Katz goes on to say that children need to grow to trust themselves and others.[6]

Children also must feel secure in their environment and, as they grow older, they must feel secure enough to venture out from the home. A secure environment allows for comfort and support and gives young children permission to be themselves, to explore, to consider options, to make mistakes, to accept consequences of mistakes yet still maintain a sense of personal empowerment. A secure environment permits easier adjustment to new situations as they arise. A secure environment likewise permits the sharing of experiences while still maintaining the important sense of being a unique, competent individual.[7]

For healthy development, young children must feel free of guilt and uncertainty, and they must be allowed to develop at their own pace. They need to be accepted, affirmed, and loved, and to be confident in that love. They must have a sense of self that says, "I can learn."

Katz reminds us that caregivers such as teachers, parents, and librarians

> should plan an environment in which children can try new ideas and skills, and apply what they have learned. They need to accept and value each child. It is necessary to make provision for each child to grow and flourish at her or his own rate and pace in a safe, supportive environment where the child feels some ownership and empowerment.[8]

Although all of these developments are important, in terms of using biographies with young children it appears that two—moral development and creativity—stand out because they so easily encompass others. Moral development incorporates reasoning, the ability to consider information and to make decisions, and to develop trust in others and the group.[9] From a social perspective, moral development in children is important in a world that is becoming more complex, where traditional values are often subject to review and questioning. Moral and social values and how these are defined have become political in some countries, including the United States, and these arguments are affecting curriculum design and the production and publishing of materials for youth.

Our basic understanding of how young people develop moral understanding is largely through the works of Piaget and Kohlberg. Overviews of these two scholars' works are available in *A Piaget Primer: How a Child Thinks* by Dorothy G. Singer and Tracey A. Revenson (Plume Books, 1996) and *Moral Reasoning: A Teaching Handbook for Adapting Kohlberg to the Classroom* by Ronald E. Galbraith and Thomas E. Jones (Greenhaven Press, 1976). Piaget's approach was to present moral dilemmas to children through playing games and questioning them regarding how they might respond to these issues. He found that young children differ from older children in how they view moral questions. The child's cognitive development and informal interactions with other children determine much of what they consider right or wrong. Young children do not describe moral reasoning in detail because such concepts lie beyond the grasp of most young children.[10]

Kolhberg wrote that young children at the basic level of moral reasoning, which he called "preconventional thought," arrive at moral decision based on avoiding punishing and satisfying one's immediate desire. Moral thought is very egocentric, and not reasoned out. Conventional thought, the intermediate stage of his moral hierarchy, is characterized by young children thinking in terms of pleasing others and doing what is helpful. They want to be good boys and girls and to help the group. Although most preschool children are not at the conventional level of reasoning, they can be exposed to moral thinking that will help them reach this stage.[11]

Within democratic societies, certain moral values persist and are necessary for a just society, and children as young as three years of age can understand some of these basic moral concepts. Social psychologists advise that when we consider moral values as applied to young children, we sometimes confuse moral values and conventional conduct. Conventional conduct refers to the rules governing good behavior such as classroom rules. For children this might be hanging up one's coat, sitting correctly in a chair, and observing rules relating to access to the playground. Generally, these involve very few moral issues. On the other hand, moral values relate to a higher order of behavior such as understanding basic concepts of justice, fairness, and human rights. We are told that when conventional rules are broken, there is little to do but explain what the rules are and that they must be obeyed for the good of the group. When moral rules are broken, a more direct intervention is necessary whereby the teacher, parent, or caregiver must carefully explain to the child what they mean so that he or she can better understand the importance of fairness and justice.[12]

Research indicates the male and female children see moral values differently, but these values are not inferior to each other. When faced with moral dilemmas, young male children seem to place more values on justice while females give more importance to caring and maintaining relationships.[13]

BIOGRAPHY AND MORAL DEVELOPMENT

There are several ways that biography can contribute to moral development. As we have seen, learning to use reason and logical thinking is important for the young child, and biography offers information about social convention and social issues. Biography can be used as a frame-of-reference to help children understand wrong actions, how to right wrongs, and how to use reason to judge appropriate consequences and/or punishments for wrong behaviors. Discussion of moral dilemmas from biographical literature can also help children understand moral conflicts. Reading biography and talking about how people make mistakes and how they come to terms with those mistakes helps children understand that we as individuals are not consistently good or bad.

Biography presented in various ways can help young children in their moral development. Questioning, dramatic play, creative dramatics, and role play are useful tools. After reading a biography, asking children questions about how they would feel if they were in that "person's shoes" allows the children to develop perspectives about other people's lives. Biography can be used in creative dramatics and role plays whereby a biography can be read to children, questions posed, and then children are asked to act out something about the biographical characters. For example, decide to give a birthday party for Abraham Lincoln as a young man in Illinois, and ask the children to plan and reenact the party as they would imagine Lincoln would have wanted.

Understanding intention and motivation is important in moral development. Biographies can be used here as well. Read an appropriate biography and discuss the characters' reasons and intentions for taking certain actions. Puppets can often be used to help visualize and re-create these situations.

Biography can also be used to celebrate moral behaviors by pointing out how the characters in biography helped others, how they saw the needs of others and took action, and how they often put the needs of others before their own. Biography can provide good models for children by asking how they can emulate admired characters' traits in biography such as kindness, fairness, and helpfulness. As young children mature, real moral dilemmas faced by characters in biography can be discussed. Such dilemmas are often found in the current mass media or news; but these dilemmas need to be concrete and not abstract situations or maxims.

BIOGRAPHY AND CREATIVITY

The need to develop creativity in the young is an important educational goal in most modern, Western societies. In the West, creativity is often viewed as allied with individualism.

There is some debate as to what fosters creativity. Some social observers contend that the way a society is constructed plays an important part in fostering creativity. Does a particular society value uniqueness and striving for the new? Does the society reward those who are creative? What types of creativity are expected and rewarded? Some believe that a society that is too controlled by dogmatic religion or governmental theories that emphasize allegiances to a social theory such as communism will hamper creativity. Others believe that economic conditions are better predictors of creativity in society. If a society is always at the brink of poverty and starvation, then that society is not likely to have the human energy or resources to offer much in the way of creativity. Closely aligned with this is the idea that a society must be safe from outside attack, so that its people do not need to be in fear of destruction.

William Duff in the seventeenth century hypothesized that human creativity was the product of many influences including heredity, society, biology, and psychology. By the twentieth century, scientific research had generally concluded that creativity was a biopsychosocial process just as Duff had suggested.[14] Today educational theories hold that although some elements of creativity are biologically based, the environment can be manipulated to promote creativity.

In the school environment, peers play a role in fostering creativity as do teachers. Research evidence suggests that creativity is promoted when creative children are taught in homogeneous ability or creativity groupings. Research suggests that creativity can be limited or redirected by peer pressure. Teacher behaviors also play a role in creativity. Some research indicates that teachers who are perceived as likeable, encouraging, interested in children, enthusiastic, courteous, business-like, and professional tend to produce classes that are more creative. Other research has shown that some teachers can sometimes disfavor creative children in the classroom. They can view creative children as worrisome and hard to control. Such teachers do not generally appreciate the playfulness, humor, and independence often found in creative children. Teachers that permit a more open classroom over a more traditional one often produce more creative children.[15] Flexibility of space, materials, resources, and the use of small group work, independent reading, critical inquiry, curiosity, exploration, and self-directedness also promote creativity. The lessening of the authoritarian approach to teaching and grading is also a factor in promoting creativity.

Several factors come to mind when we consider creativity in terms of biographical materials for young children. Studies show that cultural diversity within a society promotes creativity. The creation of biographies for children of people from various cultural, social, sexual, and national backgrounds has greatly increased since the 1960s and 1970s, encouraged by the cultural reconfiguration wrought by those eras in many Western societies.

Civil disturbances akin to those of the 1960s and 1970s often encourage creativity. Creativity is often encouraged if those disturbances are directed at states and governments and the perceived inequalities promoted by governments. Biographies written for children about and by persons who challenged governmental policies and institutions based on civil and human rights offer great examples of people who are creative and raise significant moral questions. Nobel Peace Laureates Martin Luther King Jr. in the United States and Nelson Mandela in South Africa inspired and continue to inspire creative works from people around the world.

The rise of political national states and national identities also encourage creativity. Creative energies are often released when nations in their search for identities and special symbols ask and permit citizens to become involved in this national identity process. National heroes and governing philosophies and documents that support a nation's ideas of government are sought out, identified, and promoted as a means of telling the world how unique the nation is among other nations.[16] Biographies for young children often focus on national heroes as a part of this national process. For example, Carol M. and John W. Butzow examined how, through the depiction of American heroes in selected picture books for children, American heroes have influenced American history, life, attitudes and culture.[17] Chapters 6, 7, and 8 discuss these phenomena in more detail.

Role Models, Biography, and Creativity

Families can offer excellent role models and sources for creativity. Again, research has shown that creative parents and grandparents can have a positive influence on their children and grandchildren. Within families, creative generations appear to generate later generations of creative individuals. Of course, this is reinforced by an individual's "creative precociousness."[18]

Models for Observation

Consequently, the more creative models children have opportunity to observe within the home and school, the more likely they are to be creative. Conversely research has shown that if children follow too closely models available to them in the immediate environment, their creativity can be lessened.[19]

Nevertheless, biography of family members as well as biographies of other people who are creative can serve as models. Biographies of artists, musicians, scientists, inventors, explorers, teachers, sports champions, civil rights activists, and others offer an abundance of biographical models.

SCAFFOLDING: LEARNING FROM BIOGRAPHY

Biography promotes learning in so many areas—history, psychology, social life, customs, and multiculturalism. It has always been one of the mainstays of curriculum and instruction. Nevertheless, it must be presented to young children in ways that they can accept and learn from. Scaffolding as a teaching-learning process offers this.[20]

What is scaffolding? In the mid-1970s researchers began to look at the interactions between parents and their children in terms of how parents promoted learning. Underlying this was Russian-born theorist Lev Vygotsky's social/cognitive theory that offered a means of explaining and studying how children learn. (See chapter 4.) This theory helped forge a relationship between learning and teaching, and as stated, it provided a theoretical framework of scaffolding.[21]

Scaffolding as a term was coined by theorists Wood, Bruner, and Ross in 1976 as a means of describing the playful interaction of parents and their children as parents helped their young children learn tasks that would not be possible in terms of the child's cognitive abilities without parental help.[22] It is also described as a process whereby the teacher or parent interacts with a child or with children as they move toward independence. Using an analogy from the building trade, it means that parents and other caregivers build a scaffold whereby the child is helped to reach a certain point in learning. When that stage is met, the scaffold is removed or built a little higher so the child can then proceed on to the next stage of learning. This process is different than that used in the traditional classroom where the teacher asks, "What can children do independently?" or "What can they do on their own?" Scaffolding asks, "What can the child do with assistance?"[23] Teachers must build a logical framework for the progression of skills.

Biography seems to be a natural ally in scaffolding. Scaffolding is based on careful observation of children, and it responds to what the teacher or parent sees the child trying to do. Because learning is so rapid in most young children, scaffolding must be based on what the child is doing today, not yesterday. Scaffolding when applied to biography with young children is based on providing the right biographies for children when and where they need them.[24]

When the objective is to promote reading, authorities Adrian and Emily Rodgers advise that the book should not be too easy, but should be challenging enough to promote the principles of scaffolding. In other words, the book must be challenging enough to generate errors in reading. Errors then act as a means of promoting self-correction. Some errors must be present in the learning process to permit scaffolding to occur. But it must not be too difficult, thus leading to frustration.[25]

Selection of biography for young children requires the same type of care. Although the task of reading biography text is important, biography also offers opportunities to explore. If the biography is to be read as a means of teaching reading, it must be based on literacy strategies;[26] if biography is presented to enhance other social and cultural needs, it too must be presented in ways that offer means of discussion and reflection with guidance from teachers and other caregivers.

State-mandated knowledge and skills tests, such as the Texas Assessment of Knowledge and Skills (TAKS) program, provide some direction as to how biography can be integrated into learning expectations.[27] Using the TAKS tests as an example, biography used with young children can help connect experiences and ideas with others who have encountered similar situations. Biography helps young children reflect on their own family traditions and histories (often oral histories) that connect with customs, regions, and cultures often revealed in biography. Biography can also promote interpretation through discussion and writing using speculating, questioning, and reflection as process. Biography can be used to promote cultural and social understanding through music, art, and drama.[28] Without doubt, biography can certainly help in discovering new knowledge and increase the learning of facts and skills.

In addition to using biography as a way to encourage speculation, questions, and reflection, biography can serve as an avenue to writing as it can act as a model for the recording of ideas and reflections. As a support for writing, biography can help refine ideas and help produce written documents based on biographical concepts.[29]

George Washington's Teeth, by Deborah Chandra and Madeleine Comora, with illustrations by Brock Cole (Farrar, Straus and Giroux, 2003) offers some examples of how biography can be used in scaffolding. A reviewer in *Publishers Weekly* wrote:[30]

> Chandra and Comora string together spry stanzas describing the dental difficulties that plagued George Washington. Rhyming verse explains how the general's rotten teeth gradually fall out during the Revolutionary War: "George crossed the icy Delaware/ With nine teeth in his mouth./ In that cold and pitchy dark,/ Two more teeth came out!" Cole complements this verse by rendering a sly watercolor twist on Emanuel Leutze's famous painting George Washington Crossing the Delaware, in a full-spread treatment: Washington still stands in quiet dignity, but the boatmen are grinning. By the time Washington is elected president, just two teeth remain in his mouth. Kids will love the details, such as the way Washington uses a pair of his molars to fashion a mold from which the dentist makes a set of dentures. [carved from hippopotamus ivory and shown in a photograph in the afterword]

First of all, learning is social, and the sharing of this story with others, either individually or in a group, is a social occasion. Talking about Washington and his teeth promotes dialogue with interaction and expression (play, drama, writing, painting, conversation). Although based on history, *George Washington's Teeth* offers a sense of common identity with self and home (e.g., everyone has issues with tooth care) and can help build a sense of reality while still learning facts of history. It is also an entertaining way to introduce children to life narratives and the idea of a life unfolding over time. In this biography, the child and teacher or other caregivers can engage in a dialogue about history that provides true facts and at the same time challenges children through scaffolding to look at facts as opposed to lore (e.g., Washington's false teeth were not made of wood). The young child also can be asked to consider how lore develops, the reasons for such lore, and how the historical record can correct such mistakes.[31]

Another book that offers biographical information appropriate for scaffolding experiences is *Barrio: José's Neighborhood,* by George Ancona (Harcourt Paperbacks, 1998) (grades 1–4). A review by Dina Sherman,

Brooklyn Children's Museum, New York, from *School Library Journal* describes this photo essay as focusing on

> the neighborhood of a young boy in San Francisco. Through text and photographs, Ancona takes readers on a tour of Jose's mostly Latino community known as El barrio and introduces them to various shops and foods as well as to the many customs that are part of his daily life. Celebrations including Carnaval, Day of the Dead, Halloween, and the boy's birthday party are described. Some difficult issues are touched on: illegal immigration, the problem of gangs, and even AIDS as a teacher is remembered at school. Ancona's trademark photographs are clear and bright and beautifully capture the many flavors and colors of the barrio. The text is sprinkled with Spanish words that are defined in the glossary. This title successfully captures images of a particular place as seen through the eyes of a child.[32]

Scaffolding opportunities here exist in terms of encouraging children to discuss and reflect on immigration, gangs, AIDS, and the role of cultural traditions and celebrations, and neighborhoods and family life in urban environments.

LEARNING, BIOGRAPHY, AND THE MASS MEDIA

In the 1950s, as television was making its way into homes, promoters of the new media used its ability to disseminate educational and positive cultural values to children as one means of ensuring its acceptance by the public. Nevertheless, programming for children had not changed much from what had been heard on radio. Action-adventure, westerns, old movies, animal shows such as *Lassie*, and cartoons became standard fare for television. With the advent of cable television in the 1980s, this type of programming changed somewhat. Cable networks such as Nickelodeon and Disney emerged and devoted most of their programming to children. Similarly other cable networks such as Discovery, the Learning Channel, USA, TBS, the Family Channel, and Lifetime offered children's programs. Their formats consisted of game shows, puppetry, magazine-format news presentations, live-action drama, and children's films. Magazine and news formats using by many of these programs often presented biographical features.[33] Special programming frequently featured biography or suggested biographical contexts. For example, in 2005 Nickelodeon offered "The Brothers Garcia," which it described as:

> When the kids outnumber the parents, you know your family's in for some nutty times. And when three of those kids are the boisterous Brothers Garcia, you can bet things are nutty MOST of the time! Larry, George, Carlos, Larry's twin sister Lorena and their parents are a close-knit Hispanic-American family who live in San Antonio, Texas. Told from the

point of view of the youngest brother, Larry, the show is a quirky comedy about the sometimes wacky, but always welcoming world of the Garcias.[34]

Disney has also produced biography-inspired films such as *Pocahontas* (Disney Gold Classic Collection, 1995). Dough Thomas, a reviewer, wrote:

Calling it "historical" is a stretch, but Disney created a very natural look at the two cultures. The Native American characters are handled especially well, and kids should be intrigued by their world; the movie is a far different lesson from the one their parents and grandparents learned. Disney has discovered a few things, though: you don't have to kill to solve your problems, and you can end the film without a happily-ever-after, illustrated by a touching final visual. [ages 5 and older][35]

Over the years the Peabody Award has recognized excellence in children's television programs. Although the awards do not always feature biography for very young children, since 1990 a number of awards for children's programming have gone to informational or educational programs that have biographical content.[36] These include *Captain Kangaroo*, 1957 and 1972; *Big Blue Marble*, 1975; *3-2-1 Contact Extra: I Have AIDS: A Teenager's Story*, 1988; *Children's Express NEWSMAGAZINE: Campaign '88*, 1988; Fox Children's Network: *1993 Public Service Campaign*, 1993; and *Ann Frank*, 2001.[37] The Children's Television Workshop is also recognized for its high quality children's programs, many of which have featured biographical information. These include *The Electronic Company, Encyclopedia, Nick News, Mr. Rogers' Neighborhood*, and *Sesame Street. Sesame Street* is generally credited with revolutionizing children's programming in the United States and elsewhere.[38]

Better children's programming has always seriously considered how children learn and process information. *Sesame Street* is a fine example of this child-centered approach. Research has shown that these shows can teach skills and educational concepts such as reading and math skills. Children's programming can also enhance children's pro-social behaviors and values including self-control, tolerance, helpfulness, sharing, and acceptance of differences. *Mr. Rogers' Neighborhood* is the classic example of pro-social programming.[39]

Although these attributes are present in television, in terms of cognitive development, children may not always be ready to understand their meanings. Viewing television, even programs intended for children, requires a set of complex tools. These include, among others, selective attention to events, perception of events and how those events are organized, the making of inferences, the separating of major events from secondary, comprehending sequence of events, and understanding inferences and causations. In fact, story comprehension skills so necessary for biography, such as understanding points of view and comprehending flashback or reflections, are generally not well mastered until about age ten.[40] Caregivers who use biography with young children must clearly understand these limitations and develop ways of addressing these in cognitively appropriate ways.

Children's periodicals are also avenues for biographical information. Although not as popular as they were during the nineteenth century, good quality periodicals are still being published and offer biographical information for the young child. Among these are *American Girl* (ages 8 and up); *Boy's Life* (ages 7–17); *Boy's Quest* (elementary ages); *Chickadee* (ages 6–9); *Cobblestone* (ages 9 and above); *Discovery Girls* (ages 7–12); *Disney Adventures* (elementary and middle school grades); *Faces* (ages 9 and above); *Kids Discover* (ages 6–12); *Nickelodeon* (ages 6–14); *Ranger Rick* (ages 7 and up); *Sesame Street Magazine* (ages 2–5); *Spider* (ages 6–9); *Sports Illustrated for Kids* (ages 8 and up); and *Your Big Backyard* (ages 3–7). *Children's Magazine Guide* (Greenwood Publishing Group) provides indexing to sixty-five popular magazines including those just mentioned as well as the "Biography Today" series (Omnigraphics, Inc.). The *Guide*'s website provides links to reviews and descriptive information for most of the magazines that it indexes (www.childrensmag.com/MagIndexed.html). The *Guide* now offers an online subscription (as of the fall of 2005). As with biography found in television and other forms of mass media, biographical materials in these periodicals must be designed with the developmental stage of their readers in mind.

SOCIAL BEHAVIOR, VALUES, AND BIOGRAPHY

Biography has also been a vehicle for conveying social values and expectations to the young with the hope that the information will influence in positive ways the lives and behavior of children. Chapter 7 looks in some depth at how a nation needs and creates its own national biography, encasing within that biography honored, national values.

Kyoon Kwon studied the biographies read by children in Knoxville, Tennessee, in the early to mid-1980s and found that the values contained in a selection of those biographies centered around being capable, ambitious, helpful, courageous, cheerful; having self-control; exhibiting a sense of accomplishment; being socially recognized; having a comfortable life; being secure within a family; leading an exciting life; and being happy. Values that were rarely covered in the selection of books read included exhibiting wisdom and being obedient, honest, clean, logical, broadened, and forgiving.[41] Social observer Christine Duthie believes and demonstrates in her writing that biography for young children can be used effectively in helping children focus on values associated with social issues and human experiences, values with historical significance, and values relating to current social concerns.[42]

Values from the lives of heroes are the focus of Vera Frye's *Learning from Heroes* (Volume 1). She believes that the positive characteristics of heroes can inspire children to emulate those character traits. In her work with children, she uses personalities such as Bill Cosby and Abraham Lincoln as examples. She suggests that such heroes can help to develop a sense of caring, civic virtue, courage, concern for the environment, honesty, peaceful living, respect for others, and responsibility.[43]

The positive impact of biography on behavior has often been assumed, but we have very little research data to support this. Bibliotherapy is one way to test this assumption. Bibliotherapy has been used rather extensively to test the effects of reading of fiction on behavior and attitudes, but its use with biography appears to be limited. Using biography in conjunction with developmental bibliotherapy appears to be the most logical form of reading-based therapy for school library media specialists and public youth librarians to use.

[D]evelopmental bibliotherapy uses imaginative and educative (did active) literature with people who are viewed as being normal. The development process is designed to help people maintain good mental health and to promote self-actualization and normal development. Developmental bibliotherapy can be conducted by knowledgeable people in the helping professions such as teachers, nurses, and librarians.[44]

Researcher Dewayne Green studied the effect of bibliotherapy on the self-concepts of Mexican American children. Although biography was not the immediate focus on his study, he did note that several bibliotherapeutic approaches did improve children's feelings about self-concepts, feelings of happiness and satisfaction, perceptions of their popularity, and their feelings about their physical appearance and attributes. He concluded that teachers, along with others, can cooperate in developing effective bibliotherapy programs.[45] Although his study involved children ten and eleven years old, this approach needs further testing using biography-based bibliotherapy with younger children.

SELECTION OF MATERIALS

Charlotte S. Huck and her colleagues provide some basic guidance for the selection of biography for children, many of which apply directly to biographies for young children. Among others, they state that the biographies must have an appeal and interest to young children today; and that biographies help children understand their own lives. The biography must in some way help children understand both the past and the present; it must be accurate and authentic; and if fiction is used, it must add to the story in a truthful way. The authors should provide notes and bibliographies appropriate to the age and audience for which the biography is written. They caution that serious omissions and distortions of facts and personality traits must be avoided.

In terms of how a character is presented, they ask that the true character of the individual be drawn and that hero worship be avoided. They suggest, rightly so, that biographies must have an overriding theme, but the theme must not be oversimplified and manipulated.

Picture books are essential if young children are to have access to good biography.[46] Pictures can help create character, refine historical settings, underscore historical realities, and encourage aesthetic appreciation through fine artwork. Without question, illustrations in biographies for young children "carry a substantial part of the interpretation."[47]

In an essay in *The Horn Book*, critic Betty Carter reflects on some of the major concerns just mentioned and reminds us that although biography is often tied to fiction because of its narrative, it must have an allegiance to history. Without this connection, biography becomes only a commentary on contemporary culture. (That being true, in this book, biography is presented as a part of contemporary society.) Carter contends that biographies must help children understand the historical context and period in which a life was lived. At the same time, readers must be helped to understand that the writing of biography is influenced by the historical contexts and values in which it is written. This is a sophisticated concept and one that is not likely to be realized by the very young, yet it is a very important aspect of information literacy, learning, scaffolding, and it is always a goal well worth striving to attain.[48]

In Carter's view, biography must be truthful and not perpetuate myths; biography must present an author's point of view, and it must not overdevelop characters and events. Didacticism, pronounced commemoration, and propaganda are often enemies of good biography for children. Yet biography must have a good story to tell and, as Huck suggests, be built around an underlying theme.[49]

For Carter, illustrations in good biography for children do more than expand the text; they become a central part of the narrative. Effective illustrators of children's biography know how to use color, size, placement, and even paper texture to create elements of personality and characters and historical contexts.[50]

Good biography for children must encourage curiosity and lessen the need to conform to a standard view of a person. Carter suggests that explanations of resources used to research the biography can promote curiosity as well as lay foundations for the development of information literacy.

Good biography, even for the every young, must reveal weaknesses that help define the personality and explain his or her actions. We know that Lincoln was a troubled man during the Civil War. How can children's biography portray this? Carter suggests through direct words. Amy Cohn and Suzy Schidt in *Abraham Lincoln* (Schmidt, 2002) accomplish this when they simply state: "He slept in snatches, walking the streets at night, stopping by the telegraphy office at all hours for the latest news."[51]

Pictures books such as *Roberto Clemente: Pride of the Pittsburgh Pirates*, by Johan Winter, illustrations by Raúl Colón (Atheneum, 2005) conveys Roberto's personality, spirit, and public acclaim through line drawings and textured colored pictures. A review by Bill Ott in *Booklist* says this about the art:

> Soaked in pastoral greens and browns, Colon's evocatively grainy, soft-focus illustrations, rendered with a mix of watercolors, colored pencils, and litho pencils, capture perfectly the worlds in which Clemente was most at home: the tropics and the baseball diamond. Baseball history brought vividly to life for a younger audience.

A different approach by illustrator Whitney Martin is given in *George Foreman: Let George Do It* (Simon & Schuster, 2005). Using bold and colorful caricature figures, children learn about the unusual family life of George Foreman, boxing champion and family man. On the other hand, the art presented in *Mother Teresa*, by Charlotte Demi Hunt (Margaret K. McElderry Books, 2005), is a combination of art styles ranging from cartoon-like pictures to religious iconic presentations and Indian art motifs. This biography is also a good example of a theme-based biography built around values of Catholicism and an intense admiration for the life of Mother Teresa.

Although picture book biographies are meant for children, some may not serve well as read-aloud materials. Some of these present detailed information that will not read well to a group of children. Nevertheless, the information and concepts are worth sharing. A way to do this is to present the biography as you would tell a story, summarizing the important points and showing selected pictures from the biography to illustrate elements of the life. *A Picture Book of Samuel Adams*, by David and Michael Adler (Holiday House, 2005), offers authentic biographical information, but its information is complex and might be better presented to young children in a storytelling format. The same can be said for Judith St. George's *Take the Lead, George Washington*, illustrated by Daniel Owens (Phiomel Books, 2005). Using exaggerated cartoon illustration, the life of Washington is presented in detail, and we see an engaging and likeable Washington emerge; but for young children, this biography might be better told than read. On the other hand, *Odd Boy Out: Young Albert Einstein*, by Don Brown (Houghton Mifflin, 2004), with its pictures (perhaps a bit too subdued for a large group) and simple narrative, could be read aloud easily.

PUBLISHERS AND PUBLISHING

Publishers certainly play a role in the kinds of biographies that are made available to children. Like any other business, publishers pay attention to popular market demands, reading interests of this market, and school curricula and subjects taught in schools. We see this in the vast amount of biographies published about persons who are celebrities in entertainment and sports. We also see this in biographies of national heroes that are part of the school curricula. Sometimes there are mismatches between the needs of the curriculum and mandated testing of young children and the types of biographies being published that are available at age-appropriate levels.

Publishers have also shown interest in social and cultural movements, and they have responded by publishing biographies that reflect those interests. Cynthia Chin-Lee's *Amelia to Zora: Twenty-Six Women Who Changed the World* (Charlesbridge, 2005), with illustrations by Megan Halsy and Sean Addy, is an example both of reader interest and curricula needs calling for more and expanded information about women in society. Marisabina Russo's self-illustrated *Always Remember Me: How One Family Survived World War II* (Atheneum, 2005) addresses the need for historical information that explains the broader historical context of World War II for young children. This picture book offers a personalized view of an extended family and their fight for survival during the Holocaust.

Fictionalized biography is well accepted by publishers, and we can expect to see this trend continue. On the other hand, professional educators are insisting more and more on the authenticity of biography, and publishers are being pressured to make sure that their biographical products can stand this test. Carter offers a good example of fictionalization that has no place in biography written for children. She questioned, among others, how author Stephen Krensky in his *Abe Lincoln and the Muddy Pig* (Aladdin/Simon, 2002) could write that Lincoln's speaking abilities were appreciated by both humans and pigs.[52]

Illustrations in picture book biographies must also stand the test of authenticity. Carter tells of reviewing Elizabeth Partridge's biography of Woody Guthrie, *This Land Was Made for You and Me* (Viking, 2002) in text-only galley copy and was concerned about the interfusions of references to other folksingers that seemed out of context to Guthrie's life. She was only able to see in an expanded copy of the book how the illustrations and captions expanded the historical text. These illustrations included photographs of other personalities such as Leadbelly, Joan Baez, and the Weavers, along with copies of Guthrie's letters, drawings, and handwritten lyrics. Carter believed that it was those illustrations that raised the book from a good one to a great one.[53]

In fact, all biographical picture books, through their illustrations and other cueing patterns, help children learn what is real from that which is imagined. Anne Bustard's *Buddy: The Story of Buddy Holly* (Simon & Schuster, 2005) is an excellent example of information that is authentic, is well researched, and separates facts from myths. The illustrations by Kurt Cyrus are based mostly on actual family pictures of Buddy, and they succeed in reinforcing reality and sense-making in young readers.

Because children's biographies are sold primarily to the educational market, educators such as teachers, school library media specialists, and public youth librarians can exert influence on the types of biographies that are placed on the market. Although not focused completely on biography for young children, Morgan Reynolds Publishing Company (www.morganreynolds.com) illustrates how publishers respond to teachers and school library media specialists' demands for improved biographical products. Their line of publications is directed at grades 6–12 as well as grade 5 and younger readers through their "First Biographies" series. A statement in their 2005 catalog addressed to school library media specialists and teachers suggests that their new line of full-color biographies for secondary-school students will not only meet the needs for school reports, but will provide in addition to the text interesting and enlivened information through sidebars. Included in each book's design are period photographs, maps, paintings and portraits, clean and easy-to-read fonts, suggestions for further reading and source materials, and age-appropriate websites.[54]

Such comments appear to indicate that publishers are indeed listening and responding to school library media specialists and teachers regarding the needs for better, well-rounded, and better designed biographies for youth. Authors and illustrators can also be influenced by contacting them at trade shows and conventions as well as through email messages and regular "snail" mail and expressing to them what is needed in terms of subject, content, and illustration.

As mentioned above, period photographs are frequently used by publishers to enliven their books. Figure 3.1, a photograph of Mary Todd Lincoln in her inaugural ball gown, is an example of both historical context as well as original source materials. This image is part of the collection of the National Archives in Washington, D.C. Such authentic presentations in biography can prove fascinating for many readers—young and old.

TECHNIQUES FOR USING AND PROMOTING BIOGRAPHY WITH THE YOUNG

Research coming from mass media offers school library media specialists and public youth librarians a wealth of guidance and information about how to effectively use biography with youth. As with television, attention is the first key to using biography with young children. Attention leads to comprehension. Research has shown that gender plays a role in how children pay attention to message such as biographical story. Although boys and girls do not differ in comprehension, they do differ in what gains and holds their attention. Boys appear to be more visually orientated, while girls are more auditory— attracted to the story as read aloud. The same information may be comprehended, but boys will comprehend this visually while girls will gain this information by what they hear. Boys are also more attentive to action or animation than are girls.[55] This suggests that when presenting biography to young children, one must consider the group's gender composition and construct the presentation around these characteristics.

Formal design and presentation features can help young children attend to a biography session. Design and presentation factors are used to help guide the listener. They help structure and organize content by marking breaks and changes in content; and they help make connections between separated

Figure 3.1
Mary Todd Lincoln, dressed in her inaugural ball gown. National
Archives, Civil War Series, 111-B-5 864.

events. Consider them much like "punctuation, capitalization, paragraphing, and chapter headings."[56] Visual cues such as pictures in biographies and how they are shown to children are important design elements. Biographical books having clear, non-abstract pictures with primary colors as well as presentation methods used by school media specialists and youth librarians will help capture and engage young children's attention.

Techniques used in children's television programs such as color, camera panning, auditory cues (voice, music, singing), camera cuts, and camera zooms can be adapted for story time using biographical material. For example, when using *George Washington's Teeth*, one might pan to the place in the book where George Washington is standing with pride as he crosses the Delaware River on his way to face the enemy. Pan to make sure that all see this image. At an appropriate time, *cut* to the important visual cue of the actual picture of George Washington's false teeth and *zoom* (carry the picture around) so that all in the group can see this.

In presenting any biographical story, auditory cues such as voice inflections and characterizations can help gain and hold attention. Music and interactive singing work well too.[57]

What the child comprehends from a biographical presentation is determined by age. In viewing television, preschoolers and children to age 7 or 8 do not retain much of the central content, and they recall only isolated events and do not focus on the plot. In terms of biography for these ages, the presenter might use the design format of the successful *Sesame Street* program. *Sesame Street* uses isolated events and information that emphasize characteristics of a person or small group of people. This approach is probably better than attempting to read or tell a complete biography. In other words, consider the presentation as a "magazine presentation" whereby only isolated events and descriptions of characters are given rather than presenting the biography as a whole, no matter how simple and pictorial the biography may be.[58] *Martin's Big Words: The Life of Martin Luther King Jr.*, by Doreen Rapport (Jump at the Sun, 2001), works well in this kind of situation.

As with television, comprehension based on print biography will relate to several important personal characteristics. These include a child's knowledge of the format (story, narration); general appeal to the child's expectations and knowledge about situations, events, sequences based on his or her earlier experiences; and the child's prior knowledge of book and story conventions. Although age is important in determining comprehension, relevant background and accumulated (prior) knowledge and skill at information processing are also important.[59] These elements imply that the child is best served first by their being exposed to reading and books as pleasing forms of narrative dialogue. Early and more varied environmental experiences with this and other forms of information increase young children's level of experiences and prepare the way for more sophisticated comprehension of biographical narratives as they grow older.

Children seek to make sense out of what they see and what is presented to them. To do this, they need to know what is real and what is fictional. As with television, biographical book materials can provide clues and guideposts. Children will use their own experiences to judge what is real and what is not. Good biographical picture books, through their illustrations and other cueing patterns, can help children with this task of discerning what is real from that which is imagined.

As mentioned earlier, there is a long tradition of fictionalizing biography for children. This is based on the assumption that pure biography will not be interesting to children or that it is too difficult in concept for children to comprehend. Among others beliefs, advocates often hold that biography must be encased in exciting, fictional environments to hold the attention of children. The argument is also made that this is an engaging way for "biographical and imaginative identity to become fused in a powerful, intimate, and often poetic way."[60]

That may well be true, but at the same time fictionalized biography must have enough format cues to help children separate fiction from truth. This is especially true for young children who tend to perceive isolated events and to stereotype that information. That is, they encounter information and then place that information into a familiar context based on prior experiences and/or understandings; but this categorizing of information is often subject to error.[61] For example, upon hearing the myth that George Washington cut down the cherry tree, a young child might then say that he or she too cut down a cherry tree while visiting with grandfather. In reality the child may have taken a walk with grandfather into the woods and helped grandfather clear away brush. Another example is that a few years ago a grandmother and acquaintance of the author told of hearing her six-year-old grandson tell about an episode of food poisoning in his school cafeteria. The actual incident was minor with only a few children becoming slightly ill, but in the grandson's recounting of the event to his grandmother, six children died.

PRESENTATIONS OF BIOGRAPHY

Creative Dramatics, Music, Read-Alouds, and Booktalks

In helping young children make sense of stories and helping them to separate fact from fiction, several techniques can be used. These include creative dramatics, scripted dramas, dance and movement, music and song, booktalks, and read-alouds. All of these approaches offer format cues and should be well crafted so that they can point the way to good sense-making.

According to Kevin M. Reese creative dramatics for young children (K-6) is

structured, goal-oriented playing. Through Creative Dramatics (CD) we help the kids explore their imaginations, learn how to communicate ideas, and learn how to feel comfortable with themselves and their role in society. The emphasis is on creation—not performance. Our belief is that sometime around the 2nd or 3rd grade, society conditions children into not utilizing their imaginations—it stresses rational and logical thinking. Through CD, we try to keep them in touch with their imagination (or help the older ones remember how to use it again).[62]

He suggests several ways of doing this; and these suggestions, with modifications, can help in presenting biography to children.

Actors' Tools. This exercise is designed to help children understand how actors create drama through tools such as their own bodies, voices, and imaginations; and he relates these to the idea that all work or employment has special tools. In this exercise, children are asked to identify and describe the tools that their parents use in their work. For biography, this might be adapted into something like "Tools for Work" and ask children to identify and describe tools that were used in a biography just read or shared with the group.[63] Ask children to identify and describe the tools the dentist used to make George Washington's false teeth. Another adaptation might be to ask the children to look for tools of work in a biography about to be read to them.

Film vs Stage. In this exercise, the idea is to help children understand the difference between film and stage presentations and what is expected of an audience. For example, the audience is expected to be polite and to respect both the actors and those in the audience—just as in story hour. Ask children what is different from seeing a movie and seeing a stage play. Help those who have not seen a play or perhaps a movie understand what that is. Once this difference is understood, ask the children if they have ever seen a play or movie about a famous person and what did they remember about the film or play. Remind them that everything we see on film or stage is not always true.[64] Ask them what was real about what they saw—encourage them to think about clothing, settings, technologies, and transportation. Ask them to think about what might not have been true—how the actors talked (speech) and how they acted (moved), and what might have happened in the film that did not seem true. At this point there is no need to make corrections, other than to remind them that everything we see or read is not always true.

Animal Study (favorite animal). Ask the children in this exercise to think about their favorite animal and to describe it, either with voice or action.[65] For biography ask the children what kind of animal a famous person might have had as a pet. What would George Washington's favorite animal have been and why?

First Sound in the Morning. Have the children identify and act out the sound that they first hear in the morning (for class management it might be best to ask for a volunteer, and then have the other children guess what the sound is). After that, ask the children what kinds of sounds a person in a biography might have heard.[66] What sound or sounds might George Washington have heard as he woke up on the day he went to his dentist for his false teeth?

Walking Exercise. Ask the class to take a walk around the room in a thoughtful manner, and as they walk ask them to imagine what a famous person might have seen on their walks.[67] What might George Washington have seen as he walked to his dentist on the day he went for his false teeth?

Talking about Biography. Talking about biography is important and this can be aided by associating creative dramatics with biographical performances. Arrange for a puppet show or small biographic drama to be preformed. After seeing the performance ask the children something about the performance—their favorite parts, characters, and asks them to tie some of the parts together. Ask them about the sets and costumes. If an actual performance is not possible, read a biography and ask the children to help plan a performance such as a puppet show based on the book. If the children are very young or if time is limited, you might suggest that they design a scene around a small part of the book.

Improvisation and Scenes and Monologues. Improvisation and the creation of a monologue or scene from biographical materials are appropriate for older children. Based on facts given in the biography, children can develop and perform a brief monologue based on the book. Also children can develop a scene from a biography and perform it for the group. A monologue can run from thirty to sixty seconds while a scene should not be longer than three minutes.[68] This allows children to draw their materials from the biography, concentrating on what is true.

For older children, ages six and older, improvisation and theater games can be used along with biographical materials.

History Lesson. In this exercise, ask children to take an object mentioned in a biography under study and have them tell the history of the object based on some basic research (have reference materials readily available or have a printout of basic information). Ask the children to come before the group and discuss their selected object—who invented it and why it was invented, and how it has been used and changed throughout its history. Do not be too concerned about facts; what is important is to have the discussion be imaginative, but logical in terms of the biographical and historical context.[69]

Point of View. Ask two or three students to take part in an interview based on information in a biography studied by the group. Have a child play one of the characters found in the biography and have another play an interviewer. Ask the group to select one or two incidences in the biographical story and have the dyad play out the interview based on the selected events. After the interview ask the group to add comments about the interview—how accurate were the questions and responses, what other questions could have been asked?[70]

Talk Show. Ask one of the students to play the host of a talk show, and have another play a character is the biography. The interviewee does not need to be the main character, but he or she might be a secondary personality mentioned in the biography. Perhaps a Washington grandchild or stepchild could be played with the interviewer asking them questions about being related to such a well-know person in American history. A variation on this is the *Family Reunion* where children are asked to play certain family roles within the household of a biographical personality. Ask them to pretend that they are all related to a biographical personality and that they have all gathered for a family reunion, and ask them to interact with each other, telling each often what they liked (or disliked) about their famous relative. Again, try to encourage the children to be logical in their interpretations, based on the biography.[71]

More Methods. Other types of creative drama that can be used in the study of biography include *Primitive Society*, where a group acts out how a biographical character might influence the development of a primitive community—how might he or she lead the group? *Soup Kitchen* is where a group of biographical characters find themselves in a soup kitchen as all have fallen onto hard times. Ask a child to develop a scene whereby he or she, playing a biographical personality, explains why he or she helps out in the kitchen or has come to depend on the kitchen for food. Again, try to encourage the scene to be logical to the personality of the character. *What's Next?* is a role play where the teacher or the school library media specialist asks the audience to suggest a conflict situation and asks a child to play out how a biographical personality might solve or react to the conflict based on information provided in the biography under study. In *Service Desk,* ask a child to play an agent at a service desk at a large department store, and have another child play a biographical character. The character wants to return a piece of merchandise, but the clerk does not want to accept the return. Ask them to play out the scene whereby the biographical personality tries to get his or her wishes met based on what is known through his biography.[72]

Music can also be used in similar ways with biography. Have children discuss what types of music a particular person in biography might have liked or what musical instrument he might have enjoyed playing. If the personality is a musician, have children consider the various ways that music influenced his or her life and personality. Also have children think about how music played a role in the musician's community and in the time period in which he or she lived (e.g., what were people listening to and dancing to in 1789 when Washington became president of the United States?).

Booktalks and read-alouds have been highly effective and respected presentation techniques used by teachers, school library media specialists, and public youth librarians for years. Booktalks are designed to interest an audience in reading a book or a series of books. A booktalk is not a review; it is relatively short and simple and is designed to highlight and capture the essential elements of a book so that the audience will be encouraged to read it on their own. In many ways a booktalk is a dramatic presentation, calling on the booktalker to assume many roles in presenting the talk. Booktalks can be presented to any age group, including young children.

Rosanne J. Blass offers good suggestions for using biography in booktalks and read-alouds with young children. *Molly Bannaky*, by Alice McGill (Houghton Mifflin, 1999), is the true story of a young women in Great Britain who is sentenced to several years of bondage in the New World for spilling a farmer's milk. Over time, Molly gains her freedom, marries a former slave, and has children, and one of her grandsons becomes a famous mathematician. As with any booktalk the ending is not given away, and Blass suggests that the audience be asked to guess whom this famous grandson might be.[73]

Another picture book suggested by Blass for both booktalks as well as read-alouds is *Rare Treasure: Mary Anning and Her Remarkable Discoveries*, by Don Brown (Houghton Mifflin, 1999). This is a picture book suitable for ages 7 to 12 about the first commercial fossil collectors who "dug up dinosaurs."[74] Shana Corey's *You Forgot Your Skirt, Amelia Bloomer!* (Scholastic Press, 2000) will certainly amuse children ages 5–8 as they learn how Amelia Bloomer changed fashion and introduced the word *bloomer* into American speech.[75, 76]

Kathleen A. Baxter, Marcia A. Kochel, and Michael Dahl offer numerous suggestions for other picture biographies to use with young children as book-talks and read-alouds. These include several biographies by David Adler: *Picture Book of Thomas Alva Edison* (Holiday House, 1995); *Martin Luther King Jr.: Free at Last* (Holiday House, 1986); and *A Picture Book of Harriet Tubman* (Holiday House, 1992).[77, 78, 79]

Reader's Advisory Programs

School library media specialists and public library youth librarians conduct reader advisement on a daily, if not hourly, basis. It has a long history. Early school library textbooks such as those by Ann Eaton—*School Library Service* (American Library Association, 1923)—and Lucile Fargo—*The School Library and the School* (American Library Association, 1928)—suggested that working with children in helping them find good books to read was an expected responsibility.

Reader advisement is not bibliotherapy. Reader advisement is designed to assist others to have enjoyable and worthwhile reading experiences. It is not specially directed at changing behaviors. Originally it was an educative process developed to help library users and patrons move to a higher and perhaps better level of reading and thus improve their education and cultural attainments.[80]

Today the elements of a good reader advisement program consist of selection of materials for the collection, effective interviewing and talking with children about their reading interests and needs, consultation with teachers and parents, creating an inviting environment for reading and browsing, effectively displaying materials, developing reading lists for various user groups (teachers, parents, students), developing websites and Internet links, writing annotations and reviews, mounting book exhibitions, conducting book fairs, giving booktalks, storytelling, and having read-aloud programs.[81, 82]

Crystal Faris suggests that reader advisement for youth can foster curiosity and help with brain development. She feels that reader advisement with boys can be especially useful in helping them develop and widen their personal interests, help them to establish a lifetime of curiosity and inquiry that can satisfy their needs for facts, support their development needs, and help those who do not read become readers.[83]

These suggestions certainly apply to girls as well as boys. Biographical topics that can be suggested in reading advisement with young children as well as older youth include world record holders; persons who work in various fields such as forensic medicine, the automobile industry, auto driving; sports personalities; and individuals from history, entertainment, and the arts.[84] She also suggests that the book stacks and other areas be made attractive and conducive for browsing and that nonfiction, including biographies, be marketed in appealing ways through bookstore-type displays. Based on these suggestions, biographies suitable for young children should be displayed in prominent places for easy access. Faris highly recommends keeping abreast of new publishing trends and using books suggested on listings of award winners published by various professional associations such as the American Library Association and the International Reading Association as well as others.[85]

In her consideration of reader advisement within a school library media environment, Marcia Kochel echoes many of the same suggestions as Faris. She mentions that one of the problems with promoting nonfiction (and we can include biography here) is that most teachers almost exclusively assign and/or suggest fiction to students.[86] Mark Dressman of the Center for Writing Studies at the University of Illinois at Urbana-Champaign in his book *Literacy in the Library* (1997) suggested that the favoring of fiction over nonfiction might be an issue based on the female gender of the school library media specialist. This idea was based on his study of Austin, Texas, school librarians (i.e., the local designation for school library media specialists). Using a critical theory approach, he concluded that when advising boys on reading, female librarians generally encouraged boys to read fiction rather than nonfiction. He reasoned that female librarians simply prefer fiction over nonfiction and naturally direct boys away from nonfiction reading.[87] The counter argument to that is that librarians know that boys read and prefer to read nonfiction, and they direct them to fiction as a means of expanding their reading experiences.

Kochel also mentions other problems associated with promoting nonfiction. She noted that it is often stereotyped in that it is considered boring, is accepted more by boys than girls, that it is too dense with information to be exciting reading, and it is too much connected to curriculum mandates.[88] With these problems in mind, Kochel believes that one-on-one recommendations are essential to good reader advisement in the school library media center. This approach is based on developing good and long-lasting relationships with readers, having a firm knowledge of nonfiction, understanding the needs and interests of readers, and knowing the collection well.[89] Although these recommendations and observations are made in reference to general school or public library youth users, they apply equally well when encouraging very young children, their teachers, and their caregivers to experience biography.

CONCLUSION

Very young children benefit from biography is many ways. They learn new information and concepts, they are encouraged to think about their own lives, they are exposed to positive values, and they learn to understand and appreciate what it means to live in and contribute to society, Biography helps them to relate to knowledge and facts that they are learning as they begin their formal education. Through biography, young children are introduced to information literacy and critical thinking skills. Most importantly, they learn to be critical thinkers as they read and hear about the triumphs and mistakes of others. Nevertheless, we must remember that young children do not think as adults and they do not construct information as adults. Patrick Groff reminds us of biography's limitations when he says that children make mistakes in their interpretations of adult activities in reading biography and that "biography tends to prematurely impose highly complex rational descriptions of life upon unprepared minds."[90, 91] Understanding this and helping young children make sense of their world through biography is one of the great joys of working with very young children.

NOTES

1. Susan Engle, "Children's Life Writing," in *Encyclopedia of Life Writing: Autobiographical and Biographical Forms,* vol. 1, ed. Margaretta Jolly (London: Fitzroy Dearborn, 2001), 204.

2. Engle, 204.

3. Engle, 205.

4. Engle, 206.

5. Engle, 206.

6. Lilian Katz, "Children," in *Early Childhood Education: What Research Tells Us* (1988), 12, http://www.sasked.gov.sk.ca/docs/kindergarten/kindneed.html (accessed May 13, 2005).

7. Katz.

8. Katz.

9. Sandra Crosser, "Emerging Morality: How Children Think about Right and Wrong," http://www.earlychildhood.com/Articles/index.cfm?FuseAction=Article&A=118 (accessed April 29, 2005).

10. Crosser.

11. Crosser.

12. Crosser.

13. Crosser.

14. W. Bernard Lukenbill, *Collection Development for a New Century in the School Library Media Center* (Westport, Conn.: Greenwood Press, 2002), 147–48, citing John Dacey, "Concepts of Creativity: A History," in *Encyclopedia of Creativity,* ed. Mark A. Runco and Steven R. Prizker (San Diego: Academic Press, 1999), 312, and M. Hadas, "A Greek Paradigm of Self Control," in *The Quest for Self Control,* ed. Samuel Z. Klausner (New York: Free Press, 1965), 201.

15. Teresa M. Amabile, *Creativity in Context: Update to the Social Psychology of Creativity* (Boulder, Colo.: Westview Press, 1996), 204–5.

16. Amabile, 219–20.

17. Carol M. Butzow and John W. Butzow, *The American Hero in Children's Literature: A Standards-Based Approach* (Westport, Conn.: Teacher Ideas Press, 2005).

18. Amabile, 220.

19. Amabile, 220.

20. Emily M. Rodgers and Adrian Rodgers, "The Role of Scaffolding in Teaching," in *Scaffolding Literacy Instruction: Strategies for K-4 Classrooms,* ed. Adrian Rodgers and Emily M. Rodgers (Portsmouth, N.H.: Heinemann, 2004), 1.

21. Rodgers and Rodgers, 1.

22. Rodgers and Rodgers, citing D. Wood and others, "The Role of Tutoring in Problem-Solving," *Journal of Child Psychology and Psychiatry* 17 (April 1976): 89–100.

23. Rodgers and Rodgers, 2–3.

24. Rodgers and Rodgers, 4.

25. Rodgers and Rodgers, 8.

26. Rodgers and Rodgers, 9.

27. Texas Education Agency, "Texas Essential Knowledge and Skills (TEKS)," http://www.tea.state.tx.us/teks (accessed May 5, 2005).

28. Texas TEKS Addressed with the "Creative Authors Program," Elementary§110.5, English Language Arts and Reading, Grade 3, http://www.tea.state.tx.us/rules/tac/chapter110/index.html (accessed Nov. 9, 2005).

29. Texas TEKS Addressed with the "Creative Authors Program."

30. "Publisher's Weekly Review of *George Washington's Teeth,*" *Publisher's Weekly,* 2002, http://www.amazon.com/exec/obidos/tg/detail/-/0374325340/qid=1131549158/sr=21/ref=pd_bbs_b_2_1/002-45221585660846?v=glance&s=books 5 (accessed May 5, 2005, and Nov. 9, 2005).

31. Janice Huber and D. Jean Clandinin, "Scaffolding Children's Identity Making with Literature," in *Scaffolding Literacy Instruction: Strategies for K-4 Classrooms,* ed. Adrian Rodgers and Emily M. Rodgers (Portsmouth, N.H.: Heinemann, 2004), 143–61.

32. Dina Sherman, "Review of *Barrio: José's Neighborhood,* by George Ancona, in *School Library Journal,*" http://www.amazon.com/exec/obidos/tg/detail/-/061311308X/qid=1131549422/sr=1-1/ref=sr_1_1/002-4522158-5660846?v=glance&s=books (accessed May 5, 2005, and Nov. 9, 2005).

33. Alison Alexander, "Children and Television," in *Museum of Broadcast Communications Encyclopedia of Television,* vol. 1, Horace Newcomb (Chicago: Fitzroy Dearborn, 1997), 351–59.

34. Nickelodeon, "The Brothers Garcia," http://www.nick.com/all_nick/tv_supersites/show_description.jhtml?show_id=bro (accessed May 6, 2005).

35. Dough Thomas, "Review of the Disney film *Pocahontas,*" http://www.amazon.com/gp/product/B00004R99J/002-4522158-5660846?v=glance&n=130&s=dvd&v=glancem (accessed May 6, 2005, and Oct. 31, 2005).

36. Alexander, 503.

37. Peabody Awards, http://www.answers.com/topic/peabody-awards (accessed May 6, 2005).

38. "Children's Television Workshop (CTW)," in *Les Brown's Encyclopedia of Television,* 3rd. ed. (Detroit: Gale Research, 1984), 113.

39. Alexander, 507.

40. Alexander, 506.

41. Kyoon Kwon, "A Study of Values and Children's Biographies" (dissertation, University of Tennessee, 1984), abstracted in *Dissertation Abstracts International* 45-A (Dec. 1984): 1578.

42. Christine Duthie, "'It's Just Plain Real!' Introducing Young Children to Biography and Autobiography," *New Advocate* 11 (Summer 1998): 219–27.

43. Vera Frye, *Learning from Heroes,* vol. 1 (Bloomington, Ind.: ERIC Clearinghouse on Reading, English and Communication, 2003), ERIC document no. ED 474 621.

44. W. Bernard Lukenbill, *AIDS and HIV Programs and Services for Librarians* (Englewood, Colo.: Libraries Unlimited, 1994), 208, citing Joyce Rubin Rhea, *Using Bibliotherapy: A Guide to Theory and Practice* (Phoenix, Ariz.: Oryx Press, 1978), 2.

45. Dewayne Arden Green, "A Study of the Impact of Bibliotherapy on the Self-Concept of Mexican-American Children Ten and Eleven Years of Age" (dissertation, University of Northern Colorado, 1988), abstracted in *Dissertation Abstracts International* 50-A (Nov. 1989): 1252.

46. Charlotte S. Huck and others, *Children's Literature in the Elementary School,* 6th ed. (Madison, Wis.: Brown & Benchmark, 1997), 558.

47. Huck, 559.

48. Betty Carter, "Reviewing Biography," *The Horn Book* 79 (March/April 2003): 165–74.

49. Carter.

50. Carter.

51. Carter, citing Amy L. Cohn and Suzy Schmidt, *Abraham Lincoln* (New York: Scholastic, 2002).

52. Carter.

53. Carter.

54. Morgan Reynolds Publishing, *Nonficton for Grades 6–12, Spring 2005 Books* "From the Publisher" (Greensboro, N.C.: Morgan Reynolds Publishing, 2005), np.

55. Rose M. Kundanis, *Children, Teens, Families, and Mass Media: The Millennial Generation* (Mahwah, N.J.: Lawrence Erlbaum Associates, 2003), 20.

56. Kundanis, 21.

57. Kundanis, 20.

58. Kundanis, 21–22.

59. Kundanis, 22.

60. Stuart Hannabuss, "Biography in Fiction," in *Biography and Children: A Study of Biography for Children and Childhood in Biography,* ed. Stuart Hannabuss and Rita Marcella (London: Library Association Publishing, 1993), 95.

61. Kundanis, 22–23

62. Kevin M. Reese, "Creative Dramatics: Workshop Handbook & Workshop Material for Creative Drama Acting Improvisation," KMR Scripts [Rev. 11/98], http://www.kmrscripts.com/cdguide.html (accessed May 11, 2005).

63. Reese.

64. Reese.

65. Reese.

66. Reese.

67. Reese.

68. Reese.

69. Reese.

70. Reese.

71. Reese.

72. Reese.

73. Rosanne J. Blass, *Booktalks, Bookwalks, and Read-Alouds: Promoting the Best New Children's Literature across the Elementary Curriculum* (Westport, Conn.: Libraries Unlimited, 2002), 96.

74. Blass, 90.

75. Blass, 91.

76. Blass, 91.

77. Kathleen A. Baxter and Marcia Agnes Kochel, *GOTCHA! Nonfiction Booktalks to Get Kids Excited about Reading* (Englewood, Colo.: Libraries Unlimited, 1999).

78. Kathleen A. Baxter and Marcia Agnes Kochel, *Gotcha Again!: More Nonfiction Booktalks to Get Kids Excited about Reading* (Greenwood Village, Colo.: Libraries Unlimited/Teacher Ideas Press, 2002).

79. Kathleen A. Baxter and Michael Dahl, *Gotcha Covered!: More Nonfiction Booktalks to Get Kids Excited about Reading* (Westport, Conn.: Libraries Unlimited, 2005).

80. Lukenbill, 206, citing Joyce G. Saricks and Nancy Brown, *Readers' Advisory Service in the Public Library* (Chicago: American Library Association, 1989), 3–8. See also Saricks's *Readers' Advisory Service in the Public Library,* 3rd ed. (Chicago: American Library Association, 2005).

81. Lukenbill, 206.

82. Marcia Kochel, "Nonfiction Advisory Services in the School Library Media Center," in *Nonfiction Readers' Advisory,* ed. Robert Burgin (Westport, Conn.: Libraries Unlimited, 2004), 158–59.

83. Crystal Faris, "Nonfiction and Young Readers," in *Nonfiction Readers' Advisory,* ed. Robert Burgin (Westport, Conn.: Libraries Unlimited, 2004), 145–47.

84. Faris, 145–48.

85. Faris, 150–55.

86. Kochel, 158–59.

87. Mark Dressman, *Literacy in the Library: Negotiating the Spaces between Order and Desire* (Westport, Conn.: Bergin & Garvey, 1997), 165–66.

88. Kochel.

89. Kochel, 171.

90. Patrick Groff, "How Do Children Read Biography about Adults?" *Reading Teacher* 24 (April 1971): 609–15.

91. Patrick Groff, "Biography: A Tool for Bibliotherapy?" *Top of the News* 36 (Spring 1980): 269–73.

4

BIOGRAPHY: LIFE IN A MIRROR

INTRODUCTION

Throughout history people have assumed that biography influences behavior and attitudes. Chapter 2 considered how biography is used in curriculum and in library programming to influence learning, value formation, human relations, and other aspects of social behavior. Likewise, other chapters in this book consider biography in terms of such attributes as political, social, cultural, and literary influences. This chapter looks more closely at some models and theories that can help us better understand the interplay of biography in helping youth understand life and the world in which they live. It will also consider how biography can offer guidance in forming positive social behavior necessary for productive human life.

MODELS AND THEORIES OF SOCIAL BEHAVIOR

As we discussed in chapter 3, young children have special needs regarding biography. That chapter focused primarily on how biography can be used to enhance special developmental, social, learning, and psychological needs. It also looked at some of the problems associated with sharing biography with the very young. A closer look at models and theories of social behavior can help us not only use biography effectively with younger children, but can enhance its effectiveness with youth as a whole.

Bandura's Social Learning Ideas

One of the most influential theorists in social behavior and the effects of media on behavior is psychologist Albert Bandura. Bandura is well known for his theory of social learning and social modeling. This concept reflects the idea that people learn from what they observe and what they experience in life. For example, for children a simple task like brushing one's teeth is learned by observation and practicing what adult caregivers demonstrate. Bandura suggested that social learning theory is applicable to studying the influence of mass media, especially television, on how people learn behaviors and attitudes.

Among other elements, television imagery depicts material values and possessions, human relationships, how problems are solved, and violence. It defines in its own way what a culture considers physically beautiful, powerful, successful; what it is to be admired; and what is to be rejected. Television influences our notion of what is stylish, what kinds of cars to drive, how to drive them, how to handle aggression, and how to behave in various social situations. Although both adults and children are influenced by television, Bandura suggested that children are especially susceptible. Children have less experience with life and cannot place television imagery into perspective.

In most cultures, children are taught to be obedient and noncritical of adult behavior. This unquestioning obedience can lead to internalizing negative examples of adults shown on television as behaviors that are not only acceptable, but even expected. Moral development in children is influenced by observations and by guidance. If children have little moral guidance or information other than what they see on television, then they are most likely to accept negative behaviors shown on television as legitimate.

Bandura's social learning theory is based on extensive clinical research in which he found that children learned significantly from mass media, especially TV. His research demonstrated that children learned both negative and positive social behaviors including aggression, cooperation, sharing, social interaction, and the delay of gratification. Nevertheless, much of this information is conveyed to young children through cartoon images, where behavior is couched in violence.

Social learning theory goes beyond mass media and television, and an understanding of how youth learn social behaviors can have significant influence on how biography is used with youth. In many societies, for younger children, biography offers models of good and valued social behaviors, but for biography to be more effective, information literacy skills must be introduced. Critical analysis and evaluation of a person's life, values, and contributions to society are essential when reading or viewing biographical materials. Youth must be encouraged and taught to consider how a writer analyzes sources of information, presents points of view, and shows political and social biases. Youth must also be able to determine biases in the life of the writer as well as his or her subject.[1]

For example, *An American Hero: The True Story of Charles Lindberg*, by Barry Denenberg (Scholastic, 1996), requires the reader to face Lindberg's attraction to Hitler and his admiration of the Nazi industrial and military complex as it developed in the 1930s. The book also requires the reader to consider Lindberg's public anti-Semitism, voiced by him in speeches well into World War II.

In fact, biographies of prominent people who came into adulthood in the 1930s present us with problems of understanding the power of time, place, and circumstances in how people construct and express their values. For example, with the early rise of Hitler and fascism, personalities such as the Prince of Wales (later King Edward VIII and the Duke of Windsor), Lindberg, architect Philip Johnson, and singer Paul Robeson admired what fascism promised the world.[2, 3, 4] An evaluation of their lives today requires that we as readers understand the social and political forces that might have influenced thinking during those times, but not necessarily to excuse it.

Bronfenbrenner's Ecological Concepts

The late Cornell scholar Urie Bronfenbrenner offers an ecological systems theory that can help us use biography with children and young adults.[5] He suggested that we live in an ecological system. In this system we learn behaviors and attitudes; and these behaviors and attitudes are influenced by experiences arising from broader social and cultural systems as well as a child's immediate surroundings. In other words, the home and immediate caregivers are important, but children are not isolated, and they observe and learn from the broad framework of culture and society that make up their ecological systems.

Advocates of Bronfenbrenner's theory see it as a powerful tool in the support of public policies that support families and youth. According to these supporters, structures are needed to provide foundations so that supportive ecological systems can grow. This foundation requires that the community, society, and culture support healthy relationships by providing values and resources that encourage positive cognitive and emotional development.

Based on the ecological model, research by Lewis and Morris (1998) offers five basic needs for positive development in children and youth.[6]

- A personal relationship with a caring adult
- A safe place to live
- A healthy start toward their future
- A marketable skill to use after graduation from high school
- An opportunity to contribute to their community

Public libraries and school library media centers are important parts of a wide range of partnerships that exist within the community that can be used to help build ecological support systems. We have ample evidence that libraries have and are continuing to build their programs and services influenced by this theory.

Biography can play a powerful role in this ecological system. Biography provides values and examples of support and comfort in a harsh world. For older readers, *What Are You? Voices of Mixed-Race People*, by Pearl Fuyo Gaskins (Henry Holt, 1999), and *50 American Heroes Every Kid Should Meet*, by Dennis Denenberg and Lorraine Roscoe (Twenty-First Century Books, 2004), offer insights into human fortitude within challenging social ecological systems.

Biography also provides examples of positive relationship, friendships, achievements and skills needed for success, and how to contribute to society and community. Eloise Greenfield's biography for younger children, *Mary McLeod Bethune* (Crowell, 1977; HarperCollins, Canada, 1995), provides such guidance in the telling of the life and contributions to American society of this African American educator and teacher.

Vygotsky's Sociocultural Theory

Another theory that can influence how we use biography with youth is socio-cultural theory. This theory holds that higher order functions develop out of social interaction. As advocated by Marxist writer Lev Vygotsky, to understand a child and his or her development we must look at the world in which the child develops. In their social and cultural life, the child participates in "activities that require cognitive and communicative functions, children are drawn into the use of these functions in ways that nurture and 'scaffold' them."[7] Vygotsky considered "learning as being embedded within social events and occurring as a child interacts with people, objects, and events in the environment."[8] In this theory, caregivers convey cultural information and expectations to children, who in turn emulate behaviors that allow them to acquire cultural meanings and to communicate within their culture. These stages are discrete and are contained in developmental zones and cycles, each of which is carefully observed and reacted to by primary caregivers. Each of these cycles must be mastered before the next one is undertaken. The caregivers therefore are involved in a cultural interactive process designed to bring children into the larger culture.

Biographies offer insight and support for youth as they learn from their cultural environments and as they move, step by step, into society and culture. For younger children, biographies that tell simple life-stories and include illustrations provide sociocultural learning. Aliki's *A Weed Is a Flower: The Life of George Washington Carver* (Simon & Schuster, 1988) provides for young children information on the value of scientific knowledge and research, individual integrity, hard work, and overcoming limitations imposed on one by society. In Lynda Van Devanter's autobiography, *Home before Morning: The Story of an Army Nurse in Vietnam* (Warner Books, 1984), older readers witness the gradual radicalization and the stress of an army nurse as she witnesses the brutality of war. The book helps older youth learn of the often conflicting roles that culture, society, and allegiance to country demand of people and the consequences that often arise from their choices.

Socio-Literary Theory

Socio-literary theory also considers the influence of culture and society on behavior, but this approach is based on literature.[9] There are three major components of this theory. Probably the most profound of these is the assertion that literature controls society. Today we see this theory in operation through many censorship attempts to control what is written, published, distributed, and read. The second idea within this concept is that literature influences society. The idea here is that literature can have a direct influence on how society develops. Professional organizations such as the American Library Association and its various divisions serving the needs of youth as well as educational organizations and schools have generally interpreted this to mean that good, well-written literature, containing socially responsible values and behavior guides can improve both individual behavior and the behavior of society in general. Recommendations from these groups appear frequently, such as the annual lists issued by the Association for Library Services for Children (ALSA), and Young Adult Library Service Association (YALSA). The Coretta Scott King Award lists also offers books often of a biographical nature that help promote social justice and equality.

Because of this aspect of the theory's long association with education, it is easy to see its close association with biography. Recommended lists of biographical materials for youth are embedded in this theory. Some recent biographical materials that have been recommended for youth that imply literary influence are: *The Voice That Challenged a Nation: Marian Anderson and the Struggle for Equal* Rights, by Russell Freedman (Clarion Books/Houghton Mifflin, 2004), *Sequoyah: The Cherokee Man Who Gave His People Writing*, by James Rumford, translated from Cherokee by Anna Sixkiller Huckaby (Houghton Mifflin, 2004), and *The Autobiography of Malcolm X*, by Malcolm Little (as told to Alex Haley) (Sagebrush, 1999).

The final concept within socio-literary theory is that literature reflects society. Taken to the extreme this might well imply that literature has no obligation other than to reflect the good and bad realities found in society. This theory has been used with considerable effectiveness by novelists such as Upton Sinclair in his novel *The Jungle* (Sharp Press, 2003; first published in 1906), attacking the meatpacking industry and unsafe food marketing practiced at that time. Muckraking journalists (now often considered investigative journalists) of the late nineteenth and early twentieth centuries also used reality writing to expose abuses of economic, political, and social power.[10]

Modern biographies suitable for youth that attempt to show the realities of life include Ilse Koehn's *Michling, Second Degree: My Childhood in Nazi*

Germany (Greenwillow, 1977); Francisco Jimenez's *The Circuit: Stories from the Life-Migrant Child* (University of New Mexico Press, 1997) and *Voices from the Fields: Children of Migrant Farmworkers Tell Their Stories* (Little Brown, 2000); Leon Tillage's *Leon's Story* (Farrar, Straus and Giroux, 2000); and Alex Kotlowitz's *There Are No Children Here: The Story of Two Boys Growing Up in the Other America* (Han A. Talese, 1991; Anchor, 1992).

Feminist Ideas

In recent decades feminist theory has greatly influenced the development of biographical materials for youth in what is written, published, recommended, and selected for use with youth.

Feminist literary theory offers a means of analyzing how women (and men) are presented to society through literature. It seems especially interested in seeing how

> gender produce, transform, and transcend social stereotypes about women and men. In this critical approach, one examines why certain cultural behaviors are gendered and how that labeling has been limiting and/or empowering to women and men in society.[11]

This theory is more fully explained in the *Encyclopedia of Feminist Literary Theory* edited by Elizabeth Kowalewski-Wallace (Garland, 1997) and in Kay Vandergrift's "Model of Female Voices in Youth Literature."[12]

Feminist-based biography for children and young adults has tended to explore history and culture for women of achievement who have been ignored or marginalized and to look at society and the way that women as a group have always been responsible and resourceful, and have contributed significantly to the world. These writings have presented women of achievement as well as women in general, ranging from ancient societies to modern life. For example, *Women in Mathematics*, by Lynn M. Osen (MIT Press, 1975), *Ditchdigger's Daughters: A Black Family's Astonishing Success Story*, by Yvonne Thornton (Dafina, 2002), *Black Women of the Old West*, by William L. Katz (Simon & Schuster, 1995), and *Into a New Country: Eight Remarkable Women of the West*, by Liza Ketchum (Little Brown, 2000) all present women who have risen above the stereotypes traditionally imposed on women.

BIOGRAPHICAL INFLUENCES ON BEHAVIOR: SOME RESEARCH GUIDANCE

Biography and its influence on behavior and attitudes have also been of interest to researchers. Scholarly research as well as action research continues to offer us insight into how we can better understand these phenomena.

Much of this research has come from dissertations as well as psychological research and social and cultural enquiry.

For example, Stephen Butterfield in his study of African American autobiography suggested that autobiographies by such personalities as Frederick Douglass and W. E. B. DuBois were forms of social resistance to the effects of white history on the black sense of self. Similarly, Kathleen Armstrong looked at Langston Hughes' autobiographical works and concluded that he based his literary metaphor and life on the black condition as he understood it. David Newquist's study of Black Hawk's autobiography, *Life of Black Hawk* (Dover Press, 1994; originally published in 1833), noted that it presented a literary vision of how he and his tribe, the Sauk Indians, viewed life.

In spite of students' interest in biography, Helen Lodge found little in terms of how biography might affect the value systems of eighth grade students who had participated in a study unit on biography. On the other hand, Elizabeth Partridge considers reading biography aloud to children who are deprived especially helpful in lifting despair from their lives.[13] Biography has also been used to help develop better self-awareness and self-esteem.

BIOGRAPHY: A REFLECTION OF HUMAN BEHAVIOR

Reading biography not only affects us as individuals, but by reading about the lives of others and how they react to life, we gain a better understanding of human nature and behaviors. Readers have a vast number and types of biographical materials at their disposal. Forms of biography are numerous and apparently there are no agreed upon classification systems. Within this broad array are included informal autobiographies such as memoirs and reminiscences, formal autobiographies, special purpose biographies, specialized forms of biography, character sketches, informational biographies, and reference sources.[14] All of these are important and help to explain the lives of people in some way. In so doing, they offer us a broad picture of our cultures and societies. Narrative biography, a form of biography, offers us an excellent means of discovering lives.

NARRATIVE BIOGRAPHY

Personal narrative biography is a form of biography that falls within several of the categories just mentioned. Narrative biography is a powerful tool in helping to shape our personal attitudes and in helping us to understand diversities of life. At the personal level, Jean Brockmeier and Donal Carbauch of the University of Toronto explain that narrative biography is a form of biography that allows one to tell his or her own biography and, as such, "gives shape and meaning to human life" and how one identifies and comes to better understand oneself in the world. Narrative biographical research includes the lives of individuals and groups and how they communicate, their linguistic behaviors, and their psychology and sociology. Along with the study of individuals, narrative biography is a study of culture, national identity (see chapters 7 and 8) and group identities such as those of Holocaust survivors.[15]

Studies in Narrative Biography

Dan Bars-On's *Fear and Hope: Three Generations of the Holocaust* (Harvard University Press, 1995) researched the lives of five Holocaust survivors and how their stories were passed on to their children and grandchildren. This study shows how family stories and narratives are communicated, shared, and interpreted over time. These narratives also reveal rich complexity of individual biographies, family history, social history, family dynamics together with similarities in adaptations and transmissions.[16]

Frieda Wong studied the narrative biographies of five second-generation Chinese American women ages 20 to 30 in terms of how they dealt with cultural stereotypes and parental expectations. Parents expected their daughters to gain financial security, practice filial piety, marry acceptable husbands, remain thin and feminine, and, for older daughters, help with caring for younger children in the family and help their parents live in the English-speaking world.[17]

Based on biographical accounts, Rachel Thomson and her colleagues reported on the mapping of young people in Great Britain as they moved toward adulthood. They were particularly interested in identifying critical moments in this transition. The researchers were especially interesting in learning how these moments might relate to social and geographical location and to the events in their lives and how they responded to them in terms of chance, opportunities available, and choices.[18]

Samuel Raphael and Paul Thompson in their editing of *The Myths We Live By* (Taylor & Frances/Routledge, 1990) present a mixture of life stories from ordinary people, including children on labor strike, family legends going back into antiquity, native Canadian Indians, Swedish lumberjacks' tales, martyrs of the Boer War, and Nazi concentration camp survivors. This study is a part of the *History Workshop Series*, and it is considered a landmark in oral history.[19] American slave narratives such as *Incidents in the Life of a Slave Girl*, by a former slave, Harriet Jacobs (Dover Publications, 2001; first published in 1861), and *Voices from Slavery: 100 Authentic Slave Narratives*, edited by Norman R. Yetnam (Dover Publications, 2000), offer provocative insight into American history and American social psychology and sociology.

Narrative biography is generally limited to a small part of one's life, and because of its first person approach, it is often popular with youth. It is a style with which many persons in public life feel very comfortable. It is also a style that individuals who experience an extraordinary event or events use to tell their stories of hardships, triumphs, and survival. Sports figures, politicians, entertainers, and ordinary people who experience unusual events produce a great deal of worthwhile personal narratives.

Examples of Narrative Biography

Published narrative biography suitable for youth include 1997 Nobel Peace Prize winner Loung Ung's *First They Killed My Father: Daughter of Cambodia Remembers* (Sagebrush Education Resources, 2001) and Judd Winick's *Pedro and Me: Friendship, Loss and What I Learned* (Henry Holt, 2000). Authors of children's and young adult books often write in narrative prose about their lives. Among these are Betsy Byars' *The Moon and I* (Simon & Schuster, 1994), Beverly Cleary's *A Girl from Yamhill: A Memoir* (Morrow/Avon, 1996), Roald Dahl's *Boy: Tales of Childhood* (HarperCollins, 2002), and Gary Paulsen's *My Life in Dogs* (Random House, 1998) and *Guts* (Laurel Leaf, 2002).

As mentioned, slave narratives are an integral part of the American narrative dialogue. Slave narratives became well established because of the work conducted by the Library of Congress in cooperation with the Works Progress Administration Federal Writers Project, as well as universities such as Fisk and Southern. In the 1930s these institutions collected, recorded, and, in many cases, published personal narratives of persons who were slaves.[20]

Perhaps less known among American narrative literature are narratives of persons who were captured by Native American tribes during the settlement of the American West. Raids and captures often occurred in Texas and other western states well into the 1870s and early 1880s by Apache, Comanche, and other tribes. Children were often victims, and they were often assimilated into tribal life and custom, and became highly prized members of the social network.

An interesting example of this is Cynthia Ann Parker (Naduah), who spent almost all of her life as a Comanche and bore several children, one of whom was her son Chief Quanah Parker, who lived for a time with his mother's brother Silas. Cynthia, however, was never able to adjust to Western society once she was found. Her story is told in *Where the Broken Heart Still Beats: The Story of Cynthia Ann Parker*, by Carolyn Meyer (Harcourt, 1992). The Quahadi band of the Comanche tribe in Texas, under Quanah's leadership, was later moved to Indian Territory in what became Oklahoma. There Quanah straddled both worlds, encouraging adaptation of many white ways such as ranching and education. While an influential citizen and leader in both Native American and white societies, he continued to hold and treasure many of his Native American traditions. He died in 1911 a very rich and honored man.[21] The two branches of the Parker family still maintain family relationships and often hold their annual reunions at the Parker homestead in East Texas at what

Is now the Fort Parker State Park.[22, 23] Nonetheless, such kidnappings had harsh consequences for the families and captured children.

For example, the following notice appeared June 1, 1868, in the *Austin Daily Republican:*

> Taken from my house by the Indians, in Legion valley, Llano county Texas on Wednesday, Feb. 5th, 1868, my son LEE TEMPLE FRIEND, aged eight . . . also my neighbor's daughter, MALINDA CAUDLE, aged seven. . . . All Indian agents or trader, or any person having an opportunity, are request to rescue the above named children.[24]

Author Scott Zesch has such a history in his own family. One of his relatives was one of the children described in the above notice. The children were eventually rescued and returned to their families, but Zesch's relative never adjusted to the white world and died a recluse in 1911. Based on family legends, interviews with his own family, and after much research, he published *The Captured: A True Story of Abduction by Indians on the Texas Frontier* (St. Martin's Press, 2004) (Figure 4.1). A review of the Zesch book in *Booklist* states that the author gives an interesting account of the "reasons for their 'Indianization,'" which for most of them lasted the rest of their lives, and discusses why they couldn't adjust to white society."

Another book on the topic suitable for mature readers and that records the aftermaths of such captures is *The Oatman Massacre*, by Brian McGinty

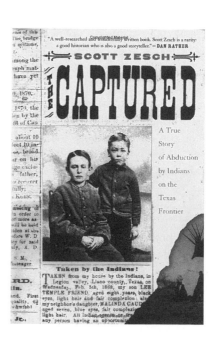

Figure 4.1
The Captured: A True Story of Abduction by Indians on the Texas Frontier, **by Scott Zesch. The pictures are not those of the captured children but are representative of children of the period. From *The Captured*, by Scott Zesch.** Copyright © 2004 by the author and reprinted by permission of St. Martin's Press, LLC.

(University of Oklahoma Press, 2005). The McGinty book tells the story of Olive Oatman, who spent many years with various western Native American tribes after her abduction as a thirteen-year-old girl living in Arizona. She returned to live for a time with her only family—her brother, who had survived the family's massacre. With facial tattoos given to her by Mohave Indians, she toured the country telling her story. She later married a man who was also a child captive, and she died in Sherman, Texas, in 1903 after a life filled with health problems and depression.[25] These two books, although not personal narratives in style and format, by recounting captives' experiences, clearly highlight conflicts that accounted for and resulted from the clash of different cultures on the American frontier.[26] Other captive narratives and experiences include *Shawnee Captive: The Story of Mary Draper Ingles*, by Nary R. Furbee (Morgan Reynolds, 2001), *The Ordeal of Olive Oatman: A True Story of the American West*, by Margaret Rau (Morgan Reynolds, 2003), and older writings by Carl Coke Rister: *Border Captives: The Traffic in Prisoners by Southern Plains Indians* (University of Oklahoma Press, 1940) and *Comanche Bondage: Dr. John Charles Beales's Settlement of La Villa de Dolores on Las Moras Creek in Southern Texas of the 1830's. With an Annotated Reprint of Sarah Ann Horn's Narrative of Her Captivity among the Comanches, Her Ransom by Traders in New Mexico, and Return Via the Santa Fe Trail* (University of Nebraska Press, 1989; first published in 1955).

Capture of whites and others by Native Americans is a recurring theme in white-based accounts. Figure 4.2 is an illustration from a book narrating several recounts of captives taken from various frontier settlements prior to 1830.

BIOGRAPHY AS LITERATURE

Literary biography contributes greatly to the world's literature. This literature includes published diaries, journals, memoirs, and both informal and formal autobiography and biography.

Diaries, Journals, Memoirs, Reminiscences

Diaries, journals, memoirs, and reminiscences have always played an important role in the development of biography. Journals, memoirs, and reminiscences are autobiographical in that they reflect what is remembered rather than presenting a chronology of a life. In them, the authors recount experiences, people, and events that have been significant in their lives. One of the most famous, if not infamous, is the memoir of Giacomo Casanova and his adventures as a rake, *The History of My Life* (Johns Hopkins University Press, 1997). On a different cultural level, musician Hector Berlioz's memoirs, *The Memoirs of Hector Berlioz* (Everyman's Library, 2002), provide insight into the musical scene in Europe in the early nineteenth century.[27]

Figure 4.2
Native Americans walking with captives. Illustration from a
contemporary narrative published in New York in 1833. Courtesy of the
Library of Congress, LC-USZ62-39381.

Although both males and females write journals and diaries, they are characterized as a feminine genre in that it is natural, spontaneous, and sometimes aligned with the culturally repressed.[28] The earliest records of journals written by women are from fifth-century Rome, ninth-century Japan, and sixteenth-century Europe. Women's journals ranged from household books to private autobiographical accounts of daily life. Women's diaries and autobiographical accounts written in the Western tradition tended to reflect the overriding social and cultural concerns of their times. Journals written in the United States and Britain were often religious in tone, reflecting the rise of religious evangelism. As nations developed, such as with the United States and Australia, and new territories were opened up for settlement, women wrote accounts of their experiences for family and friends.[29]

Although many diaries and journals remain hidden away in archives, often authors and researchers take diaries and make these accessible to children and young adult readers. An example of this is *Way West: Journal of a Pioneer Woman*, by Amelia Stewart Knight (Simon & Schuster Children's Publishing, 1993). This is Knight's account of her life going from Iowa to Oregon in 1852. Another book based on women's diaries found in archives and other places not generally accessible to the young is *Growing Up Female in America: Ten Lives*, edited by Eve Merriam (Beacon Press, 1987). Of course, Anne Frank's diary, *The Diary of Anne Frank*, is a modern classic. Other diaries and memories are being written, discovered, and published reflecting the Holocaust. These include *In My Hands: Memories of a Holocaust Rescuer*, by Irene Gut Opdyke (as told to Jennifer Armstrong) (Random House, 2004), and Jacob Boas's *We Are Witnesses: Five Diaries of Teenagers Who Died in the Holocaust* (Henry Holt, 1995).

Observations suggest that young people enjoy reading about other young people who have experienced and become a part of history. The Holocaust is just one engaging type of experience reflected in journals and diaries. Other journals and diaries suitable for young readers include Joseph Plumb Martin's *Yankee Doodle Boy: A Young Soldier's Adventures in the American Revolution* (Holiday House, 1995) and the Amelia Knight diary already mentioned.

Journals suitable for more mature readers who have an interest in history include *High Seas and Yankee Gunboats: A Blockade-Running Adventure from the Diary of James Dickson*, edited by Roger S. Durham (University of South Carolina, 2005), *Confederate Yankee: The Journal of Edward William Drummond, a Confederate Soldier from Maine*, edited by Roger S. Durham (University of Tennessee Press, 2004), and Johannes Steinhoff's *Messerschmitts over Sicily: Diary of a Luftwaffe Fighter Commander* (Stackpole Books, 2004).

A useful approach to presenting journals, letters, speeches, and memoirs to youth (including younger children) without using fiction is to select letters and journal writings of persons involved in history and events, and to place them into the context of the children's time. Milton Meltzer's books, including *A Lincoln: In His Own Words* (Harcourt Brace, 1993) and *The American Revolutionaries: A History in Their Own Words, 1750–1800* (Harper Collins, Canada, 1993), illustrate this approach. Libraries can greatly facilitate this firsthand approach to history and biography by offering their resources online. For example, the Library of Congress offers its American Memory resources.[30] The Library and Archives of Canada maintains its "Learning Centre" and a variety of other biographical rich resource materials including multicultural and aboriginal resources and services, the Portrait Gallery of Canada, and the *Dictionary of Canadian Biography Online*.[31] The National Library of Australia has maintains its "PictureAustralia" site whereby pictures held in its collections can be searched by keywords and its Online Exhibits that reflect useful biographical, historical, and cultural information about Australia.[32] Often museums and universities offer their resources to the public. For example, several years ago the University of Texas at Austin established a site that it called "Utopia." This was an effort made by the university to offer its vast resources, including biographical materials, to Texas and the world through its website (http://utopia.utexas.edu).

Fictionalized diary accounts can often introduce journals and diaries to young readers. The 1980 Newbery Medal winner, *A Gathering of Days: A New*

England Girl's Journal, 1830–32, by Joan Blos, is such a journal (Simon & Schuster, 1990), and the 1998 Newbery Medal winner, *Out of the Dust*, by Karen Hesse (Scholastic, 1997) allows readers to use fiction to understand some of the personal suffering of people in the American Plains states during the Depression and the Great Dust Bowl of the 1930s. Scholastic Publishes the "History Diaries" of fictionalized journals based on the experiences of young adults throughout historical periods. Each diary in the series is built around a teenager who tells his or her story in a chatty, personal way, with the events embedded in the backdrop of a specific time period. Scholastic's diary series sets include *The Royal Diaries*, *My Name Is America* (adventures of boys and young men), and *My America*, and *Dear America The Royal Ballet School Diaries*, also published by Scholastic, offers fictionalized accounts of pupils in the competitive English Royal Ballet School.

Autobiographies

Laura Marcus rightly argues that autobiography offers us insights into the minds of persons from the nineteenth and twentieth centuries who have greatly influenced who we are today. She contends that autobiography, along with biography, are important as we study public and private issues important to nations and societies.[33] We see that today, as cultural and social issues arise, leaders often use autobiography to set forth their beliefs and agendas for social reform and change. Some of these are controversial in that they raise social conflicts that society has had difficulty facing and resolving. *Nigger: An Autobiography*, by Dick Gregory (Buccaneer Books, 1993), the previously mentioned *Autobiography of Malcolm X*, and *Black Boy: A Record of Childhood and Youth*, the narrative autobiography of author Richard T. Wright (Harper/Collins, 2005; originally published in 1945), are other examples. These works are classics in American autobiographical writing showing the dark side of racism and violence. *Black Boy* in particular personalizes a young black man's struggle for personal dignity as he decides to leave the Jim Crow South of his birth and to begin a new life in the north.

BIOGRAPHY AND LITERARY STYLES

Literary biography is biography that lies between objectivity and subjectivity and becomes the mainstream of literary biography as art. This biographical literature is faithful to the individual and his or her place in life, and through literary style and methods, it seeks to truthfully present lives as lived. It does not distort or falsify, and within these boundaries, literary styles vary.

Some authors use vivid narratives, dialogue, dramatic scenes with documentation such as letters and diaries, and manipulate their evidence by offering interpretations based on their own insight and research. Some of these may stop just short of fictionalization. Other writers are careful not to manipulate their data and rely only on documents.

Fictionalized biography is often confused with literary biography. In fictionalized biography, documents are invented, scenes and conversations are constructed, and even events are developed from the author's imagination. Research is often based on secondary resources, and little scholarly research is evident. The attempt here is to blend the novel with biography, and in so doing the author is not limited by historical reality. During his life, novelist Irving Stone (1903–1989) wrote many such novels. Among his best known novels are *The President's Lady: A Novel about Rachel and Andrew Jackson* (Rutledge Hill Press, 1996; first published in 1951), his accounts of artists Vincent Van Gogh, in *Lust for Life* (Arrow Books, 2001; first published in 1958), and Michelangelo, in *The Agony and the Ecstasy: A Novel of Michelangelo* (Arrow Books, 2001; first published in 1961). These and his other works stand as primary examples of this type of approach to writing biography within a fictionalized context.

As noted, fictionalized biography has always played an important role in providing biographical information to young. The argument here is that fiction in biography is necessary to encourage young children to read and/or be interested in biography. Charlotte Huck and her colleagues justify the use of fictionalized biography with children as long as it remains true to the documented historical record. They maintain that while invented dialogue or background is allowed, it must be true to the time, place, and personality.[34]

Biography as literature extends well beyond the boundaries of literary studies as we find some of the great biographical literature in various fields such as the social sciences, political life, social life and culture (including entertainment and sports), and the sciences. These areas are well populated with the various forms of biographical writings as mentioned earlier. For example notable examples are Garrett Mattingly's *Catherine of Aragon* (AMS Press, 2005; first published in 1942), *Madame Curie*, by her daughter Eve Curie (Da Capo Press, 2004; first published in 1937), and *Victoria*, by Lytton Strachey (Harcourt/Harvest Books 2002; first published in 1921). Because of its psychological understanding of Victoria and her close associates, and its beautiful prose, it is considered the definitive biography of Victoria. Strachey's *Eminent Victorians* is another of his fine literary biographies (Continuum International Publishing Group, 2005; first published in 1918). The history and development of biography as great literature was discussed in chapter 1 and is considered further in chapter 5.

EXPERIENCING BIOGRAPHY

Biography offers many opportunities to reflect on personal experiences and to understand the significance of broad human and cultural life. Information literacy is important to help youth better use biography. Among others, biography requires careful attention to accuracy, documentation, understanding points of view, how points of views are stated, and how data are analyzed and interpreted. But to experience biography fully, it must be made personal and intimate. School library media specialists, teachers, and youth librarians in public libraries have long recognized this and have provided avenues for youth to experience biography in many ways. At one level is understanding that each person and family has a biography that is unique and special. Beyond that comes a sense of community based on an understanding of how biography is central to community life and history. Youth need to also understand how biography helps to define their society and their culture. Many of these suggestions made in the following discussions are based on curriculum needs and directives, but with some modification, public librarians serving youth can make good use of these as well.

Personal Reflections and Journal Writing

Learning about Self

Journal writing is used widely in curriculum and instruction as well as in psychological therapy. In therapy, it offers a means of self-examination and reflection. It can also be used to develop an improved sense of self and self-esteem; and it can help develop a sense of purpose and direction.[35] As a therapeutic process, this involves placing one's thoughts and feelings into words. Journal therapy focuses on emotions and seeks to foster a better understanding of one's internal life. By writing one's concerns into a journal, personal growth often occurs and problems are better solved.[36]

Although not used as psychological therapy, curriculum use of journal writing is helpful in learning content as well as in helping youth understand themselves and others. In literature classes, journal writing has been effectively used to help youth better understand the writing process as well as to help them associate writing with literature and personal experiences.

One form of journal writing is the personal dialogue journal where the student writes and the teachers reads and reacts to what is written. This type of journal allows students to write about personal concerns based on subjects considered and/or read in class. In their personal writing they use comparisons, analogy, description, and argumentation. In this process, they not only deal with subject content, such as conflicts in literature, but they are also involved in biographical writing.[37]

Journal writing is used with young children as well. The following list of journal "prompts" illustrates how journal writing is a biographical tool no matter the age of the student. In this process the teachers offer suggestions, or "prompts":[38]

- If I were the teacher, I would . . .
- If I could give one piece of advice to any person in history, that advice would be . . .
- Describe a dream that you had recently. Provide as many details as possible.
- The best lesson my grandparent (or parent or any relative) ever taught me was . . .
- [on the day after the Grammy Awards are announced] Do you think the right artists won? Why or why not?
- Tell five things you'd like to do on your next birthday.
- In 20 years, I will be . . .
- Tell about an event in your life that has caused a change in you.
- I was most angry when . . .
- If you could design one room in a house to suit only your needs, what would it look like? [Challenge kids to be as fanciful as they like. For example, would someone have a desk made of chocolate?]
- Describe your perfect vacation.
- My worst mistake was . . .

For older, secondary students:

- Imagine a friend of yours is considering whether to take steroids. What would you tell that friend to persuade him or her not to do that?
- Do you believe in love at first sight?
- If you and your best friend could have a free limo for twenty-four hours, where would you go and what would you do?
- You have the freedom to travel to any city or country in the world. Where would you go and why?
- What would you do if you were president of the United States?
- You have an extra $100,000 to give away; you cannot spend it on yourself. What would you do with the money?
- The qualities that make a best friend are . . .
- If you were an insect, what kind would you be and why?
- Describe your room at home in detail. What are you proudest of and why?
- [using a current local controversy] Do you agree with the decision? Why? Would you change anything about the situation?

Learning about Others

The interviewing of others allows biographical concepts to develop naturally. Interviewing can be done with young children as well as other youth. Teacher Frank Miller developed a unit of study entitled "Biography Buddy: Interviewing Each Other" in which he outlined how second and fifth grade students could interview and write about each other in brief biographical sketches. Not only is the unit designed to promote collaboration between age groups, but it introduces biographical concepts and biographical references and techniques.[39]

One of the complaints of modern life is that the young know very little about older people in their communities and even in their own families. Teachers in training Annette Packard and Michelle Grant offer a lesson plan designed to introduce young children to older people living around them or associated with them. The grade levels for this unit are 2, 3, and 4. In addition to introducing the concepts of older generations, the unit focuses on teaching basic concepts of sociology, language arts, and reading. Similarly, it introduces the process of interviewing. The children are first provided with basic concepts concerning generations through instruction using books and films. The main focus of the unit is to introduce students to generations older than themselves so the students learn to value them. After instruction in interviewing, the children develop an interview instrument, then go out into nursing homes in the community to interview older people living there. After the interviews are completed and formatted for presentations, children are then allowed several other opportunities to explore older generations, such as developing posters and other types of graphic presentations showing their own families, and inviting their grandparents to visits or, perhaps, as guest speakers for the class.[40]

The use of oral history as a teaching methodology is well established in secondary schools as well. In describing oral history in the teaching of American history, Carl R. Siler states:

> Oral history is a stimulating classroom activity and an exciting process designed to increase student involvement in a United States history class and improve student understanding of the historical topic. Further, oral history involves students directly in a method of historical inquiry, which includes the organization and presentation of data acquired directly from another person.[41]

These remarks apply in all areas of study where students are asked to investigate and gather information directly from people as primary sources. One of the best known oral history projects involving secondary school students is that developed by Eliot Wigginton in his highly successful Foxfire project and publications concerning the folklife and people found in the southern Appalachian Mountains of the United States. The project was begun in 1966 by Wigginton and his students in Rabun Gap-Nacoochee schools as a class project and has now grown into The Foxfire Fund, Inc.[42]

Family Histories and Stories

Family history and genealogy can also tie young people to their communities and offer them a sense of identity, and provide a means of connecting with the culture, history, and stories of their families.

Nelda Helt developed a lesson plan for teaching genealogical research and recording methods to secondary-school students in grade 11. The primary aim of the unit was to personalize history and to help students understand that history was not just a list of names and dates, but involved the actual lives of people. To make this connection, the unit was designed to introduce them to family history and to help them appreciate and communicate with older generations. The unit helps students understand economic, social, and political issues that played and continue to play roles in defining a family's history. In addition, the unit was constructed to help students learn something about the countries of their family origins and to help them understand the processes of immigration and cultural assimilation.[43]

All families have stories. Some of these may go back into antiquity while others are recent. Whatever the age, they are all important to biographical study and family identity. In her unit Helt suggested that students begin to seek out and record family stories and to document these in various ways. Images (see Figure 4.3), stories, and other items can be used. Some examples are:

- Family portraits and albums that present visual histories (portraits of great grandparents, family gatherings and celebrations)
- Experiences of family members in wars, such as World War II, the Korean War, and more recent wars (Great Uncle Joe was a prisoner of war in Korea.)
- Famous or well-known family members such as members of state legislatures, mayors, etc. (Grandmother was the first woman mayor in our town.)
- Stories of work experiences (Granddad's first job as a bank teller)
- Travels of family members (Great Grandmother's Trip to South Africa, 1930)
- Special skills and/or hobbies of family members (Great Uncle Jack helped build the Empire State Building.)
- Hardships and how they were met (Great Granddad had a hard time making a living in the Depression driving a gravel truck.)
- Legends that have survived in family stories (e.g., coming West in a covered wagon, descended from Scottish nobility, origins of family names)
- Childhood remembrances of older generations (Great Grandmother attended school in a one-room country schoolhouse with only a wood-burning stove to keep warm.)

Figure 4.3
Pictures from family albums and portraits provide biographical
insights into family and self-identity. Private collection. Drawing by
Richard Hendler.

Biography and Community

Senator Hillary Rodham Clinton uses the old African proverb "It Takes a
Village to Raise a Child" in her book *It Takes a Village: And Other Lessons
Children Teach Us* (Simon & Schuster, 1996) to introduce her concepts of
community responsibility for child rearing and child care. Biography helps
cement together the fabric of caring, responsibility, and commitment to
community. School library media specialists and public librarians serving
youth have an important role to play in this relationship between community
and youth by ensuring that community biographies are available to youth.
Traditional ways of doing this are through vertical file systems, portrait files,
and the school archives. Computer technology now provides a vast array of
biographical materials in digitized formats as more and more libraries, museums, and archives place their holdings on the Internet. Biographical material
is now so plentiful on the Internet that most youth need to be taught how to
access it, evaluate it, and use it properly. Because some of this material is not
appropriate for young children, library media specialists and librarians both

in schools and in the public library will need to carefully screen much of the material before it is provided to students.

Organizing this vast array of materials for access is necessary. There are many approaches to such organization, but this is not the place to consider these procedures in depth. Lukenbill's *Community Resources in the School Library Media Center: Concepts and Methods* (Libraries Unlimited, 2004) offers some suggestions.

Students can use local biographical materials for special projects including histories of events and personalities that have played keys roles in the development of the community, including the local school. Cultural and historical information about individuals and families should also be made a part of the biographical program.

A unit in the ninth grade English Language Arts program for Michigan schools offers an introduction to life stories that can be adapted to highlight local biography. In this unit, students are instructed to read personal life stories based on memoirs, biographies, autobiographies, diaries, and journals and to write in their own journals about the various themes and issues faced in people's lives. In doing this, students are encouraged to think about common elements that most people face in their lives. This theme can be used to ask students to consider how local situations have affected people's lives and what common life elements are found in their communities. Local newspapers and published historical records such as city and county histories can serve as resources for this inquiry. Figures 4.4, 4.5, 4.6, and 4.7 all illustrate that biographical information is widespread in most communities.

Along with celebrations and government officials, work roles in the community can also provide understanding and insight into a community's collective biography.

In many communities, biographical books dating from the late nineteenth and early twentieth centuries exist and chronicle the lives of early settlers in communities. These were products of publication companies of the time that often sent their representatives into local homes to gather biographical and genealogical information about residents as a means of selling these books to residents on a subscription basis. Today they provide valuable information in developing a sense of the history and biography of a community. Many of these books have been republished by specialized companies such as Higginson Book Company (www.higginsonbooks.com) and the Local History Company of Pittsburgh, Pennsylvania (www.thelocalhistorycompany.com). The "AcqWeb Directory of Publishers and Vendors—History Publishers" maintained by Vanderbilt University Law School offers a list of many such publishers that offer materials of local interest (http://acqweb.library.vanderbilt.edu/pubr/hist.html).

Specific examples of this type of local material include *Vernon County Black Settlers: The Correct Location of the Black Americans in the Forest Township*, by Orville T. Waldron and Beverly M. Waldron (O. T. Waldron [Sparta, Wis.],

Figure 4.4
Local biographical information is found throughout the community:
African Americans celebrating Emancipation Day, Austin, Texas, 1900.
PICA 05476, Austin History Center, Austin Public Library.

Figure 4.5
City council, Austin,
Texas, 1910–1919.
PICA 00126, Austin
History Center, Austin
Public Library.

ca. 2000); *Early Settlers, Clinch County, Georgia*, by MariLee Beatty Hagenes (M. B. Hageness [Anniston, Ala.], 1995); and *History of Olmsted County, Together with Biographical Matter, Statistics, Etc.: Gathered from Matter Furnished by Interviews with Old Settlers, County, Township, and Other Records, and Extracts from Files of Papers, Pamphlets, and Such Other Sources as Have Been Available* (Olmsted [Minn.] County Historical Society, ca. 1987).

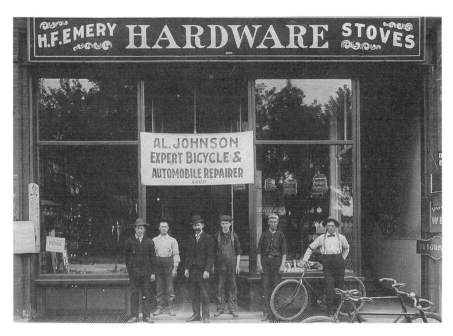

Figure 4.6
Workers and owner, bicycle and automobile repair shop, Fargo, North Dakota, ca. 1900. Private collection.

Figure 4.7
School teachers, Williston, North Dakota, ca. 1900. Private collection.

Regional biographical volumes in the "Who's Who" series published by the Marquis Company provide current information on persons of regional and professional prominence (www.marquiswhoswho.com/products/productlist_main.asp). Local heroes and celebrities also play a large role in the biographical program of the school library media center and public library. Information about notables such as sports teams and sport heroes, entertainers, and other local public figures needs to be collected and presented to youth in interesting ways. An active collection program of local biographical information is fundamental. Readily available sources include local school and town newspapers and publications, obituaries, published local histories, organizational and business histories, and family genealogical materials.

Oral History and Oral Traditions

"Oral history is the practice of collecting, preserving, and interpreting information about the past through the study of both individual and social experiences in story form."[44] The formal, academic approach to oral history began in the United States in the 1930s and 1940s.[45] During this period, the Library of Congress, The Works Projects Administration, as well as other academic institutions were very active in recording slave narratives, Western lore, local histories, and other forms of folk culture, and the world's first oral history archives was founded at Columbia University in 1946.[46] As mentioned earlier, much of this material is available through the Library of Congress' American Memory website.

Today oral history is well established as an important academic discipline and as an effective teaching tool. Teacher Elaine Seavey in 1994 outlined her concept of how to use oral history and techniques in teaching history and writing to students in grades 8, 9, and 10. She was particularly interested in combining literature, composition, English, and editing. Students were instructed to look into their local communities through reading local newspapers, local histories, and any fiction that might have been influenced by the local community. Instructions were given on how to conduct oral histories, using experiences found in the "Foxfire" series (Turtleback Books). She also suggested to students that they interview persons in the local area about their lives and experiences and research the histories of sites in the local area. Once this initial research was completed, students were instructed to develop and edit publications based on research and writing skills learned in English.[47]

Oral history techniques are useful when studying biography, but this technique should not be taken lightly as it does require skill to successfully execute a project. The Oral History Society of Great Britain describes oral history in the following way:

- Oral history is the recording of people's memories. It is the living history of everyone's unique life experiences.

- Oral history records people's experiences on audio- and videotape. It is a vital tool for our understanding of the recent past. No longer are we dependent only on the written word.

- Oral history enables people who have been hidden from history to be heard, and for those interested in their past to record personal experiences and those of their families and communities.

- Oral history is new and exciting because it is interactive: it is shared history and a rare chance to actually talk to history face to face.

- Oral history preserves everyone's past for the future.[48]

The society also provides training and offers useful publications on oral history including *Talking in Class: Oral History and the National Curriculum,* by Allan Redfern (Oral History Society [Colchester, Great Britain], 1995). Other important oral history organizations include:

Associations

- Oral History Association (United States), http://omega.dickinson.edu/organizations/oha
- Canadian Oral History Association, www.ncf.carleton.ca/oral-history
- International Oral History Association, www.ioha.fgv.br

National Libraries

- National Library of Australia Oral History Collection, www.nla.gov.au/oh
- National Library of New Zealand Oral History Centre, http://tepuna.natlib.govt.nz/ abouttp/abkilbirnie/about.html
- Library of Congress WPA Federal Writers' Project Life Stories (United States), http://lcweb2.loc.gov/ammem/wpaintro/wpahome.html

Research Centers and Resources

- British Library National Sound Archive Oral History Collection/National Life Story Collection, London, www.bl.uk
- BBC Education, History, 20th Century Vox, www.bbc.co.uk/education/20cvox
- Indiana University Oral History Research Center, www.indiana. edu/~ohrc
- John F. Kennedy Library Oral History Project, www.cs.umb.edu/~serl/jfk/oralhist.htm

- Kellogg African American Health Care Project, www.urnet.com/kellogg/theoral.htm
- Regional Oral History Office, Bancroft Library, Berkeley University, www.lib.berkeley.edu/BANC/ROHO
- Smithsonian Institution Archives, www.siris.si.edu
- Southern Oral History Program, University of North Carolina at Chapel Hill, www.unc.edu/depts/sohp
- Survivors of the Shoah Visual History Foundation, www.vhf.org
- 1968: The Whole World Was Watching, www.stg.brown.edu/projects/1968
- J. S. Battye Library, Library and Information Service of New South Wales, Australia, www.liswa.wa.gov.au/oral.html
- New Zealand Historical Branch (Oral History), http://inform.dia.govt.nz/internal_affairs/businesses/hb_pro/profile.html
- Yad Vashem: The Holocaust Martyrs' and Heroes' Remembrance Authority, Jerusalem, Israel, www.yad-vashem.org.il

Oral history groups and associations are often found in local communities. These centers generally provide resources and instructions, and they often have ongoing projects that are built around the assistance of volunteers and resource contributors. For example, the Austin History Center in Texas, a division of the Austin Public Library (www.ahca.net/ahc.htm), relies on the community for many of its oral history projects. One project that the center has just completed is *The Blue Bellies Are in Austin: Readings from the Travis County Slave Narratives,* a film based on slave narratives housed in the center (www.ahca.net/slavenarratives.htm). The center also has an active publication program, much of which is biographical in nature. For example, a recent *Writing Austin's Lives: A Community Portrait Written by the People of Austin* (University of Texas Humanities Institute and Waterloo Press, 2004) presents 127 visions and personal experiences of all sorts of people who were and are an important part of Austin at the beginning of the twenty-first century. Another of its useful biographical resources is its *Austin & Travis County: A Pictorial History, 1839–1939*, edited by Katherine Drake Hart (Encino Press for the Friends of the Austin Public Library, 1975, reprinted by Waterloo Press, n.d.). Included here are sepia reproductions of rare images of families, individuals, and sites in Austin and Travis County. Waterloo Press, which is a division within the center, also offers posters and prints of images and artifacts found in their collection.

Universities in local areas frequently have departments of oral history where instruction and ideas can be obtained that will be helpful to both public librarians and school library media specialists. The Institute for Oral

History at Baylor University in Waco, Texas, is a good example of such resources (www3.baylor.edu/Oral_History). Among other resources, it provides "The Oral History Workshop on the Web," where basic information about oral history interviewing can be found (www3.baylor.edu/Oral_History/Workshop.htm).

PROGRAMMING FOR BIOGRAPHY

Missions, Goals, and Objectives

We have already seen how biography is used extensively in curriculum and instruction in school environments. These examples are driven by curriculum needs and student achievement. Aside from that, they also meet the social, cultural, and recreational demands placed on schools. Although the public library has a different role than that of the school library media center, public library programs for youth have always served the school curriculum in various ways. Nevertheless, public library programs have their own unique missions, goals, and objectives to meet, and their biographical programming drives those demands.

The mission statement of the Orange County (California) Public Library is similar to many mission statements of American public libraries. It reads:

> To provide a framework for the delivery of relevant resources meeting their educational, cultural, civic, business and life-long learning needs to residents of all ages of member communities through a network of locally focused libraries in which knowledgeable, service-oriented staff members offer access to information, books and other materials in a variety of formats using contemporary technology, and which encourage and foster reciprocal community involvement to educate, inform and enrich the lives of a diverse population.[49]

Children's and young adult services in public libraries must reflect the mission of their parent institution through their programming and services, and their overall plan of operation. Although the public library in many cases serves the same audience as schools, the circumstances of their relationship to the school-youth population is different. Needs of the client group or audience differ as the environment moves from school to public library.

The public library generally meets the biographical curriculum demands placed on it through homework help, bibliographic database provisions, reference materials (both in-house and online), and programs such as term paper workshops and computer instruction and information literacy instruction. Public libraries also provide biographical information in ways that best meet the needs of their client groups. For example, guest appearances of people of interest to youth, such as authors, local personalities, and celebrity personalities, are popular as they are specifically focused biographical programs.

For example, the Marion County Public Library in Ohio offered the "American Girl" program in February 2005 for grades K–5, which featured fictional information about a girl who grew up during the Great American Depression (www.marion.lib.oh.us/kids/kzprograms.htm). The "American Girl" series is a popular book series that is designed to interest young girls and to teach them history in fun ways. The series attempts to show children how the world has changed but how elements of human relationships— family, friendship, feelings—have remained the same. A section of each book gives historical information about the time in which the fictional character of a particular book lived. The series is well illustrated to provide a picture of life in the times of the characters (www.bookloversden.com/series/girls/ AmGirls/AmGirl.html). A popular spin-off of the "American Girl" series is the doll that goes with each of the books. For teens, the Marion County Public Library developed a contest whereby contestants were challenged to identify and match celebrity couple breakups (www.marion.lib.oh.us/ Teens/teenstart.htm).

Recognizing the appeal of television, popular culture, and celebrities, the Orange Country (California) Public Library provides access on its teen web page to "Teen Television," which links to celebrity sites, music, and television (www.teentelevision.com). Similarly, Baltimore County (California) Public Library provides linkage to popular cultural biographical information of interest to teens, including local music personalities (www.bcteen.info/ entertainment/music.html).

Styles of Presentations

Biographical information can be presented in several ways. Story hours and read-aloud programs can include the reading and/or telling of accounts based on real people's lives, struggles, accomplishments, and adventures. In a similar way, booktalks and media talks can offer the same types of coverage. Book clubs and thematic discussion groups can also increase interest and understanding of biographical information. Genealogical, local history, and oral history workshops can provide a base for biographical inquiry. Writing workshops can also be a part of biographical program. These types of workshops can not only include biographical research methods, but also provide instruction on how to develop a personal biography through journal and diary writing. This type of workshop can also encourage participants to prepare biographical information products such as PowerPoint presentations, project or poster exhibits, family albums, personal web pages, and other forms of information delivery. These types of offerings also provide opportunities for public librarians to teach critical thinking and analytical skills, especially as related to biographical presentations through the mass media.

Biography and Atmospherics

Careful consideration must be given to the environment in which biographical programs are presented. Attention to good lighting, adequate space, good seating, and necessary supplies and equipment is essential for success. In addition, the space should be designated as a special place for children and/or young adults. Design features such as colors, furniture, art, and wall decorations should be used generously. Providing these elements is fundamental to successfully promoting biographical programs and materials to children and young adults.

Evaluation

No program can go without evaluation. One of the important concepts to consider in evaluation is outcomes. That is, what effects will your programs and services have on your audience? This might be measured in changes in attitudes, behaviors, immediate and long-term actions, and beliefs. In terms of a biographical program, careful consideration should be given to what kinds of behavior outcomes you want your programs to have.

Do you want to see an increase in biographical materials being checked out of the library?

Do you want evidence of an increased knowledge of biographical information about important individuals?

Do you want to see a better understanding from your audience in terms of the role of biography in culture and society?

Do you want your audience to assume a more critical way of looking at how biography is presented to them?

Do you want to see a more critical appraisal of biographical materials as presented in the mass media?

With such questions in mind, a biographical program can then be developed to affect positive behavior and attitude changes. Ways to measure these are important. Measurements must go well beyond the counting circulation and attendance at programs; it must assess actual behaviors and attitude changes in the audience. The Institute of Museum and Library Services (IMLS), through their various programs, endorses such measurements, and the United Way of America offers useful information and resources about outcome measures (http://national.unitedway.org/outcomes).

IMLS also provides examples of actual outcome measures used successfully in some of the programs that they have funded (www.imls.gov/grants/current/crnt_obe.htm). The following is a list of outcome measures adapted from public library programs that can be used in youth biographical programs.[50]

- Attitude/perception change about biographical materials (e.g., from negative to positive)

- Personal efficacy (self-esteem, confidence building) in the use and understanding of biography and how it influences lives and culture

- Increased skill levels (increase in information literacy skills; better use of critical skills; better knowledge of how to access biographical materials in various formats)

- Learning gains (aside from information literacy, increase in social and cultural information gained from biographical materials)

- Social networking (better socialization skills developed through information and interaction with biographical materials and those who can supply such materials—librarians, teachers, bookstores, friends, organizations, etc.)

- Status change (moving from lower learning and social networking status to a higher level based on biographical materials)

Measurements of outcomes can include staff observations, comments from children and youth who are part of the program, comments from teachers and parents, formal evaluations from staff and participants, selected interviews and focus groups, and informational anecdotal evidence. Measurements need to be structured in such a way that they can be placed into a statistical format. This approach to evaluation is discussed further in *Community Resources in the School Library Media Center: Concepts and Methods,* cited previously.[51]

CONCLUSION

The influence of biography on human behavior is profound and complex. An understanding of social theories can help school library media specialists and public youth librarians better appreciate this pervasive influence and how they can help youth in constructive ways to contemplate the world in which they exist. Such theories as Bandura's social learning theory, Bronfenbrenner's ecological theory, and Vygotsky's sociocultural theory, as well as various theories of literature and its interplay in society, can help us better define the role of biography in the lives of youth. Beyond that, an understanding of the types of biography—narrative biography, journals and diaries, various types of autobiographical and biographical writings, oral histories, family histories, local history—can bring into focus how people express their lives in writing, in film, and in actual life, and in how they view their various experiences. From there, developmentally and culturally appropriate programs offered by schools and public libraries can help solidify this important bond between biography and human behavior.

NOTES

1. Summer Pierce, "Class Bios of Albert Bandura," http://www.utexas.edu/coc/journalism/SOURCE/j363/bandura.html (accessed Feb. 1, 2005).

2. Rob Evans and David Hencke, "Hitler Saw Duke of Windsor as 'No Enemy' US File Reveals Intelligence Report Throws New Light on Former King's Ties to Führer," *The Guardian* (Jan. 25, 2003), http://education.guardian.co.uk/higher/artsandhumanities/story/0,,883183,00.html (accessed Nov. 3, 2005).

3. "Charlayne Hunter-Gault Engages Philip Johnson about His Influence on Architecture and His Controversial Life," PBS interview, http://www.pbs.org/newshour/bb/environment/johnson_7-9a.html (accessed Nov. 3, 2005).

4. Rob Nagel, "Paul Robeson. Contemporary Musicians," Sept. 1992, http://homepage.sunrise.ch/homepage/comtex/rob3.htm (accessed Feb. 6, 2005).

5. The Psi Café: A Psychology Resource Site, "Urie Bronfenbrenner," http://www.psy.pdx.edu/PsiCafe/KeyTheorists/Bronfenbrenner.htm (accessed April 21, 2003).

6. M. Dean and W. Huitt, "Neighborhood and Community," Aug. 1991, citing R. Lewis and J. Morris, "Communities for Children," *Education Leadership* 55 (1998): 34–36, http://chiron.valdosta.edu/whuitt/col/context/neighbor.html (accessed April 21, 2005).

7. Julia Scherba de Valenzuela, "Socioculture Theory," http://www.unm.edu/~devalenz/handouts/sociocult.html (accessed Feb. 22, 2005).

8. Scherba de Valenzuela.

9. M. C. Albrecht, "The Relationships of Literature and Society," *American Journal of Sociology* 59 (March 1954): 425–26, 431–32.

10. [Spartacus Shoolnet], "Muckraking," http://www.spartacus.schoolnet.co.uk/Jmuckraking.htm (accessed Feb. 23, 2005).

11. W. Bernard Lukenbill, *Collection Development for a New Century in the School Library Center* (Westport, Conn.: Greenwood Press, 2002), 38–39, quoting Dino F. Felluga, "Undergraduate Introduction to Critical Theory," http://omni.cc.purdue.edu/~felluga/theory.html (updated as http://www.cla.purdue.edu/academic/engl/theory/index.html) (accessed Nov. 3, 2005).

12. Kay F. Vandergrift, "Journey or Destination: Female Voices in Youth Literature," in *Mosaics of Meaning,* ed. Kay Vandergrift (Lanham, Md.: Scarecrow Press, 1996), 17–47.

13. Elizabeth Partridge, "The Creative Life," *School Library Journal* 48 (Oct. 2002): 42–43.

14. "Biography," in *Encyclopædia Britannica,* Encyclopædia Britannica Online, http://search.eb.com/eb/article?tocId=51200 (accessed Feb. 23, 2005).

15. "Biography," in *Britannica Student Encyclopedia,* Encyclopædia Britannica Online, http://search.eb.com/ebi/article?tocId=9273218 (accessed Feb. 24, 2005).

16. Carolyn S. Ellis, *PsycCRITIQUES* (2004, unpaged), review of Dan Bar-On *Fear and Hope: Three Generations of the Holocaust* (Cambridge, Mass.: Harvard University Press, 1995), PsycINFO Database, accession no. 2004-17624-027 (accessed Feb. 4, 2005).

17. Frieda Wong, "Experiences of Successful Second-Generation Chinese American Women with Cultural Stereotypes and Parental Expectation" (dissertation, University of Massachusetts, Amherst, 2003), abstracted in *Dissertation Abstracts International,* 64-B (April 2004): 5243.

18. Rachel Thomson and others, "Critical Moments: Choice, Chance and Opportunity In Young People's Narratives of Transition," *Sociology* 36 (May 2002): 335–54.

19. Raphael Samuel and Paul Thompson, *The Myths We Live By* (New York: Routledge, 1990).

20. W. Bernard Lukenbill, "Marketing *Gone with the Wind* in an Age of Social Conflict," in *Strategic Marketing in Library and Information Science,* ed. Irene Owens (Binghamton, N.Y.: Haworth Information Press, 2002), 211.

21. Brian C. Hosmer, "Parker, Quanah (ca. 1845–1911)," *Handbook of Texas* Online, http://www.tsha.utexas.edu/handbook/online/articles/PP/fpa28.html (accessed June 5, 2005).

22. "Parker Family Reunion," http://www.rootsweb.com/~okkingfi/family.htm (accessed June 5, 2005).

23. Hosmer.

24. Mike Cox, "Stealing Glances into Frightening Frontier Days," *Austin American-Statesman,* June 5, 2005.

25. Cox.

26. Cox.

27. "Biography," in *Encyclopædia Britannica,* Encyclopædia Britannica Online, http://search.eb.com/eb/article?tocId=51207 (accessed March 2, 2005).

28. Rachel Cottam, "Diaries and Journals: General Survey," in *Encyclopedia of Life Writing: Autobiographical and Biographical Forms,* vol. 1, ed. Margaretta Jolly (London: Fitzroy Dearborn, 2001), 269.

29. Sarah M. Edwards, "Women's Diaries and Journals," in *Encyclopedia of Life Writing: Autobiographical and Biographical Forms,* vol. 2, ed. Margaretta Jolly (London: Fitzroy Dearborn, 2001), 950.

30. Library of Congress, "American Memory," http://memory.loc.gov/ammem (accessed April 21, 2005).

31. Library and Archives of Canada, http://www.collectionscanada.ca/education/index-e .html (accessed April 21, 2005).

32. National Library of Australia, http://www.nla.gov.au (accessed April 21, 2005).

33. Laura Marcus, *Auto-Biographical Discourses: Criticism, Theory, Practice* (Manchester, UK: Manchester University Press, 1999).

34. Charlotte S. Huck and others, *Children's Literature in the Elementary School,* 6th ed. (Madison, Wis.: Brown & Benchmark, 1997), 555.

35. Phil Rich, "Journal Writing and Self Help," http://www.selfhelpmagazine.com/articles/growth/journalwrite.html (accessed Feb. 17, 2005).

36. "Writing Therapy," http://www.wholehealthmd.com/refshelf/substances_view/1,1525,745,00.html (accessed Feb. 17, 2005).

37. "Journal Writing Every Day: Teachers Say It Really Works!" http://www.education-world.com/a_curr/curr144.shtml (accessed Feb. 17, 2005).

38. "Journal Writing Every Day."

39. "Journal Writing Every Day."

40. Annette Packard and Michell Grant, "Developing Relationships with Older People," An Educator's Reference Desk Lesson Plan, Lesson Plan #:AELP-SOC0002, (1994), http://www.eduref.org/Virtual/Lessons/Social_Studies/Sociology/SOC0002.html (accessed Feb. 17, 2005).

41. Carl R. Siler, *Oral History in the Teaching of U.S. History* (Bloomington, Ind.: ERIC Clearinghouse for Social Studies/Social Science Education, 1996), ERIC document no. ED 393 781.

42. "The Foxfire Tradition," http://www.foxfire.org/whatis.html (accessed April 22, 2005).

43. Nelda Helt, "Genealogy Research," An Educator's Reference Desk Lesson Plan Lesson Plan #:AELP-HIS0005 (1994), http://www.eduref.org/Virtual/Lessons/Social_Studies/History/HIS0005.html (accessed Feb. 17, 2005).

44. Mary Marshall Clark, "Oral History," in *Encyclopedia of Life Writing: Autobiographical and Biographical Forms,* vol. 2, 677–79.

45. Clark, 677.

46. Clark.

47. Elaine Seavey, "A Team Approach to Oral History," An Educator's Reference Desk Lesson Plan, Lesson Plan #:AELP-HIS0013 (1994), http://www.eduref.org/Virtual/Lessons/Social_Studies/History/HIS0013.html (accessed Feb. 17, 2005).

48. Oral History Society, "What Is Oral History?" http://www.oralhistory.org.uk (accessed Feb. 17, 2005).

49. Orange County Public Library, "Mission Statement of the Orange County Public Library," http://www.ocpl.org/about-mission.asp (accessed Jan. 31, 2006).

50. Joan C. Durrance and Karen E. Fisher with Marian Bouch Hinton, *How Libraries and Librarians Help: A Guide to Identifying User-Centered Outcomes* (Chicago: American Library Association, 2005), 121–30.

51. W. Bernard Lukenbill, *Community Resources in the School Library Media Center: Concepts and Methods* (Westport, Conn.: Libraries Unlimited, 2004), 58–61.

5

BIOGRAPHY AND LITERATURE

INTRODUCTION

Previous chapters in this book have briefly considered attributes relating to literature and society. This chapter continues this discussion by giving more attention to the roles that biography plays in aesthetics and in fine literature. Among other topics, it will consider various issues and problems related to writing literary biography; writing literary biography of interest to youth; writing regional biography; small presses and university publishers, and their contribution to literary biography; and film, television, and audio productions of literary value.

BIOGRAPHY AND FINE LITERATURE

This discussion uses the term *literary biography* to refer to biographical works that meet high standards of literature. Often the term *literary biography* is used to refer only to biographies of writers and authors generally associated with imaginative literature, such as novels, dramas, and poetry.[1] Nevertheless, biographical writing by persons who are not identified as imaginative authors can also be considered literary biographies because of the skill shown in the writing and the attention given to literary devices in developing the biographical narrative.

In her classic work, *Living with Books*, Helen Haines correctly associated biography with psychology, history, imaginative literature, art, history, science, and all other areas of thought. She wrote that biography

> presents life in the experience of living, it turns the abstract into the concrete, gives us not the thought alone, but the personality of the thinker, not the record of the deed alone, but the nature of the doer.

***

The universality of its relationship to literature and to life, its power of inspiration, its appeal to innate, unquenchable human curiosity concerning human character and experience, have given biography a place second only to fiction in the affection of readers.[2]

Further, she noted that biography offers an easy link or bridge from the reading of fiction to nonfiction for young persons.[3]

Lytton Strachey is generally considered one of the first modern-day literary biographers based on his works *Eminent Victorians* (1918), *Queen Victoria* (1921), and *Elizabeth and Essex* (1928). In these biographies he rejected the Victorian notions of biography with its mass of materials, poor writing styles, and overall lack of design and presentation of materials. He insisted that a biographer has the "right to select material artfully, to present it in a carefully crafted style, and to expose the foibles and inner lives of his subjects."[4] He departed from the traditional notion that actions reveal character. To him, the biographer must strip the subject from its outward self-directed, protected covering and search for the truth of character in the recesses of a person's life. Strachey insisted that he imposed nothing, and insinuated nothing about a life, that he simply exposed the life: "*Je n'impose rien; je ne propose rien; j'expose.*"[5]

To Strachey, truthfulness in biography required that he consider the psychology of his subjects as well as the personal selflessness, ambitions, egotisms, and sexualities found in their lives. To do this, he used literacy devices such as created scenes, conversations, metaphors, and physical mannerisms, often suggesting these attributes contributed to or shaped his subjects' behaviors and even achievements. Apparently he was little concerned with the conflicts and tensions between a biographer's right to shape and select materials and the need for objectivity.[6] Following these concepts, Strachey established for himself a respected and honored place in modern English language literature.

The Literary Autobiography

Autobiographical writing also is a part of biographical literary expression. It can be produced by professional writers or it can emerge from the life experiences of amateurs. Elements that make autobiography fine literature are the same aspects of all good literary writing. Stephen Shapiro in his essay "The Dark Continent of Literature: Autobiography," written in 1968, stated that these elements begin with a narrative structure and themes related to how a person views his or her life and then build through literary devices found in all good literature. Shapiro maintained that fine autobiographical literature flows from narrative styles that embrace descriptions, pace and momentum, metaphors, reflections, characterizations, skillful use of language, dialogue, dramatic scenes, and synecdoche.[7]

Autobiography as Social Discourse

Recent poststructuralist and feminist critics have supported the idea that autobiography need not be considered as fine literature at all, preferring that it be viewed as social and cultural artifact and discourse. The emerging idea seems to be that fine autobiography can include all of these, but individual autobiographies must always present structural and thematic complexity.[8] Examples of this type of autobiography read by young adults are Maya Angelou's autobiographical works, including *I Know Why the Caged Bird Sings* (1969).[9]

PROBLEMS IN CRAFTING A LITERARY BIOGRAPHY

Biography often takes on the characteristics and values reflected in academic traditions. Such construction often poses problems for the general reader as well as for children and young adults. The argument is made that good biography, skillfully written, can act as a bridge between academic discourse and the general reader. Selected examples that are well written using good literary standards, show responsibility for intellectual honesty, and appeal to young readers are discussed later in this chapter.

Authors of good literary biographies face many problems. John Batchelor writes that good literary biographers must always be accurate in what they present, but they must also be allowed to create a work of art. They must choose their subject with care, and then they must select and organize their materials in ways that will reveal details and associations. In doing this they must remain objective and maintain a distance between themselves and their subject and materials.

Problems in biography writing are many, ranging from whether to present subjects as heroic or simply as persons influenced by events of his or her times, to how much detail to include.[10] This is especially critical for biographies that are suitable for youth. For youth, depending on the age and maturity of youth readers, too much detail can include excessive descriptions and analysis of events, too much attention to secondary characters, and too much attention to documentation and citations.

Like all good biographers, authors of fine literary biographies for youth must be cultural historians, sociologists, and even psychologists. In addition, they must be literary critics, novelists, archivists, archaeologists, political analysts, and willing sleuths. They must be aware of documentation limitations and the urge to create or fill in the missing links with their own devices and imaginations. They must understand that even the subject's reflections of his or her remembered past may not be accurate. Biographers must likewise guard against becoming too emotionally involved with their subjects. They must always seek to balance objectivity and personal engagement. That is not to say that biographers cannot respect or even love their subjects, but the biographer must always understand that human foibles are at play and influence all lives.[11]

The writer must understand that various cultures see and use biographies in different ways. In most English-speaking countries biographies tend to stress individualism; but this approach may not be the case with other cultures, including some Western nations. For example, traditionally German biographical writings may emphasize hard work, devotion to a cause, systematic thinking, and philosophical traditions over hero worship or personality cults.[12]

Other practical matters that all biographers face, and this certainly includes writers of biographies for youth, are limitations on time, expenses of travel, access to archives, interviews with living persons, and the cooperation of the subjects themselves or their descendants. Copyright issues must also be faced in terms of reproduction rights of documents. For example, some archives, literary agents, governments, and executors of estates hold considerable power over what can and cannot be reproduced.[13]

LITERARY BIOGRAPHY FOR YOUTH

Biographies for Younger Children

Invincible Louisa: The Story of the Author of Little Women, by Cornelia Meigs (Little, Brown, 1995; originally published in 1937) won the Newbery Medal in 1938 as the most distinguished book published for youth in the United States during the preceding year. It has remained in print almost continuously since its publication. The book recounts Louisa's life as a young woman and the struggles with poverty and other family and personal hardships. By today's standards, some children might find this book slow and too reflective; nevertheless, it is a fine piece of writing for children ages 9–12.

Candace Fleming's *Ben Franklin's Almanac: Being a True Account of the Good Gentleman's Life* (Atheneum/Anne Schwartz Books, 2003), for ages 9–12, tells the story of Franklin based on large themes such as "Boyhood Memories" and "Tokens of a Well-Lived Life" intertwined with Franklin's prose, observations, and reminiscences. A *School Library Journal* review commented that this was a "superlative example of the biographer's craft" that produced

> an authoritative work of depth, humor and interest, presenting Franklin in all his complexity, ranging from the heroic to the vulgar, the saintly to the callous.

Charlotte S. Huck and her colleagues suggested a number of illustrated biographies suitable for young children, including the 1984 Caldecott Medal winner, *The Glorious Light: Across the Channel with Louis Blériot, July 25, 1909*, developed and illustrated by Alice and Martin Provensen (Penguin Putnam Books, 1987); *Thomas Jefferson: A Picture Biography*, by James Giblin and illustrated by Michael Dooling (Scholastic, 1994); and the biographies of Ingri d'Aulaire and Edgar Parin d'Aulaire, including the 1940 Caldecott Medal winner, *Abraham Lincoln* (Sagebrush Education Resources, 1987; first published in 1939).[14]

Biographies for Older Youth

Black Boy by Richard Wright (Perennial, 1998; originally published in 1945) is one of the outstanding social and literary autobiographies of the twentieth century. It is a memoir of Wright's life from ages 4 to 19. Deserted by his father, the autobiography recounts a childhood and youth in the American South of hunger, deficiency, poverty, fear, and physical abuse. Because of its picture of American racism and its sexual overtones, *Black Boy* has periodically been subject to censorship (1972 in Michigan, 1975 in Tennessee, 1978 in New Hampshire, 1987 Nebraska).[15] It was one of several books considered by the U.S. Supreme Court in the landmark *Board of Education, Island Trees Union Free School District v. Pico*, when in 1982 it ruled that the underlying motives of school boards in removing books from school libraries must be considered in terms of students' constitutional rights.[16]

Concerning the literary style in *Black Boy*, *Merriam-Webster Encyclopedia of Literature* (Merriam-Webster, 1995) says the book is often taken as fictional biography because it uses a novelistic approach and that when it was first published, many critics considered it an attack on racist Southern society. By the 1960s it was more widely seen as a statement of an artist's coming of age and of his development as a writer. Racism and his experiences with whites did play a role in the development of his persona, but these experiences were among many influences on him as an artist.

Native Son: The Story of Richard Wright (Morgan Reynolds, 2003) for grades 8 and up, by Joyce Hart, gives witness to Wright's struggle as a poor black child in the "Jim Crow" South and his rise to fame as a literary person. Explored are his involvement with the Communist Party, his anger at American racism, his acceptance in Europe, his personal love life, and, most importantly, his great influence on American writers and the American theater. A *School Library Journal* reviewer noted Hart's accessible and smooth writing style.

Another highly regarded book about Wright for older readers, grades 9–12, is Robin Westen's *Richard Wright: Author of* Native Son *and* Black Boy (Enslow Publishers, 2002). Here again we see the depth of Wright's outspokenness, references to his harsh writing style, and his criticism of racial discrimination.

Biographies of well-known authors for young adults are generally popular with readers. *The Beet Fields: Memories of a Sixteenth Summer*, by Gary

Paulsen (Delacorte Press, 2000; Laurel Leaf 2002) is young adult author Paulsen's account of his sixteenth summer, when he runs away from an abusive, alcoholic home, works in beet fields of the upper Midwest, joins a carnival, and along the way, learns something about life. A critic commented:

> The striking cover picture of a beautiful young man's bare, muscular back foreshadows the sensuality of this brilliant autobiographical novel for older boys by the author of *Hatchet* and *Soldier's Heart*. In this remarkable book, Gary Paulsen reworks material from his own life that has appeared earlier in his novels, to tell—with simple words and Hemingwayesque cadences–the story of a summer when a 16-year-old boy became a man. [Editorial Reviews, www.amazon.com]

Another popular writer is Chris Crutcher. His autobiography, *King of the Mild Frontier: An Ill-Advised Autobiography* (Greenwillow Books, 2003), tells of Crutcher's growing up in Idaho of the 1950s and his development as an author. Autobiographically, he reveals his relationships with his parents—an alcoholic mother and a strict, controlling, and demanding father. Joel Shoemaker, in a review in *School Library Journal*, describes Crutcher's literary style and appeal to readers:

> Hyperbole lightens the mood as the author portrays himself as a young cry-baby, academic misfit, and athletic klutz, utterly without self-aggrandizement. Abrupt transitions, some convoluted sentences, and nonlinear progression may challenge some readers, but the narrative holds undeniable appeal for the author's fans and demonstrates the power of writing to help both reader and writer heal emotional/psychic wounds.[17]

Well-researched and -written books of well-known celebrities and icons such as Elvis Presley contribute to the literary values of good biography and, at the same time, appeal to the interests of youth. *Last Train to Memphis: The Rise of Elvis Presley* (Little, Brown, 1994) and *Careless Love: The Unmaking of Elvis Presley*, by Peter Guralnick (Little, Brown, 1999) are examples of this type of biography. *Booklist* notes in its review of *Last Train to Memphis*:

> Guralnick depicts Elvis as a naive yet extremely talented boy whose dream of stardom came true, leaving him a virtual prisoner of his own success. Realized through scores of interviews and hours of in-depth research, Guralnick's Elvis is ignorant of worldly matters, seemingly without artifice, but a quick study. . . . Taking pains to keep the story fresh and flowing and refraining from foreshadowing and editorializing, Guralnick lets the facts speak for themselves.

In reviewing *Careless Love,* the second volume of Presley's life, a *Kirkus* review noted:

Careless Love is about claustrophobia, insularity, and disintegration. . . . [In this volume] we miss the cultural context of the 1960s and '70s, but then, so did Elvis. The diffuseness of this life is reflected in Guralnick's narrative. Nevertheless, this sequel to his exhilarating first volume is the most meticulously researched and sympathetic, honest portrait of Elvis we are likely to see.

One of the interesting aspects of biography is that it opens doors for exploration. Once introduced to the biography, youth can always search out and find a wealth of information and experiences that appeal especially to them as individuals. Perhaps they will even discover some old, even forgotten masterpieces relating the lives of persons such as sports figures, politicians, adventurers, actors, writers, and ordinary people who have done extraordinary things. Biographies such as *Madame Sarah*, by Cornelia Otis Skinner (Houghton Mifflin, 1967); *The Story of My Life: A Memoir*, by Helen Keller (Dover Publications, 2002; first published ca. 1902); and *Up from Slavery*, by Booker T. Washington (Bedford/St. Martin's Press, 2003; first published in 1901) often await discovery by new readers.

Regional Biographies

Many states, provinces, territories, and local communities have biographies that are well written and reflect the lives of important persons who have helped to shape a regional identity. Some of these can be considered literary biographies in their own right. The development of regional biographies is often encouraged by governments that mandate that regional histories and government be studied. These mandates may be specific as to when and how students are given instructions, thus requiring that curriculum guides, directives, and resources be made available to teachers and schools.

Another influence on the development of regional biographies is the growth of university and small presses that serve very specific interest groups within their designated markets. Such presses vigorously encourage authors to research and write regional biographies that meet their marketing needs.

Fortunately, a great deal of regional biography exists. Amazon.com has a subject list that highlights these in convenient ways through its "Biographies & Memoirs" link. Under the Regional U.S. link, a search box allows specific searching by simply typing in a locality (e.g., Maine for a state, Atlanta for a city). Subject contents range from important persons at the state, province, or territorial levels to individuals who recount their experiences in their towns, villages, states, and provinces. Regional biographies are numerous, but unfortunately they are not widely reviewed in the national press. A good way to personally examine these is to attend book trade shows and professional meetings where publishers display their publications.

For younger children, regional biographies often are of persons who are important in state or provincial history or who have distinguished themselves in areas of achievement such as in sports, the arts, writing, and politics. Occasionally, significant literary biographies based on regional personalities are published. For example, *The Raven: A Biography of Sam Houston*, by Marguis James (Reprint Services Corp, 1991; originally published in 1929), falls well within this category. *The Raven* offers both good biography and fine writing. The introduction to the biography by the late historian Henry Steele Commager reads:

> This is the stuff of which legend is made, this story of the making of Texas, and Houston is one with those semi legendary characters—with Daniel Boone and Davy Crockett, with Marion the Swamp Fox and Ethan Allen. . . . In a sense he is too good to be true, this man who wrought such mighty deeds within the lifetime of our fathers and grandfathers; in a sense if he had not existed we should have had to create him.

Although frequently reissued since it first publication in 1929, *The Raven* is now available through the publisher's "United States Local History" series. Books in this series are often difficult to acquire, making them expensive, but they do serve a special need in terms of regional history and biography.

Obituaries

Obituaries are useful in building biographical collections and they are especially important in serving the needs for local and regional biographical materials. In a formal sense, obituaries are memorial articles for persons that newspapers consider newsworthy, and they are generally considered news reports. They tend to focus on persons of social, political, cultural, or economic importance. The obituaries that appear in the *New York Times* and London's *Times* are of the formal kind. Smaller newspapers and newspapers that serve regional or local areas generally do not follow this definition and report the deaths of residents in their obituaries according to established policies. On the other hand, published death announcements are brief notices that appear in newspapers serving to announce the death of a person. Large newspapers generally distinguish between the two types.[18]

Obituaries and death notices serve several purposes. They are both sources of information and a tribute to the deceased. They are also marks of individualism. That is, according to Armando Petucci, they present and honor the individual by recording publicly that he or she has lived and that his or her life was different from all other persons who ever lived.[19]

Small Presses, Regional Associations, and University Presses

As noted, most areas have publishers that provide biographical materials of geographic interest. Although many of their products may not meet the highest literary standards, they are important to culture because they provide unique biographical information.

Generally these fall into two categories: commercial and noncommercial presses. Noncommercial presses can include university presses that operate as part of a university system and/or historical or genealogical associations. Aside from offering academic and scholarly books that appeal to their markets, university presses often provide biographies that reflect state and regional interests. Likewise, state, regional, and local historical and genealogical associations frequently publish biographical materials. For the most part these associations and presses are expected through their publications to advance culture and knowledge about state, regional, and local societies and history. If at all, reviews of their publications generally appear in local and regional documents that may be hard to find at the local school and public library levels. The Internet offers access to some of these through the search terms *university presses* and *historical associations*.

Commercial small publishers located in a region may also market biographical products of interest to their clients within well-defined geographical areas. Sometimes these presses are hard to locate, and their catalogs or trade lists are limited. Their publications often go out of print frequently, and often the presses themselves fail and go out of business.

Extra effort often needs to be made to locate and contact small presses (including noncommercial publishers). There are several ways to address this problem. Book and library trade shows and conventions offer access to these presses. Generally these presses exhibit or have representatives at such gatherings and make available their trade lists and catalogs. Once these presses are located, one must develop a good relationship with their sales departments and maintain contact. One way to do this is to offer one's service in reviewing their publications for regional and local newspapers and other periodicals. These presses can be accessed through the Internet by searching the term *small presses*.

Another type of commercial press is the small press that serves a national and/or international market. This type of publisher generally provides specific types of materials to a specific type of market. As mentioned elsewhere in this book, Morgan Reynolds Publishers, located in Greensboro, North Carolina, is an example of such publishers (www.morganreynolds.com). Morgan Reynolds specializes in nonfiction, including biographies for young adults. An example of a small commercial press that caters to state interests is Halcyon Press, located in Houston, Texas (http://members.tripod.com/managing_editor/Halcyon). Along with a line of general interest books, it provides "Texana" biographies that appeal to Texas interests. Included in their inventory are biographies on public figures Barbara Jordan and Rosa von Roeder Kleberg, founder of the famous King Ranch.

Biographies in Audio Formats

Biographies recorded in audio formats have become popular in the last few decades, made possible by advances in technology that permit audiotapes and CDs to be played in various locations. Fortunately, many fine audio biographies are now available and are read either by the authors themselves or by accomplished actors and readers. BBC America offers recorded biographies, such as the drama *Eleanor—Her Secret Journey*, by Rhoda Lerman, performed by Jean Stapleton. Its "Live Oak Media" biographical series for children 4–8 has biographies of Christopher Columbus, Frederick Douglass, and Harriet Tubman.

Mature readers and listeners have available *Alexander Hamilton* [abr], by Ron Chernow, narrated by Grover Gardner (Penguin Audiobooks); and *Benjamin Franklin: An American Life* [abr], by Walter Isaacson, narrated by Boyd Gaines (Simon & Schuster). Audio productions especially of interest to children include *Anne Frank's Story* [uab], by Carol Ann Lee, narrated by Barbara Rosenblat (Blackstone Audiobooks); and a collection of fictionalized but historically accurate memories of characters from Paul Fleishman's *Bull Run* [uab]. In this recording, various narrators and actors read the lines from the book (Audio Bookshelf). A commercial audio rental source that provides both evaluations and bibliographic information is "Simplyaudiobooks" (www.simplyaudiobooks.com/processInterfaceAction.php?pId = 100).

An interesting example of recorded biographical materials is the "American Author Prose Library," originated by public radio station KOPN in Columbia, Missouri. This program was established to ensure the existence of a permanent record of current American writers. Taped interviews with American authors were recorded and made available for purchase on the educational market.[20] Today these records are held by and sold by the nonprofit American Audio Prose Library, Inc. (www.americanaudioprose.org).

Biographical Films, Dramas, and Music

Well-crafted biographies presented in both film and dramas are also a part of fine literature. The University Interscholastic League located at the University of Texas at Austin each year makes suggestions for suitable plays for performance by high schools in the league's one-act play contest. Excellent biographical dramas suggested by the league over the years have included:

- *Murder in the Cathedral*, by T. S. Elliot. This is a miracle play about the martyrdom of St. Thomas Becket, archbishop of Canterbury in 1170.
- *Luther*, by John Osborn. This play looks at Luther's struggle with his own faith and his attacks on the Roman Catholic Church and the Holy Roman Empire.

- *The Lark*, by Jean Anouilh. This drama relies less on facts, but more on understanding the joy and wonder of the legend of Joan of Arc.

- *I Remember Mama*, by John van Druter. This play is an adaptation of Kathyrn Forbes' autobiographical sketches of her childhood growing up in San Francisco, drawn from her 1943 book, *Mama's Bank Account*. This successful play was made into a film and later into a television series.

- *Mary of Scotland*, by Maxwell Anderson. This is one of Anderson's best historical biographical dramas. It broadly describes the personal and political conflicts of the Scottish queen. It presents Queen Elizabeth I, Mary's rival for the English throne and distant cousin, as ruthless in her execution of Mary to protect her own power.

The Miracle Worker, by William Gibson, and *The Diary of Anne Frank*, by Frances Goodrich and Albert Hackett, were also recommended for performance by the league, as were several biographical plays by George Bernard Shaw, including *Great Catherine* and *Saint Joan*.[21]

Other interesting and critically acclaimed literary biographical dramas include the respected *Abe Lincoln in Illinois*, by Robert E. Sherwood, and *Inherit the Wind*, by Jerome Lawrence and Robert E. Lee. Although fictionalized, this play retains the essence of the famous Scopes trial in Tennessee. Critics consider the play important even today, six decades after its first production in 1954 by a professional theater in Dallas, because it describes much of 1920s America and continues to point out conflicts in American society between opposing belief systems.

Similarly, in terms of American life, *Lost in Yonkers*, by Neil Simon, is a valued and sensitive picture of American family life in Yonkers, New York, in the early 1940s. While not completely autobiographical, it does draw upon the author's experiences as a youth growing up in New York City.

Although biography has been used over the centuries by dramatists such as Shakespeare in his historical plays (e.g., *Richard II*, *Richard III*, *Henry V*, *Henry VI*, and *Henry VIII*), literary biography today must be authentic. This is true whether biography is used to create drama, poetry, political and social discussion, or music. Opera and musical theater are good examples of diverse artistic expressions that merge into literary biography. Granted, music may be allowed more poetic license than other forms of biography, but it too must provide the true essence of the lives presented. We see this in the musical *Evita*, by Andrew Lloyd Webber and Tim Rice,[22] and in such modern-day operas as *Nixon in China*, music by John Adams, libretto by Alice Goodman,[23] and the acclaimed modern opera *Dead Man Walking*, music by Jake Heggie and libretto by novelist Terrence McNally. Based on the book *Dead Man Walking* (Vintage, 1994) by Sister Helen Prejean, the opera recounts her experiences as the spiritual advisor to two men condemned to death for murder and awaiting their execution in a Louisiana prison. The opera, like the book, confronts issues surrounding the power and role of government and capital punishment in the United States.[24]

Biographical films were extremely popular during the 1930s, with some of the world's most memorable people being presented and interpreted for popular audiences through film. These include Jesse James, Abraham Lincoln, Cleopatra, showman Florenz Ziegfeld, Louis Pasteur, Emile Zolá, Marie Antoinette, Mexican President and hero Benito Juarez, and Alexander Graham Bell. Fortunately many of the good biographical films of the past are available to us today on DVD and video.

The National Film Preservation Board was established in 1988 by the American Congress. Along with establishing the board, a law authorized the Librarian of Congress "to select and preserve up to 25 films each year to add to the National Film Registry." The selected films for the registry were to represent the best in the range of American filmmaking—Hollywood features; documentaries; avant-garde and amateur productions; films of regional interest; ethnic, animated, and short film subjects. The goal of the registry law was to ensure that deserving films were recognized, preserved, and made accessible now and in the future. To date, one hundred films have been designed as "the greatest" among all selected. Biographical films among these 100 are *Bonnie and Clyde* (1967) and *Lawrence of Arabia* (1962). Other biographical films on the list include *Butch Cassidy and the Sundance Kid* (1969) and *Knute Rockne, All American* (1940). All films selected by the Librarian of Congress for the registry are considered to be "culturally, historically, or aesthetically significant."[25]

Although biographical films continue to be produced, their popularity is not what it was in earlier times. Nevertheless, biographical films still have their place, and critically acclaimed films of the early twenty-first century that have had broad interest and critical impact have included *Pollock* (2000), *Ali* (2000), *A Beautiful Mind* (2001), *Kinsey* (2004), *Ray* (2004), and *The Aviator* (2004) *Capote* (2005), and *Good Night and Good Luck* (2005). Unfortunately because of their ratings, many recent biographical films are not easily or legally available to youth.

Quality Television Productions

Quality biographical materials can be found in television production. For the most part, but certainly not exclusively so, quality programs today are produced by government or quasi-governmental television networks.

The Corporation for Public Broadcasting (CPB) is a private, nonprofit corporation created by the American Congress in 1967. It provides much of the funding for Public Broadcasting Service (PBS). It presently describes itself as:

> a private, non-profit media enterprise owned and operated by the nation's 349 public television stations. A trusted community resource, PBS uses the power of noncommercial television, the Internet and other media to enrich

the lives of all Americans through quality programs and education services that inform, inspire and delight. Available to 99 percent of American homes with televisions and to an increasing number of digital multimedia house- holds, PBS serves nearly 100 million people each week.[26]

Following this mission, PBS programs have produced an abundance of high-quality biographical materials. Biography plays a large role in such PBS series as the *American Experience*, *American Masters*, *American Presidents*, and *Ken Burn's American Stories*. Biographical materials also are found in the program *Frontline* and individually produced programs such as *NOVA*. *The Charlie Rose Show* on PBS is an example of serious biographical cover- age, as he interviews persons who have had significant influence on society.[27] PBS's *Kids Go!* also has biographical information created in formats that pro- mote learning and fun.[28] Many of these programs are sold directly by PBS.

National Public Radio (NPR) is also funded partially by CPB. NPR's bio- graphical features are found throughout its programming from *All Things Considered*, *Morning Edition*, and *Fresh Air* to its inclusive "People and Places" featuring "Newmakers," "On Music," "On the Arts," and "On Books." Like PBS, NPR also makes many of its programs available for sale and for listening on streaming audio.[29]

Other government or quasi-government broadcasting services offer biograph- ical coverage. "The BBC World is a 24-hour news and information channel broadcasting around the world from its base at BBC Television Centre in London." BBC World is especially noted for interviews that are analytical analy- ses.[30] Aside from that, a wealth of biographical information is available from the BBC through its various programs that include special features, history, sports, entertainment, and children's programs. BBC programs involving biographies and history are extensive and can be located through its complex, but complete website (www.bbc.co.uk). Especially useful features are its "Historic Figures" and "History" links. These links provide reference information about people and events. Biographical films as well as books are also sold through its several shops, such as BBC Shop, BBC America Shop, and BBC Education Scotland.[31]

The Canadian Broadcasting Corporation (CBC), a government-independent corporation, offers a variety of biographical materials. Its shop provides books, DVDs, and VHS tapes of its various productions. The shop's biographical sec- tion is well marked and offers many fine biographical programs in both English and French. Included here are well-known international figures such as Pope John Paul II and Mother Teresa as well as illustrious Canadians such as Glenn Gould and Farley Mowat. An interesting and useful set containing biographical information is its "Canadian Experience" collection. CBC describes this set as:

A new series of documentaries that define who we are as a people and a country including *Sisters in the Wilderness*, *Year of the Hunter*, *Expo 67* and *The 13th Mission*.[32]

The Australian Broadcasting Corporation offers biographical programs highlighting international personalities and well-known Australians. Its various listings include considerable amounts of biographical materials;[33] and its "Education Resources" page is especially useful in terms of providing biographical text and graphic-based information.[34]

American commercial television also offers some good biographical information, but because they generally place less emphasis on education in terms of school curriculum needs, these products are discussed in more detail in chapter 6.

CONCLUSION

Biography as fine literature established itself in the late nineteenth and early twentieth centuries, influenced by such writers as English author Lytton Strachey. New ways of looking at the world politically, socially, and psychologically influenced the development of literary biography whereby facts of a person's life were combined with perspective and understanding, leading to a better informed interpretation of that life. Creative and even symbolic writing styles were skillfully used to develop personalities and to place those personalities within the contexts of their emotional, social, and cultural lives.

This chapter began with the words of Helen Haines, and it is fitting that we end with her words as she reminds us of the relationship of biography and literature. She tells us that the power of biography is its universality in relationships to literature and to life; and its "power of inspiration, to appeal to the innate, unquenchable human curiosity concerning human character and experience."[35] She suggested that these powers have given "biography a place second only to fiction in the affection of readers."[36] She wrote those words in the early to mid-twentieth century, and today we might wonder if literary biography at the beginning of the twenty-first century has even surpassed fiction in the hearts of many readers.

NOTES

1. Jan Pilditch, "Literary Biography," in *Encyclopedia of Life Writing: Autobiographical and Biographical Forms,* vol. 2, ed. Margaretta Jolly (London: Fitzroy Dearborn, 2001), 564–65.

2. Helen E. Haines, *Living with Books: The Art of Book Selection,* 2nd ed. (New York: Columbia University Press, 1950), 250.

3. Haines, 252.

4. Ruth Hoberman, "Strachey, Lytton, 1880–1932," in *Encyclopedia of Life Writing: Autobiographical and Biographical Forms,* vol. 2, ed. Margaretta Jolly (London: Fitzroy Dearborn, 2001), 847–48.

5. Hoberman, 848.

6. Hoberman, 847–48.

7. Bonnie Gunzenhauser, "Literary Autobiography," in *Encyclopedia of Life Writing: Autobiographical and Biographical Forms,* vol. 2, ed. Margaretta Jolly, (London: Fitzroy Dearborn, 2001), 562, quoting Stephen A. Shapiro, "The Dark Continent of Literature: Autobiography," *Comparative Literature Studies* 5, no. 3 (1968).

8. Gunzenhauser.

9. Gunzenhauser, 563.

10. John Batchelor, ed., *The Art of Literary Biography* (New York: Oxford University Press, 1995), 2–10.

11. Batchelor.

12. Batchelor, 4, quoting Jürgen Schlaeger.

13. Batchelor, 6–7.

14. Charlotte S. Huck and others, *Children's Literature in the Elementary School,* 6th ed. (Madison, Wis.: Brown & Benchmark, 1997), 559–60.

15. Nicholas J. Karolides, Margaret Bald, and Dawn B. Sova, *100 Banned Books: Censorship Histories of World Literature* (New York: Checkmark Books, 1999), 19–27.

16. Karolides, 26.

17. Joel Shoemaker, "Review of *King of the Mild Frontier: An Ill-Advised Autobiography,* by Chris Crutcher," http://www.amazon.com/gp/product/0060502495/104-42386196114349?%5Fencoding=UTF8 (accessed March 13, 2005).

18. Debra Taylor, "Obituaries," in *Encyclopedia of Life Writing: Autobiographical and Biographical Forms,* vol. 2, ed. Margaretta Jolly (London: Fitzroy Dearborn, 2001), 567–68.

19. Taylor, 567–68.

20. Bill Weathersby, "American Audio Prose Library," *Show Me Libraries* 34 (Oct./Nov. 1982): 25–27.

21. University Interscholarstic League at the University of Texas at Austin, "List of UIL Approved Plays for School Year 2005–2006," http://www.uil.utexas.edu/academics/drama/plays.html (accessed April 3, 2005, and Nov. 3, 2005). Information regarding earlier years is found in the site's archives.

22. "Evita, The Musical, The Film, The Woman," http://my.execpc.com/~reva/evita.htm (accessed April 23, 2005, and Nov. 3, 2005).

23. John Adams, "Nixon in China: Opera in Three Acts," http://www.earbox.com/sub-html/comp-details/nixon-de.html (accessed April 23, 2005).

24. Andrew Druckenbrod, "Opera Preview: 'Dead Man Walking' Confronts the Issue of Capital Punishment," *Pittsburgh Post-Gazette,* June 3, 2004, http://www.post-gazette.com/pg/04155/325999.stm (accessed April 23, 2005).

25. Library of Congress, "National Film Registry's Selections (1989–2004)," http://www.filmsite.org/filmreg2.html (accessed April 14, 2005).

26. "PBS: About Us," http://www.pbs.org/aboutpbs (accessed April 4, 2005).

27. "PBS," http://www.pbs.org (accessed April 3, 2005).

28. "PBS Kids Go!" http://pbskids.org/go (accessed April 4, 2005).

29. "NPR," http://www.npr.org (accessed April 4, 2005).

30. "BBC World," http://www.bbcworld.com/content/template_bbclinks.asp? pageid=67 (accessed April 5, 2005).

31. "BBC Shop," http://www.bbcshop.com (accessed April 5, 2005). Other available BBC resource sites include http://www.bbcamericashop.com and http://www.bbc.co.uk/scotland/education.

32. "CBC Shop Online," http://www.cbcshop.ca/CBC/shopping/home.aspx?Catalog Name=CBCBase&lang=en-CA (accessed April 5, 2005).

33. "ABC Online," http://www.abc.net.au (accessed April 5, 2005).

34. "ABC Education Resources," http://www.abc.net.au/learn (accessed April 5, 2005).

35. Haines, 250–51.

36. Haines, 250–51.

6

BIOGRAPHY, CELEBRITIES, AND MODERN LIFE

INTRODUCTION

This chapter discusses popular culture and its impact on society and how biography plays a fundamental role in defining what is accepted within the boundaries of popular culture. In doing this, the chapter considers biography as found in the mass media including print, film, and television. The role that celebrities and iconic heroes play in modern life is also discussed.

IS IT A JOHN WAYNE WORLD? POPULAR CULTURE AND BIOGRAPHY

Popular culture is both a process and a product, and it has always influenced how libraries respond to its demands. Popular culture is considered a process because it arises from life and continues to change and develop based on the events of common life. The life that sustains and nurtures it may be global, national, regional, or local. Although popular culture is often hard to define, it is generally recognized as being "the behavior patterns of the great mass of people in a given region at the present time."[1] On the other hand, high culture "is the culture of the elite and usually refers to artistic endeavors such as music, dance, theater, certain writing, architecture, etc."[2]

Popular culture as a process creates and distributes products such as film, television, music, styles and fashions, sports, cyberculture, advertising, toys, and print items (books, novels, comics, magazines). Popular culture is also reflected in issues and attitudes concerning racism, class, gender, sexuality, politics, ethnicity, and political and social processes by which groups are marginalized.

Public librarians as well as school librarians often find themselves obligated to support both popular and high culture; and this obligation has not been without a struggle. In terms of literature and literacy, traditionally public youth librarians as well as school library media specialists have often favored high culture over popular culture. Public youth librarians have embraced popular culture in an attempt to attract and keep an elusive and changing audience. Perhaps school library media specialists have had an easier time following this line of reasoning than public youth librarians because they have had to support curriculum mandates designed to encourage the development of higher cultural attainment. Although youth librarians in public libraries have had to meet some of these obligations as well, they must also meet obligations enforced by satisfying public demands. This accommodation was not easily reached, as revealed in the histories of both school and public library services for youth.

The modern school library as an integrated part of American education did not begin until well after the public library movement in the United States was well under way. Although school libraries had existed in various parts of the country, the first school library of any significant record was not established until 1906 in Virginia.[3, 4] Decades before, the public library in the United States served schools as a part of its mission.[5] One of the goals of the public library within this mission was to raise cultural and literacy standards of children by promoting good literature and good reading experiences.

The professional literature of the day gives a good indication of this struggle. Although good literature for children was beginning to appear by the end of the nineteenth century, having broken loose from much of its religious and strong didactic past, a popular literature was also emerging.[6] This literature consisted of dime novels, romances, and biographies based on popular figures of the day, including those from the American West such as lawmen, outlaws, cattlemen, ranchers, and Indian fighters. Librarians and teachers saw this literature as a threat to social order, culture, and certainly good taste.

Social critic Richard Etulain reminds us:

> Biographers and historians [of the day] often used historical figures such as Billy the Kid, Calamity Jane, Wild Bill Hickok, and Kit Carson to create the sensational heroes and heroines needed to subdue a Wild West.
>
> ***
>
> Since the West was a wild, forbidding place, only historical individuals depicted as strong-armed demigods could pave the way for western settlement.[7]

Publications that carried this often exaggerated and fictionalized information were popular with youth, but their place on library shelves was hardly secured. Dime novels, bad boy books, romance literature, and biographical materials based on popular heroes were generally excluded from collections as detrimental to the moral development of youth. Based on goals of promoting culture and refinement, many librarians of the time could not promote them with clear conscience.[8]

Popular culture today continues to influence the types of biographical materials available for youth. Biographies of heroes and celebrities are especially sought out by youth. Aside from that, heroes and celebrities have a functional role to play within culture. Popular heroes, being well known, provide members of the culture with "concrete images of what they would like to be, to become."[9] Traditional heroes or citizen heroes provide a culture with important mainstream values and bedrock beliefs. In their actions, they defend the culture.[10]

Rebel heroes are also popular. They generally are gifted and have a great love of life. Their popularity often comes because they "challenge certain mainstream cultural values."[11] They call attention to the failures of society and dare culture to live up to its ideals. They champion individual freedom, and they do not hesitate to challenge authority in their quest to set things right. In the United States we find these traits in the heroes of the American and French Revolutions and in the antislavery movement. In more recent times we find them in the heroes of the American Civil Rights Movement and in other human and political rights movement, such as those led by Gandhi and the 1991 Nobel Peace Prize–winner, Aung San Suu Kyi, in Burma.[12]

The outlaw hero also is popular. These heroes have some of the same characteristics of the rebel hero except that they cannot live within the bounds of society. They challenge all authority and emphasize individual freedom. Familiar popular culture outlaw heroes include Bonnie and Clyde, and Jesse James. Soldiers of fortune heroes generally present themselves for hire to the highest bidder. They have little respect for or satisfaction with mainstream culture.[13]

Most, if not all, cultures have celebrities. In modern societies today the public's fascination with celebrities has created a huge industrial and media complex worth billions of dollars. Celebrities are noted for one thing, and that is their fame based on talent and gifts that the public wants and admires. Most, if not all, celebrities have high media coverage. Among others, today's celebrities include movie stars, select monarchs, talk show hosts, news anchors, sports figures, politicians, and statespersons. Celebrities also include local personalities. Sometimes celebrities are held up as heroes, but to do this they must exhibit the characteristics of hero as well as celebrity. The ability to move from celebrity to hero is often tied to the psychological needs of a society at a given time. For example, the movie actor John Wayne was able to move from a role of a minor western actor to a celebrity role as a major film actor to that of a national hero. He exemplified and became an icon for the values of the culture from which he arose.[14]

ISSUES IN COLLECTION DEVELOPMENT

The mass media exerts an enormous role in the defining and distribution of mass media products. Television, film, book and magazine publishing, as well as the computer industries all play their roles in seeing that heroes and celebrities are defined in terms of cultural expectations and that information about them is made available to the public. Librarians serving youth also play a role in this distribution process in that they review, order, and stock many of these products for their users. Because the public library and the school library media center are part of this distribution network, it seems proper that we look more closely at popular culture and the biographical materials it encourages.

Books and Publishers

Most publishers of books for youth have a line or several lines of biographies. Most of these are aimed at the school and library markets rather than at mass distributions. Of course, in recent decades, the widespread openings of major book stores such as Barnes & Noble and Borders have changed this distribution pattern somewhat, thus making available biographical materials to an audience outside the influence of libraries and schools. Because of the close ties that the youth publishing industry has had with schools and libraries, much of their biographical products reflect the curriculum as well as perceived interests of their youth markets.

Chelsea House Publishers advises their perspective authors:

> Chelsea House books build solid foundations for a lifetime of reading and are regarded by students as the perfect sources for information as they write papers, perform independent study, and delve more deeply into their curriculum studies.[15]

In order to meet a wide variety of interests and curriculum needs, many publishers have developed series that reflect various interests. For example, in terms of meeting demands for information about sports celebrities, the Lerner Publishing Group, which now includes Millbrook Press, offers a number of biographical series.

> "Biography®" (developed with A&E Television Network)—A series of biographies on what the publisher claims to be some of the "world's most popular and influential people." Each in-depth profile is perfect for research and reports. Included in the series are The Beatles, Arnold Schwarzenegger, Bruce Lee, Fidel Castro, Jesse Ventura, and Oprah Winfrey.

> "Exceptional Biographies"—Reading level, grades 3–9; interest level, grades 3–12. Includes biographies of Osama Bin Laden, Ralph Nader, and Jesse Ventura.[16]

Athletes as celebrities are covered in the company's following series:

> "Amazing Athletes"—Reading level, grade 4; interest level, grades 3–4. Each biography includes "a description of a famous athlete's career from the beginning through his or her current achievements."

"Millbrook Sports Biographies"—Reading level, grade 4; interest level, grades 3–6. "Features some of sports most interesting figures," with color photographs.

"Sports Achievers Biographies"—Reading level, grade 6; interest level, grades 4–9. Introduces new and reluctant readers to athletes who have become role models through their hard work and achievements.

"New Wave"—Reading level, grade 5; interest level, grades 4–8. Biographies begin with the athlete's childhood and include how they discovered their talents. Included are statistics, action photos, and quotes.

"Sports Heroes and Legends"—Reading level, grade 6; interest level, grades 6–12. In-depth biographies of some of the hottest sports stars of all time. Includes statistics, game descriptions, and quotes from the star and teammates.

"Women of Sports"—Reading level, grade 6; interest level, grades 4–8. Collective biographies that each includes eight sports stars "giving personal information, career highlights, quotes, and full-color photographs."[17]

Like any vehicle that carries information about celebrities, these series are captive to the human failures and the public exposure of those they celebrate. For example, some of the above series carry biographies of athletes whose names have been associated in the mass media with questionable behaviors, some of which have not been substantiated in courts or by professional review boards. Such sports figures as Kobe Bryant, Sammy Sosa, and Lance Armstrong come to mind in this regard when discussing the power of mass media to profile and define the lives of celebrities.

Biographies, Interests, and Celebrities

Books about celebrities and people who do interesting things abound in today's world. Readers of all ages will enjoy *Champions: Stories of Ten Remarkable Athletes*, by Bill Littlefield, a sports commentator and novelist (Little, Brown, 1993). Littlefield brings the style of a writer and the insight of a knowledgeable sports authority to these biographies. Older readers will also enjoy Maury Allen's *Jackie Robinson: A Life Remembered* (Franklin Watts, 1987). His interpretations are based on extensive interviews with teammates, siblings, and Robinson's widow.

Music and entertainment have often been defined as the hallmark of popular culture, and it has certainly fed the public interest in celebrities and their lives. Most major entertainers have had biographies written about them. For younger readers, these include *If I Only Had a Horn: Young Louis Armstrong*, by Roxanne Orgill (Houghton Mifflin, 1997), *Ella Fitzgerald: First Lady of Song* (Carter G. Woodson Honor Book Award), by Katherine E. Krohn

(Lerner Publications, 2001), and *The Beatles*, by Jeremy Roberts (Lerner Publications, 2002). Walter Dean Myers' *The Greatest: Muhammad Ali* (Scholastic Press, 2001) traces Ali's life from his childhood and includes comments on the many controversies that surrounded him.

Older readers will find *Shout, Sister, Shout: Ten Girl Singers Who Shaped a Century*, by Roxanne Orgill (Margaret K. McElderry, 2001), informative and useful. Included here are ten influential female singers of the twentieth century. It begins with Sophie Tucker (1910) and concludes with Lucinda Williams (1990s). Along the way readers are introduced to the works and influences of such stars as Judy Garland, Bette Midler, Joan Baez, and Madonna.

Authors often become popular culture celebrities in their own right, such as Ernest Hemingway and Stephen King. In recent years J. K. Rowling has reached and even perhaps exceeded those levels of recognition. Marc Shapiro's books for young readers, *J. K. Rowling: The Wizard behind Harry Potter* (St. Martin's Press, 2001) and *J. K. Rowling: Princess of Dreams* (Blake Publishing, 2003), should more than help to continue this interest.

Political and social critics have often assumed the role of celebrities in the eyes of the public. This may happen because of their perceived allure of glamour and fantasy-like qualities (e.g., the Kennedy presidency and the "Camelot" label applied to it) or their political role in establishing new political and social orders, such as Fidel Castro. Others assume iconoclastic actions in challenging the accepted norms of culture and governments, for example, Ralph Nader (*Crashing the Party: Taking on the Corporate Government in an Age of Surrender* [St. Martin's Griffin, 2002]) and Gloria Steinem (*Outrageous Acts and Everyday Rebellions* [Owl Books, 1995]).

Sometimes little known individuals arise to face professional and personal challenges. *The Librarian of Basra: A True Story from Iraq*, by Jeanette Winter (Harcourt, 2005), presents such a challenge. It tells the story for children in grades 2–4 of how the chief librarian of Basra's central library saved the book collection just before the 2003 Iraq war.

Often groups of individuals fill this iconoclastic role, as in *Gays and Lesbians in Sports*, by Perry Deane Young and Martin B. Dubeman (Chelsea House, 1995). Covered here are tributes to David Kopay, Bill Tilden, Billie Jean King, and Martina Navratilova. *Women Who Fly*, by Lynn M. Homan and Thomas Reilly (Pelican Publishing, 1994), highlights the contributions made by Harriet Quimby, Sally Ride, and Marjorie Stinson. Another book of value is *American Women of Flight*, by Henry M. Holden (Enslow, 2003). Included here are accounts of Amelia Earhart, Anne M. Lindbergh, and Martha King.

Along with other types of celebrities (popular singers, actors and performers, sport figures), the Omnigraphics Biography Library (in various series and compilations) offers coverage of political celebrities such as Arnold Schwarzenegger, governor of California and former actor, and in some ways lesser known political leaders from around the world, such as Tony Blair, prime minister of Great Britain, and Vicente Fox, president of Mexico.[18] Scholastic's "Biography" series also selectively provides information on celebrities and/or well-known personalities such as Jesse Jackson, Michael Jordan, Nelson Mandela, and the late Jackie Robinson.

Magazines

Reading magazines and newspapers has been popular with youth for decades,[19] consistent among youth since at least 1936.[20] Magazines continue today to be the leading type of reading preferred by a wide range of youth.[21, 22, 23, 24]

Adults are rightly concerned with how magazines might influence youth and how magazine content has shaped and defined a national youth character. Diane Gruber discovered through her analysis of the popular *Youth's Companion*, published from 1827 to 1929, that in its early years it was closely aligned with conservative New England Protestantism and capitalism. Its early stories were stories of "muscular" Christianity and boy's adventure stories. As it evolved into the twentieth century, it became a mouthpiece for advertisement directed at parents and, therefore, a vehicle for the celebration of consumerism.[25] In an investigation of this magazine as well as others popular with boys in the nineteenth century, such as *Young American's Magazine of Self-Improvement*, *Our Young Folks*, and *Boys' Life*, Lorinda Cohoon found that such periodicals helped to construct and shape a sense of American boyhood in terms of expected American citizenship and gender roles.[26]

There are social and psychological reasons for the continued popularity of magazine reading. Promotional materials issued by Reading Is Fundamental point out that the popularity of magazines often rests with the fact that the articles are short, giving readers a sense of finishing a task. New technology permits attractive production designs with inviting covers. They offer entertainment and are written in an easy-to-read and brisk style centering on topics in which youth have interests. They are portable and easy to carry and can fit easily into backpacks so popular with youth today. Magazines are relatively inexpensive, especially children's magazines. In recent years "special-interest" magazines have developed. These are important because they help introduce new interests to youth and reinforce established interests.[27]

Magazine content (not necessarily magazines designed for the youth market) that appeal to youth is drawn from popular culture venues such as entertainment and sports. This content provides extensive coverage of biographical materials. For example, periodicals such as *People* and *Us Weekly* focus much of their coverage on personalities that capture youth's interest and are widely visible thorough the mass media.

The present-day growth and popularity of specialized publications such as automobile or "motor," biking, and sports periodicals have furthered the interests of boys in reading magazines. These include titles such as *Car and Driver*, *Cycle World*, *Dirt Bike*, *Dirt Rider*, *Hot Rod*, and *Hot Bike*. The content of all these magazines gives attention to popular sports figures and persons important in the various motor and cycle fields.

Although reading newspapers and magazines has been of particular interest to boys, many periodicals were published for and read by girls in the nineteenth and early twentieth centuries. These included *Aunt Judy's Magazine* (1866–1885) and *The Girl's Own Annual (1880–1940)* in England, and *St. Nicholas Magazine* (1873–1943) in the United States.[28, 29] Later advent of the "teen magazine" further encouraged periodical reading by females.

Teen magazines for girls include *ELLE Girl*, *Seventeen*, *Teen Vogue*, *J-14*, *Cosmo Girl*, and *YM*. Caution is raised by some about the cultural effects of these periodicals on youth. In recent years attention has been paid to the influence of teen magazines that attract a largely female audience. Concern is raised that teen magazines treat girls as women, that too much emphasis is placed on body images, and that the message to young girls is to be accepted as a female in today's society one must project the images of beauty as defined by mass culture, particularly the entertainment and advertising industries.

Dawn Currie found that many of these readers see models used in advertising as fantasy, but they do consider stories and advice columns as real and helping them lead normal lives. Currie noted that most of these magazines present "normal" as looking good, having boyfriends, consuming goods, and being popular. Rarely do they address how to develop a sense of self.[30] These same attributes are noted by Mary Pipher in her book *Reviving Ophelia: Saving the Selves of Adolescent Girls* (Ballantine Books, 1995).

Consumerism and body image messages are reflected in advertisements and in the types of biographical materials and the pictorial presentations that accompany these biographies. Currie noted that girls that have lower self-esteem are more influenced by these contents than are girls who are more satisfied with themselves. Similarly, Melissa Milkie found that teenage girls were very aware of these images and how they are perceived and accepted by others, especially boys. However, black girls seemed to have a social network that protected them somewhat from the negative social impact of these media images.[31]

Periodicals and magazines for girls that are less influenced by popular culture and mass media and strive for a more holistic view of the world offer good alternatives to such negative images. Periodicals and magazines such as *American Girl*, *New Moon*®, *Dream/Girl*, and *Teen Voices* contain biographical and cultural materials that are both entertaining and socially responsible, and are written in ways to meet a variety of needs.[32]

Periodicals that have primarily male readerships also project mass culture images for males that may not promote or encourage socially constructive attitudes and behaviors. For example, motor and sports magazines tend to emphasize success as mastery of power through the use of motor technology and/or sport skills. Biographical coverage in these tends to celebrate personalities who have gained success through these skills. Like teen magazines directed at females, the writing style is brisk, exciting, easy to read with pictorial images delivering and supplementing much of the information presented.[33]

Public librarians and school library media specialists often defend these mass media periodicals in terms of their ability to meet the interests of youth, to be a device to promote the reading of better materials, and to encourage at-risk readers to discover that reading is rewarding.[34] Personalities from mass culture such as entertainers and athletes need to be recognized and their biographies made available to youth, but a counter argument can be made that the presentation of these biographical materials must be carried out in ways that deliver better information about behavior and attitudes.

Television and Movies

As with periodicals, radio, television, and movies have always concerned adults in terms of how they influence youth. This continues today as the influence of television grows as a predominant cultural force in many societies today. Mary Pipher, mentioned previously, details this influence in her writings. Cable television, public broadcasting, commercial broadcasting, public access radio, and television have accelerated the need for content, and this need has greatly expanded the coverage and availability of biographical materials.

Radio came to the American population in the 1920s. Programming at first was local and was largely centered on music. Radio, aided by the decline of vaudeville, gradually increased in variety so that by the 1930s, radio was offering programs of music, comedy, and dramatic serials such as *Amos and Andy* and *The Shadow*. Personalities such as George Burns and Gracie Allen, Jack Benny, Ed Wynn, and Bing Crosby became household names, often assuming a biographical presence with the public that enforced and projected their radio personas. By 1935 a variety of radio formats had developed, including panel discussions, documentaries, human interest stories, drama, and comedy.[35]

Most if not all, of this programming, along with the popularity of films, exerted direct influence on the creation of a celebrity culture. Movie fan magazines such as *Photoplay* (1911), *Motion Picture Story* (1913), and others began to appear.[36] By the 1930s such magazines as *Silver Screen* had become a mainstay of newsstand merchandise, satisfying the public's demand for information about their favorite entertainment personalities both on radio and in films.[37] Biographical films, as noted in chapter 5, were extremely popular during the 1930s, and undoubtedly, information about their stars filled much of these magazines.[38]

During World War II, American radio focused its attention on efforts to win the war, and much of its content was for military personnel as well as for the general public. Radio programming drew upon the talents of well-known performers of the day, existing popular programs, and newly discovered military personnel. The war also promoted news reporting, news personalities, and coverage of military events. This in turn helped to elevate news reporters and personalities to the status of public figures and celebrities. Names such as William L. Shirer, H. V. Kaltenborn, and Edward R. Murrow became familiar names to Americans.[39] The film *Good Night, and Good Luck*, released in 2005 with David Strathairn playing Murrow and George Clooney playing CBS television producer Fred Friendly, tells the story of Murrow's fight with the political power Senator Joseph McCarthy and is an example of this continued interest.

Apparently during this time, libraries were well aware of the influence of radio on public taste and demands, and sought to create an audience of their own. A 1934 ALA study of public libraries that had developed radio programs found that their programming revolved around answering reference questions from the public; presenting books and other information based on general interest—popular science, short story writing, and gardening; giving background on local history and community resources; presenting book discussions and/or interviews with people who were knowledgeable about books; developing programs based on children books and literature; and presenting programs dealing with library services and behind-the-scenes library operations.[40]

In 1948 the Louisville Public Library, as part of NBC's "University Theater of the Air" series, installed a "closed-circuit radio network that permitted the main library to transmit live radio broadcasts as well as recorded programs to its 10 branches." In effect, this created a network of radio-classrooms through the city.[41]

Beginning in 1949 the New York Public Library produced a radio program concerned with teenage reading. The format of the program always centered on a panel of teenagers that reviewed and discussed books in the presence of authors and editors. Over the years such notables as Paul Zindel, Madeleine L'Engle, Marian Anderson, Nat Hentoff, Eleanor Roosevelt, John F. Kennedy, and Langston Hughes appeared on the program. The program is no longer produced.[42]

By the 1950s television began to make strong headway into American popular culture, and radio needed to find new formats in order to hold its audiences. One of radio's successful ventures was to return to music formats and to create rock-and-roll disc jockey personalities at both the national and local levels. For example, Dick Clark quickly became a national celebrity with his *American Bandstand* and its immediate acceptance as a national hit among youth. The program introduced a number of popular singers such as Chuck Berry, Jerry Lee Lewis, Buddy Holly, and Chubby Checker into the American, if not an international, teen arena.[43]

Television programs of the 1950s and 1960s followed well-established formats, and with the availability of television, its influence on personalities grew. Variety shows such as the *Milton Berle Show*, *Perry Como Show*, *Colgate*

Comedy Hour, and the *Jack Benny Show* expanded the public's interest by the many guests they featured. News and interview programs such as *See It Now* with Edward R. Murrow, *Meet the Press*, *NBC News*, *CBS News*, and the *Today* show further widened the public's range of and interest in personalities and biographical information about them. Through television, and radio to a lesser extent, entertainment, sports figures, politicians, news commentators, and others soon became very familiar to the public. Television was especially responsible for the public attention given to Lucille Ball, Elvis Presley (by way of his introduction on the *Ed Sullivan Show*), the Beatles (again through their being highlighted on the *Ed Sullivan Show*), Gracie Allen and George Burns, Richard Boone, Michael Landon, Liberace, Phil Silvers, and Rod Sterling.[44] The Corporation for Public Broadcasting (CPB) (see chapter 5), created by the American Congress in 1967 further, expanded the ability of television and radio to provide biographical information to the public.

Commercial broadcasting companies in the United States today include ABC, MSNBC, CBS, and the Fox Broadcasting Company. CBS was among the first of these, beginning operation in 1927 under the name United Independent Broadcasters, Inc.[45] These American companies offer programs that largely reflect entertainment, news, and sports coverage that appeal to popular taste. Most of these programs do have content that is biographical, but these seem not to be promoted for their educational or curricular worth. For example, in terms of biographical coverage, and along with its political and social commentary programs, MSNBC offers *Headliners and Legends*, which does not appear to be marketed in formats independent from the broadcast. MSNBC describes the program as:[46]

> From the famous to the infamous, Matt Lauer brings you the stories of the most intriguing people. Gain a new perspective on those who shape our world and affect our lives every day. Find out how your favorite stars did in their eighth grade math classes, how our leaders rose to power, or what motivated society's most notorious criminals.

CBS sells some of its programs in VHS format such as its famous *60 Minutes*, dating from 1997, *48 Hours Investigates*, and other selected programs of biographical interests.[47] ABC offers a package set of some of its *20/20* programs, covering episodes of the past twenty years. On its website MSNBC links to MSN Shopping, where educational products produced by other companies are offered for sale. Many of the companies just mentioned do offer transcripts of their programs that can be downloaded or purchased.

Today cable television offers a formidable challenge to traditional television and radio. Cable television began in the United States in 1948 in Pennsylvania. It was started simply as a means of bringing better television reception to people living in mountainous areas.[48] Cable television was started in Canada in 1952[49] and in Great Britain in 1938 with the use of wires to help improve reception. A more useful system was devised in the 1960s.[50]

Cable television now is a huge industry requiring a constant stream of content to fill the many channels available to its various viewing publics. *Open Directory Project* lists numerous channels covering such interests as the arts, food, courts and law, movies, history, science, religion, style and fashions, sports, politics, and biography (http://dmoz.org/Arts/Television/Networks/ Cable). Satellite radio is also becoming more popular, and it is promising to offer a wide variety of formats and content to its subscribers,[51] but its potential for curriculum use has yet to be determined. Nevertheless, wide-ranging biographical coverage and interviews are already a part of its program offerings.

Among many others, cable channels that seem useful to know about in terms of the variety of biographical information now offered include The Disney Channel, with *Cable in the Classroom*; The Biography Channel; and A&E. Together, they provide an abundance of biographical programming ranging from popular culture personages to people of political and historical importance. CNN's and the BBC's various channels are excellent sources for diversified biographical products. The History Channel and Discovery Channel not only provide documentaries on historical and scientific topics, but many of their topics are biographical in scope and emphasis. These programs are available in most English-speaking countries including Canada, the United Kingdom, Australia, South Africa, New Zealand, and the United States.[52] The Lifetime Channel offers biographical information through several of its venues including *Real Women* and *Women Doctors*. Its "Intimate Portraits" series provides personal looks at well-known women in entertainment as well as women in other aspects of life. *Real Families*, another one of Lifetime's programs, considers the role of women in contemporary life.

ESPN provides biographical sports coverage; and C-Span provides biographical information through its coverage of scholarly events around the country such as conferences, seminars, and book reviews and interviews with authors. At a more popular level are programs such as *Larry King Live* on CNN. King's nightly interviews presents biographical materials of persons who are public figures for various reasons. These may range from presidents of the United States and their families to royalty and persons who are involved in legal and moral issues of modern life.

In terms of its appeal and effect on youth, MTV cannot be overlooked in how it showcases and promotes personalities from popular culture, especially popular music.[53] Its values, style, and motives have often been subject to criticism by parents, teachers, and the government.

As mentioned, many of these channels offer their recorded programs for sale to the public (The History Channel, the Biography Channel, A&E, and various BBC channels), but before these products can be used in classrooms or in libraries, they must conform to licensing agreements from the producers and, in some cases, distributors. Local school policies often prescribe how such programs can be purchased and used. If there are legal difficulties in school library media and classroom use, teachers and school library media specialists nevertheless can promote suitable biographical programs through lists, bibliographies, websites, displays, books, and reading tie-ins.

MASS MEDIA, CULTURE, CELEBRITIES, AND YOUTH

The mass media, culture, celebrities, and youth all play a role in defining who we are in the modern world. Because of this complex intertwining, it is difficult to clearly see how one of these affects others and how they, in turn, affect our view of modern life and how we create and identify with heroes and celebrities. Writer Joshua Gamson believes that the public's responses are varied and contradictory. To him, the attention the public gives to celebrity is much like sport and a trivial pursuit, and offers a means or outlet for catharsis or criticism.[54] Gamson, in a previous essay, noted that in the early twentieth century biographical narrative explained celebrity in terms of merit and presented the public's expectations that their heroes be meritorious. As the influence of public institutions such as churches, schools, and families lessened, mass communication grew, and advertising advanced, becoming more psychologically and sociologically sophisticated. Audience became more powerful and demanding, and the biographical narrative moved to one of artificially manufacturing and producing celebrities.[55] Garry Wills used the images of John Wayne to analyze the politics of celebrity in American society. He found that in the case of Wayne and his films, there was a progression from representing naive virtue to acceptance of heavy and even dark responsibility, and finally to accepting individualism with honor.[56]

Gill Lines notes that sports figures have traditionally been held up as highly regarded examples of social ideals and masculine virtues. Solid values learned on the playing field were thought to transfer easily into life. Lines contends that modern mass media has intruded on these concepts and has created a damaged male sports hero. Mass media can often violate the ideals of the male sports heroes by labeling them as drunkards, illegal drug users, rapists, wife beaters. On the other hand, mass media has also created unrealistic ideas about sports heroes. Because the public pays attention to sports and the people that play them, the mass media aggressively creates images that will attract consumers. In doing this mass media plays a decisive role in determining how sports heroes are characterized and models developed. In exerting its power to mold and shape images, the mass media has largely ignored or marginalized female sports heroes. Lines maintains that these images do not necessarily reflect how young people see their heroes.[57]

Sociologist Alan Edelstein argues that the role of hero in American society has changed over the years. In former times the status of hero could be placed in three categories. The highest status was for individuals in the military, sports, politics, and entertainment. The second group included persons in business, adventure, and crime. The lowest ranking group of heroes consisted of scientists, intellectuals, artists, and moralists. Edelstein suggests that America has no national heroes aside from the "celebrity" hero. In order to have heroes American society in particular must provide a national social framework in which heroic actions can occur. It must have a consensus of core values that a hero can ascribe to and model; and it must allow its heroes to be human and have flaws yet still remain heroes.[58]

THE EFFECTS OF MEDIA ON YOUTH

With the advent of radio in the early twentieth century concern was raised about its effects on youth. Between 1900 and 1960 some 242 studies of media's effects on children were conducted. In 1925 a survey revealed that 90 percent of Chicago children attended at least one movie per week (based on a survey of over 10,000), and they selected mostly westerns and adventure films.[59]

In 1928 a series of studies supported by the Payne Fund, a private philanthropic foundation, studied the cognitive, attitudinal, and behavioral effects of movies on children. The studies found that children did learn a great deal of information from movies and that they retained it for long periods. The studies also revealed that children's attitudes about race and ethnic groups were influenced by what they saw in movies. These studies were the first to suggest that children might become more aggressive from viewing violence in movies.[60]

In the 1930s radio was one, if not the most, dominant form of mass media to reach children. A 1930 survey of New York City children found that listening to radio was one of their favorite pastimes. They also reported that they learned a great deal about history, geography, music, health, and current events. The study's investigator, Ariel L. Eisenberg, concluded that radio had invaded the privacy of the home and had bewildered parents, and that it had an invincible hold over their children.[61]

By the 1950s radio's predominant format had become music, largely rock and roll. This music raised concerns about how rock and roll, and later rap music, might negatively influence the morals and values of youth. By 1986, due to public and government pressure, the music industry began to apply warning labels to music that contained sexual or violent content.[62]

Research by Wilbur Schramm and his colleagues in the United States and Canada in the 1950s further suggested how television affected youth. Effects included becoming frightened; increasing knowledge about public affairs; adopting fads; and encouraging passivity, delinquency, and violent behaviors. The researchers noted that the child's age, intelligence, and social relationship with parents and peers conditioned how youth responded to television content. Based on their findings, they concluded that viewing television by most children, under most circumstances, is neither harmful nor beneficial.[63]

In 1982 the U.S. National Institute of Mental Health was more forceful. In issuing its *Television and Social Behavior: Ten Years of Scientific Progress and Implications for the Eighties,* the institute concluded that the scientific evidence did point to a casual relationship between violence on television and violent behaviors. Nonetheless, it noted that television can produce positive behaviors as well, including altruism, friendliness, self-control, and fear-coping skills.[64]

Research by Kimberly M. Baker found that adolescents make judgments about good and bad behaviors that they see on television in terms of their own values and beliefs. Individuals create his or her own media environment based on the context of his or her life. Baker's subjects did not acquire new information from television that changed their own values.[65]

After examining, critiquing, and summarizing research on how television influences the identity of African American male adolescents, Terry V. Day concluded that these youth ascribed to the ideology of individualism that they learned from society, including television, and that television did affect their identity through its propagation of social ideology. This identity is further reinforced by this ideology in conjunction with the social barriers placed before African American male youths. Day suggested that this relationship between television content and social ideology may indeed influence the larger public's perception that African American youth hold and exhibit anti-social behaviors and attitudes.[66]

Brij David Lunine studied the role of television and popular culture in the lives of adolescents living in Berkeley, California. She found that less affluent persons of color watched a great deal of television, while white, middle-class adolescents watched very little. She noted that family, access to television, and involvement in extracurricular activities were the primary factors in determining leisure time activities. She found that those who did watch television the most exhibited unexpected tastes, creative impulses, and varied uses of popular culture. Adolescents from minority cultures often acquired and used television produced in their native languages and cultures to foster their sense of identity. Apparently viewing of television offers pleasure and possibilities for creativity coupled with "forces of constraint and [adolescents'] overdetermination."[67]

Madelyn Gould and her colleagues, Patrick Jamieson and Daniel Romer, suggested from their review of studies of youth suicides that portrayals and reports of the mass media can influence adolescent suicides. News reports and television presentations seem to have some influence on youth suicides in terms of methods. They asserted that because youth have wide access to these media, journalists should be better educated about how to present information about youth suicide in ways that will minimize imitation.[68]

Television is frequently used by adolescents as a source of information about careers. In 1979 Suzanne Jeffries-Fox reported that television was the most cited source for career information by teenagers. She concluded from her research that television cultivates an understanding of the world and helps describe that world in terms of conventional social reality. Stereotypical impressions are a part of that realty. Television creates the most widely shared stereotypes about jobs for which it was the major source of information, and less so from occupations for which it was not the primary source of information. She concluded that beliefs derived from television may bias interpretations of information coming from other sources. In other words, information external to television must first be assimilated into already existing stereotypes fostered by television. Knowledge gained from television may have long-ranging effects because it provides the basis for interaction and reflection.[69] These are small studies of large issues; nevertheless, they do help us understand how complex the relationships are between cultural products and behaviors and attitudes.

Research evidence prompted the American Congress in 1990 to pass the Television Violence Act, which required the commercial networks to develop standards to reduce violence in children's television programs. Both cable and the American networks agreed to label violent television programs and, beginning in 1994, to reduce the violence in children's programs.[70]

CONCLUSION

As popular culture and electronic formats increase in numbers and pervasiveness in society, we can expect more concern about how they affect youth. We already see this in concerns about Internet content and how youth surf the Internet. We see this in apprehensions about violence in video games and their wide accessibility, and the growing use of electronic mail in the discussion of a wide range of topics without insightful guidance.[71] Without becoming didactic, school library media specialists and youth librarians might best consider how to reach youth in terms of fostering positive social values and character development through the use of biography that is both literary and popular. Biography offers insight into human experiences. Reading and viewing experiences can offer opportunities for the creative uses of popular culture both for personal enjoyment and social understanding.

NOTES

1. John Harmon, "Some Definitions," http://www.geography.ccsu.edu/harmonj/atlas/definitions.html (accessed March 21, 2005, and Nov. 5, 2005).

2. Harmon.

3. Internet School Library Media Center, "School Library History," http://falcon.jmu.edu/~ramseyil/libhistory.htm (accessed April 23, 2005).

4. "School Libraries," in *Handbook of Texas Online*, http://www.tsha.utexas.edu/handbook/online/articles/SS/lcs7.html (accessed Oct. 30, 2005). This discussion notes that a school library existed in New Braunfels, Texas, in 1854.

5. "School Libraries."

6. Alleen Pace Nilson and Kenneth L. Donelson, *Literature for Today's Young Adults*, 6th ed. (New York: Longman, 2001), 52–53.

7. Richard W. Etulain, "Re-imagining the Modern American West: A Century of Fiction, History, and Art," http://www.uapress.arizona.edu/samples/sam990.htm (accessed March 21, 2005).

8. Nilson and Donelson.

9. Donna R. Casella, "Introduction to Popular Culture," http://www.english.mnsu.edu/casella/humanities/Humanities2502001.htm (accessed March 21, 2005). This reference is no longer posted; contact the author directly at http://www.english.mnsu.edu/casella/cas. htm (accessed Nov. 5, 2005).

10. Casella.

11. Casella.

12. Casella.

13. Casella.

14. Casella.

15. Chelsea House Publishers, "For Authors," http://www.chelseahouse.com/c/@8UU5BEURJm0VE/Pages/editorial.html (accessed March 23, 2005).

16. Lerner Publishing Group, "Biographies" link, http://www.lernerbooks.com/cgi-bin/books.sh/lernerpublishing and http://www.lernerbooks.com/cgi-bin/books.sh/lernerpublishing.p?navaction=SeriesResults.w&navvalue=Biographies (accessed March 23, 2005).

17. Lerner Publishing Group, "Sports" link, http://www.lernerbooks.com/cgi-bin/books.sh/lernerpublishing and http://www.lernerbooks.com/cgi-bin/books.sh/lernerpublishing.p?navaction=SeriesResults.w&navvalue=Sports (accessed March 23, 2005).

18. Omnigraphics, Biography Today Library, http://www.omnigraphics.com/category_view.php?ID=2 (accessed March 24, 2005).

19. Mary K. Monteith, "ERIC/RCS Report: The Magazine Habit," *Language Arts* 58 (Nov.–Dec. 1981): 965–69.

20. Linda E. Western, "Magazine Preferences of Fourth- and Sixth-Grade Children," *Elementary School Journal* 79 (May 1979): 284–91.

21. W. Bernard Lukenbill, "The Reading Interests of Young Adults," in *Reaching Young People through Media*, ed. Nancy Bach Pillon (Littleton, Colo.: Libraries Unlimited, 1983), 25.

22. Doreen O. Bardsley, "Boys and Reading: What Reading Fiction Means to Sixth-Grade Boys" (dissertation, Arizona State University, 1999), abstracted in *Dissertation Abstracts International* 60-A (Sept. 1999): 653.

23. Magaretha M. Joubert, "The Reading Interests and Reading Habits of Afrikaans-Speaking Teenagers in Pretoria (Master of Information thesis, University of South Africa, 2002), abstracted in *Masters Abstracts International* 42 (Aug. 2004), 1114.

24. Constance Schultheis, "A Study of the Relationships between Gender and Reader Preferences in Adolescents" (MLS research paper, Kent State University, 1990), ERIC document no. ED 367 376.

25. Diane Gruber, "Much of Their Tuition: The Historical Matrix of Youth, Consumerism, and Mass Culture as Illustrated in the Pages of the *Youth's Companion*, 1827–1929" (dissertation, Purdue University, 2002), abstracted in *Dissertation Abstract International* 64-A (Jan. 2004): 2533.

26. Lorinda Beth Cohoon, "Serializing Boyhoods: Periodicals, Books, and American Boys, 1840–1911" (dissertation, University of Southern Mississippi, 2001), abstracted in *Dissertation Abstracts International* 62-A (Jan. 2002): 2420

27. Reading Is Fundamental, "Getting the Family Excited about Magazines," http://www.rif.org/parents/articles/magazines.mspx (accessed April 1, 2005).

28. Charlotte S. Huck and others, *Children's Literature in the Elementary School*, 6th ed. (Madison, Wis.: Brown & Benchmark, 1997), 99.

29. The Elizabeth Nesbitt Room Nineteenth Century Juvenile Magazine Collection. "*The Girl's Own Annual (Girl's Own Paper)*," http://www.library.pitt.edu/libraries/is/enroom/juvenile/girlsown.html (accessed April 2, 2005).

30. Dawn Currie, "Teen Magazines—Will They Harm Her?" http://www.parenting-bookmark.com/pages/DC01.htm (accessed April 1, 2005). See also her *Girl Talk: Adolescent Magazines and Their Readers* (Toronto: University of Toronto Press, 1999).

31. Melissa A. Milkie, "The Social Psychological Impact of Gender Images in Media: A Multi-Level Analysis of Girls, Peers Networks, and Media Organizations" (dissertation, Indiana University, 1995), abstracted in *Dissertation Abstracts International* 56-A (May 1996): 4560.

32. Currie, "Teen Magazines—Will They Harm Her?"

33. W. Bernard Lukenbill, "'Motomania' Motorcross Racing Materials," *School Library Journal* 31 (Oct. 1984): 103–7.

34. "Teenage Boys and Reading Theme Issue," *Teacher Librarian* 30 (Feb. 2003): 9–31.

35. Ronald Garay, "Radio Entertainment," in *History of the Mass Media in the United States: An Encyclopedia*, ed. Margaret Blanchard (Chicago: Fitzroy Dearborn, 1998), 564.

36. "Film History before 1920," http://www.filmsite.org/pre20sintro3.html (accessed April 16, 2005).

37. Popular Mechanics.Com, "Science Research, Your Place in Time," http://www.popularmechanics.com/science/research/1281886.html?page=2&c=y (accessed April 2, 2005).

38. Popular Mechanics.Com.

39. Garay, "Radio Entertainment," 564.

40. Faith Holmes Hyers, *The Library and the Radio* (Chicago: University of Chicago Press, 1938), 60–82.

41. Clarence H. Graham and William Hodapp, "Television's Town Hall," *Library Journal* 74 (March 15, 1949): 409–10.

42. Ruth Rausen, "Teen Age Book Talk," *Voice of Youth Advocates* 5 (March 1983): 14–17.

43. "Dick Clark," http://www.history-of-rock.com/clark.htm (accessed April 4, 2005).

44. "Classic TV," http://www.fiftiesweb.com/tv50.htm and http://www.fiftiesweb.com/dead/dead-people-w.htm (accessed April 4, 2005).

45. "Broadcast Archives [CBS Section]," http://www.oldradio.com/archives/prog/cbs.htm (accessed April 5, 2005).

46. "MSNBC [Home Page for News]," http://www.msnbc.msn.com (accessed April 5, 2005, and Nov. 5, 2005).

47. "CBS OnLine Store," http://store.cbs.com (accessed April 5, 2005).

48. About Inventors, "Cable Television History," http://inventors.about.com/library/inventors/blcabletelevision.htm (accessed April 5, 2005).

49. Civilization.Ca, "Watching TV," http://www.civilization.ca/hist/tv/tv02eng.html (accessed April 5, 2005).

50. Digital Spy, "History of Cable TV in the UK" (updated Oct. 4, 2005), http://www.digitalspy.co.uk/cable/history (accessed April 5, 2005, and Nov. 5, 2005).

51. Lorne Manly, "Satellite Alters the Sound of Radio," *New York Times*, April 6, 2005. Available at *International Herald Tribune* Online, http://www.iht.com/articles/2005/04/05/business/satradio.html (accessed April 7, 2005) and http://www.iht.com/cgi-bin/search.cgi?query=Satellite+Alters+the+sound+of+radio&sort=swishrank&submit=Search (accessed Nov. 5, 2005).

52. Cable Channels: The Biography Channel, http://www.biographychannel.com; Disney's *Cable in the Classroom*, http://psc.disney.go.com/disneychannel/cableintheclassroom/index.html; CNN (home page), http://www.cnn.com; Lifetime: Television for Women, http://www.lifetimetv.com; The History Channel, http://www.historychannel. com. All links re-accessed Nov. 5, 2005.

53. Cable Channels: C-SPAN.ORG, http://www.c-span.org; *Larry King Live*, http://www.cnn/CNN/Programs/larry.king.live; MTV, http://www.mtv.com. All links accessed Nov. 5, 2005.

54. Joshua Gamson, *Claims to Fame: Celebrity in Contemporary America* (Berkeley: University of California Press, 1994).

55. Joshua Gamson, "The Assembly Line of Greatness: Celebrity in Twentieth-Century America," *Critical Studies in Mass Communication* 9 (March 1992): 1–24.

56. Garry Wills, *John Wayne's America: The Politics of Celebrity* (New York: Simon & Schuster, 1997).

57. Gill Lines, "Villains, Fools or Heroes? Sports Stars as Role Models for Young People," *Leisure Studies* 20 (Oct. 2001): 285–303. See also her "The Sport Star in the Media: The Gendered Construction and Youthful Consumption of Sports Personalities," in *Power Games. A Critical Sociology of Sports*, ed. J. Sugden and A. Tomlinson (London: Routledge, 2002), 196–215.

58. Alan Edelstein, *Everybody Is Sitting on the Curb: How and Why America's Heroes Disappeared* (Westport, Conn.: Praeger Publishers, 1996).

59. Kim A. Smith, "Mass Media and Children," in *History of the Mass Media in the United States: An Encyclopedia*, ed. Margaret A. Blanchard (Chicago: Fitzroy Dearborn, 1998), 349.

60. Smith, "Mass Media and Children," 349.

61. Smith, "Mass Media and Children," 340–50.

62. Smith, "Mass Media and Children," 340–50.

63. Kim A. Smith, "Children's Television Programming," in *History of the Mass Media in the United States: An Encyclopedia*, ed. Margaret A. Blanchard (Chicago: Fitzroy Dearborn, 1998), 133.

64. Smith, "Children's Television Programming," 135.

65. Kimberly Middleton Baker, "Adolescents and the Meanings They Make from Television" (dissertation, New York University, 2000), abstracted in *Dissertation Abstracts International* 61-B (Jan. 2001): 3876.

66. Terry V. Day, "Television and the Identity of African American Male Adolescents" (dissertation, The Wright Institute, 2000), abstracted in *Dissertation Abstracts International* 61-B (March 2001): 4977.

67. Brij David Lunine, "Creativity and Constraint: The Role of Television and Popular Culture in the Lives of Adolescents" (dissertation, University of New Mexico, 2004), abstracted in *Dissertation Abstracts International* 65-A (Oct. 2004): 1420.

68. Madelyn Gould and others, "Media Contagion and Suicide among the Young," *American Behavioral Scientists* 46 (May 2003): 1269–84.

69. Suzanne Kuulei Jeffries-Fox, "Television's Contribution to Young People's Concepts about Occupations" (dissertation, University of Pennsylvania, 1979), abstracted in *Dissertation Abstracts International* 39-A (April 1979): 5784.

70. Smith, "Mass Media and Children," 136.

71. Smith, "Mass Media and Children," 350.

7

BIOGRAPHY AS SOCIAL DIALOGUE

INTRODUCTION

This chapter considers biography an important part of social and cultural dialogue and community discourse. It continues the discussion that was begun in previous chapters by paying more attention to the influence of biography in modern political life, culture, and the mass media. It considers the development of a national biography and how elements of both history and current affairs influence and shape a sense of national identity through biography. Because modern mass media gives focus to national character and identity and is very much a part of forming and sustaining a sense of national biography, this chapter will likewise look at biography in film and how historical as well as social and cultural messages are transmitted through these important means. The final part of the chapter discusses how these elements can play an important part in school library media center programming.

CREATING A NATIONAL BIOGRAPHY

All nations have a national biography. Often a nation's biography is presented and codified in august, scholarly reference works such as the *Dictionary of National Biography* (DNB) for Great Britain and countries closely tied to it through history. Oxford University Press, publisher of the DNB, describes it in this way:

> The stories of 50,000 men and women who shaped the history of the British Isles and beyond, from the earliest times to the year 2000. [Fifty thousand biographies] and 60 million words record the lives of the men and women who shaped all aspects of British history, from the explorer Pytheas of the fourth century BC to modern figures.

The statement goes on to say that this work, published in a completely new and revised edition in 2004, is the work of 10,000 expert contributors from all over the world, 450 specialist advisors, and a 50-strong editorial team.[1] Because the work looks at people who have influenced British history, it has traditionally included the famous (e.g., Queen Victoria), the legendary (e.g., Robin Hood), and the infamous (e.g., Guy Fawkes).

The Dictionary of American Biography (DAB) gives similar attention to important Americans and others closely associated with the development of the United States. It serves as the national biography record in the United States. Published by Charles Scribner in 1989, the DAB is described as:

> a 20-volume set record[ing] the lives of 19,173 celebrated women and men who have made significant contributions to American life. Included are 19,173 biographies covering people who died through 1980 in 10 base volumes and 10 supplements. In addition, a comprehensive index to the entire set is available. Explorers, artists, scientists, inventors, business leaders, criminals, political figures, diplomats, and outstanding individuals from over 700 fields of endeavor are chronicled in signed biographies by specialists.[2]

Both these reference sets are necessary in larger school and public libraries. For smaller school library media centers and public libraries, the *Concise Dictionary of American Biography*, 5th ed. (Scribner, 1997), is suitable.

The listings of subjects covered in the DNB and DAB are noticeable for their variety. Biographies range from men and women of laudatory stature to criminals. That is one of the hallmarks of a national biography—it reflects national identity, character, and national conflicts.

Most countries have a unifying force that holds a nation together. This may be allegiance to a sovereign such as the king or queen in Great Britain; the idea of commonwealth and traditions of law and established order for Canada and Australia; and for the United States, the Constitution and the ideology of democracy as set by its founding fathers.

Biblical Israel is an example of forces that often shape a national biography. Jewish literary and feminist scholar Ilana Pardes, in her book *The Biography of Ancient Israel: National Narratives in the Bible*, outlines some of the attributes of how a national biography was formed for Israel.[3] Some of her illustrations are useful in helping us to better understand the importance of the idea of national biography and how it shapes our thinking about our nation and our society. These ideas are important for school library media specialists and public librarians serving youth to know and understand as they build biographical collections and present programs based on biographical themes for their users.

Pardes says that it is important to understand how a nation is born in narrative terms. A metaphor or a series of metaphors is used to justify a nation's birth and its continued existence. The metaphor is based on a sense of the nation being created by divine and special intervention from a spiritual source. This metaphor, defined by this special, unique national character, enforces a feeling of singularity and sets it apart from other nations. But this feeling of being special is not enough. A national biography is needed to support and reinforce the metaphor and the nation's calling to a place of honor among nations. The metaphor must be personalized with the lives of people who exemplify the highest qualities of the nation's calling.

Personalities are needed to build a national biography. In order to strengthen the prevailing metaphor, the personalities that come to make up the national biography must speak with a distinct voice, conveying a collective voice of strength and strong will. The personalities of the national biography must reinforce the ideas of the nation's miraculous birth, the communion of the national spirit, unity, and continuity. The idea of continuity is especially important in times of national crisis and uncertainty. Nevertheless, a nation is never perfect, and personalities that make up its national biography are not perfect. These personalities may reflect hidden desires, collective anxieties, human weaknesses, and all the drama and suspense of life.

A national biography is based on a collective memory as it attempts to reflect an imagined nation. In reality this memory is fragmented, slippery, and qualities of its memory may be faulty. The imagined communities found in national biographies are among the most powerful sources in creating nationalism. Strategies are carefully, if not unconsciously developed to advance both nationalism and national biography through reflections on national origins, belonging, distinctiveness in the world, quests for noble causes, and struggles to survive. National biography also reflects the psychology of a nation. Psychology of a nation is its collective behavior and mental characteristics. Nations can exhibit characteristics of racism, xenophobia, sexism, and other forms of fear and hatred as well as a sense of humanity, openness, justice, fairness, and trust.[4]

National biographies written for youth tend to reflect many of the elements of a nation's national biography. Questions of how individualism is viewed within a nation and how youth are encouraged and expected to develop their identities, values, and loyalties in accordance with national purposes and goals are systematically presented in biographies for youth.

In creating a national biography, Pardes notes that the narrative must be strong and clear, and reflect the identity and values of a nation. The development of nationalism and its complex need to promote group solidarity, loyalty, and pride is often the foundation of a national biography.

In the United States, the development of Jacksonian democracy gives insight into how values of a nation become inherently linked to a national biography. During the 1820s and 1830s the ideals of modern democracy were forcefully taking shape in the American mind. Popular literature of the time celebrated the United States as an almost perfect nation, offering equality, prosperity, unlimited opportunities for all people, charity and support for the poor, lessening of class distinctions, honoring of the working classes, intolerance for excesses in behaviors such as the use of alcohol, and support of capitalism and business opportunities. The value of education and the celebration of the nation's past and the people that forged the nation and national character were very much apart of this literature.[5]

Historian Ann MacLeod illustrates an emerging and conflicting value in American society when she notes that a great deal of the popular literature published in the first quarter of the nineteenth century in the United States was pacifist in nature.[6] In children's literature, war and the glories of war were not celebrated. Of course the American Revolution was an exception. Nevertheless some writers of the period, such as Joseph Alden in his *Old Revolutionary Soldier*, depicted American soldiers as plunderers and murderous brutes.[7] Nevertheless, on the whole the American Revolution, in the spirit of nationalism of the period, was justified as a good cause based on democratic principles and the freedom that it promised.

MacLeod writes that as a soldier, Washington was not criticized for his war record by antiwar writers of the time. He was praised as a good man with high morality in his character and motives.[8] The creation and rise of George Washington as a national hero is a signature example of the development of an American national biography and the archetype personality needed to forge this biography.

Parson Weems' biography of Washington, published in 1808, is an early example of the emerging character of national biography for children. His biography was designed to present Washington to children an as exemplary role model.[9] Weems (Figure 7.1) was an independent book salesman who traveled the Mid-Atlantic and southern states from 1794 to 1825. His biography of Washington is now considered "invented" biography, as it introduced readers to the fanaticized story of Washington chopping down a cherry tree and not lying to his father about the deed. This biography is typical of much of the biographical writing for children that lasted into the early twentieth century. As time progressed, writing became less didactic than that written by Weems, but national personalities particularly continued to be idealized and presented as flawless personalities, with much of the interpretations couched in fiction.[10]

The growth of national biography in Great Britain, the various principalities of Germany, and other Western countries was similar to that in the United States in that nationalism and the search for identity played an important role in defining each nation's idea of biography. Legendary figures such as King Arthur, Robin Hood, and Richard the Lion Hearted (Richard III) exemplify this biography in Great Britain.

Children's literature and biography for children in nineteenth-century Britain was closely tied to imperialism and maleness. That is, male strength

Figure 7.1
Parson Weems, a biographer of
George Washington; famous for
his account of Washington
chopping down the cherry tree.
Likeness drawing by Richard H.
Hendler, based on an image
supplied by Parson Weems, LLC
and published with permission.

was seen as a national characteristic necessary to conquer and to control the empire. In fiction as well as in biography; this requirement meant that individuality, doubt, and humanist consideration by the ruler must be subjected to the greater need of controlling the empire. In the eyes of popular as well as literary minds, absolute truth lay with God and king.[11] Literary critic Jean Webb states that "God and country, certainty, the power of knowledge of right, and English Imperialism [served] as unquestionable guides in the great quest."[12]

British Heroism: or, Biographical Memories of Some of Those Renowned Commanders, Who Have Extended the Glory of the British Union to the Remotest Parts of the World, published in 1800 by J. Wallis of London, is a collective biography written for children and illustrates how a national concept of biography was used to reinforce national values in young British children. Without question, biography soon became an established part of youth literature, and its growth in quantity, if not quality, continued throughout the nineteenth century in Great Britain and the United States. In their respective countries, J. C. Edgar in Great Britain and Laura Richards in the United States contributed greatly to biography for children during this period.[13]

Periodical literature for both children and adults during the nineteenth century played an important role in expanding the concept of national biography. Periodicals during the nineteenth century, especially during the latter half of the century, helped with social control and with inculcating values in the populations of many countries. Social critic Matthew Schneirov argues that by the end of the nineteenth century American popular magazines such as *Harper's*

Monthly, *Century*, and *Atlantic Monthly* had moved away from the idea that they were arbitrators of high culture expressed in literary, artistic, and philosophical terms of the middle and upper classes to one of energy and vitality reflecting the needs and desires of an emerging America.

This America was encased in competitive individualism and distaste for class distinction, extreme wealth and/or extreme poverty, unbridled individualism, and uncontrolled economic forces. This periodical literature promoted consumerism, capitalism, and support for certain political causes; and it fostered a mistrust of certain institutions. In so doing, popular periodicals of the day helped bring important issues to the attention of the masses, gave legitimacy to certain values, and helped form a broad national consciousness.[14] These periodicals presented their issues and stories with vigor and vitality, well fitted to their goals of forging a new American identity.

Biography was very much a part of the robust approach to journalism. In fact, *Cosmopolitan* magazine carried more biographical articles than any other popular periodical of this time.[15] Characteristic of these periodicals was what journalism historian Matthew Schneirov calls "martial ethic and other manly virtues." Biographical subjects were generally presented as heroic and engaged in state-building and war-making. The biography of Napoleon, published in *McClure's* between 1894 and 1895 and written by Ida Tarbell, is an example of such presentations. Tarbell's positive analysis of Napoleon celebrated his rebelliousness, dominance, fearlessness, strength of will and character, and his ability to compel obedience in others. In terms of his grand statesmanship, she compared Theodore Roosevelt to him.[16]

The industrialists or "captains of industry," as they were often called, were popular biographical subjects. Schneirov maintains that by presenting these industrialists as almost superhuman, a national biographical mythology was created. These heroes were not seen as products of their parents; their success was not tied directly to heredity, parental personalities, or to child-rearing practices. Rather, success was presented as nothing but individual characteristics of perseverance, the ability to craft a personal environment, and the ability to build and to create. Even those born to wealth and privilege could become "self-made" men through willpower, hard work, persistence, and the ability to take advantage of opportunities that came their way. Throughout these accounts, we find words like *force, decisive, great physical power, genius, prophetic, masterful, unhesitating, dominating, commanding figure, diligence,* and *persistence.* By downplaying the opportunities that wealth and power afforded most of these industrialists, and by celebrating personal qualities that were far from the ordinary, these biographies conveyed the impression to the general reading public that every person could emulate these values for their own success.[17]

Women of this time who wrote about women contributed significantly to the development of a national biography. Through their research skills and insight as women and social observers they enriched national biographical writing. For example, during the nineteenth century American feminist Sara Josepha Hale published the monumental *Women's Record: All Distinguished Women [from Eve till AD 1850]* (1853), and in England Clara Lucas Belfour contributed her *Moral Heroism: or, The Trials of the Great and Good* (1846).[18]

Of course children and youth periodicals and books were very much a part of the forming of a sense of national biography. Along with dime and penny novels, mass-produced magazines of the nineteenth and early twentieth centuries in both the United States and England celebrated heroes as did adult magazines and books. As mentioned in chapter 1, in his youth President Ronald Reagan read and admired many of the men who were featured in biographical materials of the time. Reagan says that he read biography and was "a sucker for hero worship." His heroes were soldiers, U.S. presidents, athletes, and "achievers and self-made men who became captains of industry and public service." Lou Cannon, one of Reagan's many biographers, described him as a man who lived in a world of heroes, who themselves lived lives of adventure and high morality.[19]

Periodicals such as *Youth Companion* (1827–1929), *Juvenile Gazette* (1827–1828), *Parley's Magazine* (1833–1844), *Youth Magazine* (1834–ca. 1838), and others tended to publish stories and themes extolling expectations for high moral behavior and responsibility to family and country. Naturally, biographical materials carried in these periodicals reinforced these values. For example, "Life in the Woods" appeared in the July 19, 1848, issue of *Youth Companion* and celebrated Thoreau's life of frugality. "Willie Lincoln" was published in the July 1865 issue of *Our Young Folks* and discussed the recently assassinated Lincoln's relationship with his oldest son. "My Own Life and Adventures," by Robert Merry (Samuel Goodrich), serialized repeatedly in *Robert Merry's Museum* (1841–1872), drew upon the remembered childhood and moralized adventures of Goodrich, the periodical's editor.[20]

Other types of magazines read by youth were also available during the nineteenth century such as *Young America's Magazine for Self-Improvement* and the weekly *Buffalo Bill Stories* (1906–1910). Although moral by the standards of the time, they offered a bit more adventure and entertainment, and social information. *Young America's Magazine for Self-Improvement* was geared to improving the lot of working-class males,[21] while magazines such as *Buffalo Bill Stories* and its continuation, the *New Buffalo Bill Weekly* (1912–1919), addressed the needs for adventure expected by its readership.

Biographies and the adventures of such figures as Buffalo Bill (William F. Cody) (Figure 7.2) and Wild Bill Hickok (James Butler Hickok) were popular with a wide range of readers from all classes. They offered exciting characters who accomplished almost superhuman tasks and exploits.[22] The *New*

**Figure 7.2
Buffalo Bill inspired a
sense of adventure and
generated interest in the
American West.** Courtesy
of the Library of Congress,
LC-USZ62-111800.

Buffalo Bill Weekly and *Buffalo Bill Wild West Series* are good examples of the intermixing of fiction and reality in periodicals as well as books.

The need for more realism and vicarious experiences was further satisfied through "bad boy" books. Bad boy books first appeared in 1870, introduced by Thomas Aldrich's *The Story of a Bad Boy*. Following a biographical approach, this book was built around what was then seen as boys who did not conform to the expected behavior of middle-class youth. These boy characters were flesh and blood, imperfect, tough, and able to survive in the world. The Aldrich book was so different from what had preceded it that it was sometimes praised by critics of the day for its originality. One critic especially commended it for its realism in terms of showing how boys really lived and its lack of teaching (e.g., didactism). Bad boy books were often serialized in popular youth periodicals of the day.

St. Nicholas Magazine, considered one of the better magazines for children during the later part of the nineteenth century and early twentieth century, concentrated largely on providing good fiction and biography for youth. The contents in *St. Nicholas Magazine* reflected a middle-class, humane world; and its high standards of writing and literary form undoubtedly influenced the development of better written biography for youth.[23]

Collectively, both real and fictionalized biography of the types of literature just reviewed along with adult periodicals of the day suggest that such publications helped form the elements of a national biographical concept for youth in the United States, England, and other countries.[24]

BIOGRAPHY AS POLITICAL DISCOURSE AND HOW IT SHAPES CURRENT THINKING

As we have seen in previous discussions, political biography is not new. It has been with us since the beginning of recorded history and probably before formal writing was ever invented. Political biography is inclusive in forms. It includes many types of writing such as memoirs, reminiscences, letters, diaries, and journals. Political biography and autobiography has several purposes. The best known of these forms is probably biography that is meant to justify and promote a political personality and career or to help ensure the success of a political philosophy. *Every Man a King: The Autobiography of Huey P. Long* (Da Capo Press, 1996; originally published in 1933), about the famed Louisiana governor and senator, is an example of this. Biographies that appeared in the former *Great Soviet Encyclopedia* (Большая Советская Энциклопедия) (3rd. ed., 1969–1978, 30 vols.) offer more examples. The more recent autobiography by former U.S. president Bill Clinton, *My Life* (Vintage, 2004), is an excellent example of an early twenty-first-century political biography.[25]

New York Times Book Review editor Barry Gewen, in an essay in the *Review*, wrote that American political biography has always been in flux, ranging from a narrow, nationalistic perception on to more recent writings authored by "a school of multicultural historians" that emerged in the 1960s." The nationalistic point of view followed a standard of historical writing coming out of earlier decades that saw the United States as a perfect nation. However, the multiculturalists from the 1960s opened up a "golden age" of social history and biography through their research and analysis of ignored groups—such as women, minorities, gays and lesbians, and workers. Nonetheless, Gewen contends that at their extremes, many of these writers were narrow and judgmental of American society, often labeling it racist (blacks), imperialist (Mexican Americans and Native Americans), and exploitative (workers). He further suggested that multiculturalism "curdled into political correctness."[26]

As a reaction to these negative views and what he feels were exaggerations and distortions, Gewen held that the American popular reading public, especially in the 1990s, wanted a reaffirmation of the country's fundamental national values and was more than ready for new, interesting, and readable biographies about national heroes such as Washington, Hamilton, and the Adams family. Authors David McCullough, Ron Chernow, and Walter Isaacson have all published biographies that were popular and became best sellers; for their writings, McCullough and Chernow have won National Book Awards, and McCullough has won two Pulitzer Prizes.[27]

Gewen noted that the early twenty-first century introduced new influences on how both American history and American biography were written. These newer trends were caused by globalization and the disaster of 9/11.

Globalization and 9/11 forced Americans to see the United States in a larger world context, freed from its traditional, isolationist, and provincial context. He predicted that American history and biography in the future would be written as one "single stream in a larger global current."[28] He concluded his essay with these somber words: "The major lesson the new historians must teach is that there is no longer any safe haven from history's horror story."[29] This continues to be a lesson for not only historians, but for teachers and school library media center specialists as they seek to teach youth to be better informed and critical users of information.

Although Gewen's words and advice are important, we must remember that popular political biographies read by children and young adults tend to be those that evoke interest, identification, and empathy. Biographies and writings of Eleanor Roosevelt are examples of this type of personality. This factor is well illustrated by Mary Winget's biography *Eleanor Roosevelt* (Lerner, 2000).

Political biography for children and youth also includes what Gewen might call multiculturalism—biographies that are concerned with social and cultural issues such as gender, race, nationalism, class, and oppression. Personalities such as Nelson Mandela (*Peaceful Protest: The Life of Nelson Mandela*, by Yona Z. McDonald [Walker, 2002]) and Booker T. Washington (*Up from Slavery* [Norton, 1995; originally published in 1901]) fall into this category. These types of biographical writings are important because they either directly address political affairs controlled by government or they influence and often direct political discussion and debate.[30] Gewen's concern with extreme multiculturalism was that it sometimes exaggerated and misrepresented historical and social realities.

Political biography likewise includes resistance writing and writings from various subcultures. This biographical form seeks to address social and political wrongs by deliberately challenging repressive forces in society that have traditionally controlled and/or repressed groups in society. Biography of this type has been described as a form of cultural intervention. Feminist writing, writings about and by African Americans and others affected by the African diaspora, writings concerning various native peoples such as Native Americans and aborigine people in Australia are very much a part of this biographical legacy. Important works here include *Sojourner Truth: Ain't I a Women*, by Pat and Frederick McKissack (Scholastic, 1994, 1999), *We Are Your Sisters: Black Women in the Nineteenth Century*, edited by Dorothy Sterling (W. W. Norton, 1997), *Strong Men Keep Coming: The Book of African American Men*, by Tonya Bolden (John Wiley & Sons, 2000), *The Life and Death of Crazy Horse*, by Russell Freedman and his associates (Thomas Allen & Son, 1996), *In a Sacred Manner I Live: Native American Wisdom*, edited by Neil Philip (Houghton Mifflin, 1997), and *Harvesting Hope: The Story of Cesar Chavez*, by Kathleen Krull (Harcourt & Brace, 2003).

Sexual minorities such as gay, lesbian, and transgender people are very much a part of political biography. Books of a political biographical nature especially useful for youth include *Out Spoken: Role Models from Gay and Lesbian Community*, by Michael Thomas Ford (Morrow/Avon, 1998) and *Being Different: Lambda Youths Speak Out*, by Larry Dane Brimner (Scholastic, 1996).

We should not forget that ordinary people are very much a part of the political process. Biography of this type addresses real life experiences of minorities; working-class people; women; migrant workers; and lesbians, gays, and transgender people. These biographies that present ordinary people going about their lives also address situations of racism, colonialism, sexism, and other forms of repression and exploitation. These biographies not only serve to open up political debate within democratic society, but form a record of experiences that promotes analysis of how individual people cope with institutional, societal, and governmental repression. They likewise give support to group identity and solidarity.[31, 32] Examples here include *We Shall Not Be Moved: The Women's Factory Strike of 1909*, by Joan Dash (Scholastic, 1998), *Into a New Century: Eight Remarkable Women of the West*, by Liza Ketchum (Little, Brown, 2000), *Persepolis: The Story of a Childhood*, by Marjane Satrapi (Knopf, 2004), *Black Indians: Hidden Heritage*, by William L. Katz (Simon & Schuster, 1997), *When Heaven and Earth Changed Places: A Vietnamese Woman's Journey from War to Peace*, by Le Ly Hayslip with Jay Wurts (Penguin, 1993), and *Voices from the Fields: Children of Migrant Farmworkers Tell Their Stories* (Little, Brown, 2000).

Biography can also include a variety of narrative works such as fiction, poetry, drama, and essays. Although not always discussed as biographical statements,[33] such works often help reinforce the importance of biography as a form of social dialogue.[34] Examples include *Carver: A Life in Poems*, by Marilyn Nelson (Front Street, 2001), *The Miracle Worker*, by William Gibson (Simon & Schuster, 2002; various editions available), *Inherit the Wind*, by Jerome Lawrence and Robert E. Lee (Pan, 2000; various editions available), and *Evita*, by Andrew Lloyd Webber and Tim Rice (Morrow/Avon, 1979; various editions and formats available).

BIOGRAPHY AS JOURNALISM AND REPORTING

Most serious adult biographies before 1975 were written by academics and scholars. However, since 1975 a new type of biography has appeared, capturing the public's interest and contributing to social dialogue. These new writers often come to biography from journalism and investigative reporting. According to critic Steve Weinberg, academic biographers trained as historians were rather nonjudgmental in terms of private lives and personalities. Investigative journalism, for the most part, has no such tradition, and these journalists feel it is their obligation to assess personality, intellect, emotional status, and the moral character of their subjects.[35] Although there is a danger of abuse, and we do have many examples of recent investigative biography that might be called "muckraking" in research and approach, quality investigative biography adheres to rigid standards of writing and reporting. Weinberg lists the following as the prevailing standard for good journalistic biographical writing:

- A life is told chronologically.
- A writer presents the subject in the context of his or her time.
- A good writer refrains from injecting personal hindsight into the life of the person being discussed.
- A writer maintains a sense of sympathy or empathy for the subject, or at least recognizes antipathy and lets facts speak for themselves.
- A biographer injects psychological analysis sparingly.
- A writer recognizes and seeks to explain the complexity of human behavior. Motivations are complex, and the good and bad must be seen in the context of the subject's perceptions—but not necessarily justified.
- When gaps in the record must be filled in, a writer is honest with readers as how those gaps were closed.
- A biographer checks out all facts and never relies on secondary sources.
- A writer makes hard decisions about the length of a book or article.
- A good writer avoids traps of illogic and writes with style as well as substance. Style can include geographical descriptions, physical descriptions of persons, dialogue, imagery, symbolism, irony, contrast, and view points as they change from situation to situation or person to person.[36]

Although these may be directed at journalists, they are sound and certainly apply to good biographical writing for children and young adults.

Biographies of investigative reporters make excellent reading in their own right. Their biographies help us better understand their society and the social and cultural problems that they faced. For example, *Nellie Bly: Journalist*, by Elizabeth Ehrlick (Chelsea House, 1989) shows how Bly, using investigative reporting, exposed the blight of the mentally ill and brutal factory working conditions in late nineteenth-century America. *Ida M. Tarbell: Pioneer Women Journalist and Biographer*, by Adrian A. Paradis (Scholastic Library Publishing/Children Press, 1985) records how Tarbell worked to expose the dishonest and heavy-handed business practices of the Standard Oil Company, leading directly to its restructuring by the federal government.

BIOGRAPHY IN FILM

We live in a media-driven age. Films and television dominate our cultural and social life. Biography is very much a part of film culture, and for that reason most agree that we must pay close attention to how biography is presented through these media, and how presentations can affect children and youth.

Biography has been a part of film culture since the beginning of the film industry in the twentieth century. Between 1927 and 1960, some 300 biographical films were produced. The 1970s witnessed a watershed of biographical and autobiographical films. Similar to books, filmed biography addresses issues and needs associated with history, memory, nationalism, and personal identity. Like books, film biography offers a means of expression for groups marginalized by reason of race, gender, ethnicity, sexuality, and class. Biography is also a means whereby nations and regions can assert their claims to special identities. Some critics hold that in some ways film biography can well challenge print and other media in creating powerful biographical images and statements.[37]

Problems of biographical interpretation must be considered here. It is wise to consider how such social and cultural issues as gender, class, and stature are portrayed. How honest will the film adaptation be to real life? What liberties will the producers, writers, and cinematographers take? Will the interpretation overplay or avoid issues of controversy? Will film interpretations of women be subjected to patriarchal and rigid social expectations? For example, how might the life of the ill-fated movie star Veronica Lake be treated based on her autobiography and other books about her? A review of her life shows how exposed and open her life might be to various interpretations:

> One of Hollywood's sultriest sirens of the 1940s, Veronica Lake steamed up movie screens with her fragile beauty and exotic hairstyle. A heartthrob of millions during her heyday, she was the hottest ticket around starring in 27 motion pictures. Off screen Lake's life was a disaster—a controlling mother, three failed marriages, extramarital affairs, a secret abortion and downward spiral due to alcoholism and mental illness—ending up broke, destitute and forgotten.[38]

The importance of biography in television cannot be overlooked. As mentioned in chapter 1, television in the 1950s, often called the golden age of television, produced a number of noteworthy biographical and historical programs. These include Walter Cronkite's *You Are There* (1953–1957), *Eyewitness to History* (1961–1962), *Twentieth Century* (1957–1967), and Edward R. Murrow's *See It Now* (1951–1958). Biographical and historical documentaries of the early 1960s challenged American sensitivity with accounts of farm labor exploitations and the emerging homosexual subculture. Edward R. Murrow's contributions through his program *Person to Person* (1953–1959) succeeded in solidifying the rich and famous in popular culture.

Aside from these programs, television then and now often blurs the distinction between reality and fiction. Examples of this are found in the popular celebrity-based programs based on the fictionalized lives of Desi and Lucy Arnaz, George Burns and Gracie Allen, and Ozzie and Harriet Nelson.

Today's configuration of biographical outlets found on television include talk shows, news magazine programs, game shows revolving around personal lives (e.g., dating, newlyweds), and interview programs. Content can range from the serious to the lighthearted, including topics such as exercise, health information, domestic issues, and romance.

Some critics maintain that the popularity of biographical programs featuring both the famous and the ordinary is based on our human need for intimacy and community that is becoming increasingly hard to find and maintain in the modern, urban world. Biographical programming for television offers a powerful sense of social dialogue and a means of helping individuals evaluate and structure they own lives.

Although entertainment-driven, talk show hosts of the late 1950s and 1960s (Jack Parr, David Susskind, Johnny Carson, and others) met some of these needs by reinforcing the close relationship between audience and subject or guest. As noted, these shows were generally entertainment and celebrity-focused, where the audience was expected to be very passive and noninteractive. Phil Donahue introduced audience participation in his innovative show *The Phil Donahue Show*, where he encouraged the audience to interact with his guests. He was also successful in introducing controversial topics that had not been widely covered previously.

Today this type of programming continues and is reinforced by biographical coverage found on various cable networks. These include CNN Profiles, Specials, and some of their other programs (www.cnn.com), productions of E! Entertainment, (www.eentertainment.com), Court TV (www.courttv.com), the Biography Channel (www.biographychannel.com), and PBS, with such notable productions as those by Ken Burns and others (www.pbs.org). Some, if not all, of these programs and channels have websites where additional biographical materials and instructional materials are available.

The major commercial and/or national broadcasting news programs likewise have websites that offer biographical coverage including Fox News (www. foxnews.com), NBC News (www.nbc.com/nbc/NBC_News), ABC News (www. abc.net.au/news), CBS News (www.cbsnews.com), BBC (www.bbc.co.uk), the Canadian Broadcasting Corporation (CBC) (www.cbc.ca), and the Australian Broadcasting Company (ABC) (www.abc.net.au).

The Internet also has a profusion of biographical information, including sites hosted by little-known individuals, sites maintained by various types of persons who can be considered public personalities, and sites devoted to honoring and celebrating public figures such as film personalities. Biographical information is also maintained through official website outlets such as the White House (www.whitehouse.gov) and royal families such as those in Great Britain (www.royal.gov.uk), Denmark (http://kongehuset.dk), and the Netherlands (www.koninklijkhuis.nl/UK/welcome.html). Various official governors' and ministers' offices in the United States and elsewhere also maintain official websites.

FILMED BIOGRAPHY IN THE CLASSROOM AND LIBRARY

Film as an effective means of mass instruction was recognized by the United States government in World War I. The country's armed forces were faced with the enormous task of educating and training large groups of people in such diverse areas as weaponry, health, and the prevention of sexually transmitted diseases.[39]

Educational films for classroom use were introduced prior to World War II. As early as the 1920s the first standards for school libraries recognized the value of film materials for instruction.[40]

Film can be used in a variety of ways: to enhance cultural and historical awareness, to increase cognitive skills and information, and to foster and improve critical thinking. Filmed biography meets many of these needs both within the context of classroom instruction and the context of library programs and services. Film products have a role to play in improving visual literacy; fostering improved logical thinking; and increasing knowledge about history, society, and current affairs.

LOGICAL AND CRITICAL THINKING APPLIED TO BIOGRAPHY

Logical thinking can be divided into two parts: formal logic (based in philosophy) and informal logic or critical thinking. Critical thinking uses "reason in the pursuit of truth" and the "ways truth can be preserved as we make inferences—[i.e.], one or more statements to support or justify another statement."[41]

In developing logical skills, it is necessary to understand the vocabulary of logic and arguments—a basic term in this vocabulary is *true value*. True value is a statement that can be either true or false, but the value is often unknown. Statements of truth are one issue, but how these statements are presented is another issue. Viewpoints may or may not comprise statements of truth, and viewpoints are determined by the context in which the statements are presented.

In biography the reader has the right and even obligation to ask whether the interpretation given by the writer is based on established facts and how those facts are presented in terms of the context of the subject's life.[42]

Peddlers or providers of statements and consumers of statements present another concept in logical and critical thinking. A peddler may be an individual or writer of biography that has a particular point of view that he or she wants the reader to accept, and the consumer of the statement is a reader who needs convincing.[43] The rash of biographies coming from publishers during the late twentieth and early twenty-first centuries are good examples of peddlers with points of view concerning famous personalities. These authors include well-known biographer Kitty Kelley and others who have written books about Bill and Hillary Clinton, the Bush family, and various members of the British royal family.

Peddlers of biography take on many roles indicating that they have the authority to write biography. They may present themselves as investigative journalists; social, cultural, and political commentators; legal authorities; and academic scholars and researchers. They may justify their work based on the traditions of rigorous academic research; they may claim they have access to documents and persons of influence and knowledge that others do not have; and they may justify their work based on their past experiences and positions in places of power and influence.

Depending on their overall goals and objectives, biographers may use various means of writing to persuade or "peddle" their wares. They may write with academic authority and brilliance; they may tell an interesting story with narrative clarity; they may even write in accusative and even inflammatory ways, or they might present their biography as chatty gossip.

In reading the biography, the reader or "consumer" must ask several questions. For example: Is the biography, as a whole, true or false based on what the reader already accepts as true or false, or is it probably true or false based on what the reader takes as probably true or false? The reader can decide on the truth of the biography based on personal experience or knowledge, the internal consistency of the biographical argument, and consistency with regard to established facts.[44]

Reader-response theory may help us understand this concept better. Louise Rosenblatt's ideas concerning reader responses were discussed in chapter 1, and these concepts relate well to an overall consideration of the role that biography might play in the logical thinking of youth as they explore biographical concepts.[45] Recall the two basic theories Rosenblatt suggests: the first asserts that readers are in dialogue with the text, relying on it to inform and direct them as they process information and narration (the phenomenological view); the second asserts that readers' prior and existing political and social backgrounds establish conditions as to how the text will be read and processed (the political or ideological view).[46]

In using biography to encourage critical thinking, students should be encouraged to see the biography as an argument to be either accepted or rejected. In critical thinking terms, the biography is an argument about a person's life, and within that argument is the collection of statements on which the argument is based. The foundation of the argument is its supporting statements. Both the argument and its supporting statements must be justified on known evidence.

When applying critical thinking skills, a reader of biography must reconstruct the argument in which he or she extracts the essential statements from the context of the presentation. For example, a biographer who is overly sympathetic for his or her subject may present an exciting narrative and well-written story but may gloss over some of the, unsavory yet essential facts of a person's life. To be a critical reader of biography, the reader must also assess (look at the raw data or facts) and evaluate statements for their basic truths based on known truths and facts.

Evaluation is looking for the truth or falseness of biographical argument; but evaluation also must consider how clearly the argument is presented and whether the argument and its supporting statements are too vague and in need of further defense or refinement. Identification of fallacies in biographical argument implies that some of the statements may be presented in such ways that the reader or consumer of the biography may likely accept the overall argument without adequate justification based on known facts.

Biographies of Thomas Jefferson describing his alleged intimate relationships with his slave Sally Hemings are examples of how this type of argument might be presented and either rejected or accepted by readers. *Jefferson and His Children: The Story of One American Family*, by Shannon Lanier, edited by Kate Klimo (Random House Children's Books, 2000), illustrates this well. This is an account by Lanier, one of the Jefferson African American descendants who accepts his descent from Thomas Jefferson based on DNA and circumstantial evidence, and travels the United States meeting his relatives from both sides of the Jefferson lineage, some of whom reject his claim, while others accept it as fact.

BIOGRAPHY IN THE SCHOOL LIBRARY MEDIA CENTER

As we know, biography is used across the curriculum. Chapter 2 provides both a lengthy discussion concerning its use in the curriculum and examples of how biography can be applied to classroom teaching and instruction. The school library media specialist will also find biography useful in teaching a variety of information literacy skills. "Biography Writer's Workshop" with Patricia and Fredrick McKissack is available through Scholastic Books, and it offers excellent guidance for students (http://teacher.scholastic.com/writewit/biograph/; http://teacher.scholastic.com/lessonplans/).

The McKissacks take the students through the major steps involved in writing biography and introduce them to the concept of writing drafts. They also give information as how to select a subject. They advise students to select someone in whom they are interested, followed by conducting basic but simple research, then moving on to bibliographic research work, especially through recent books, newspapers, magazines, and Internet sources. They suggest that materials written by the individuals about their own lives are valuable sources as are audiotapes and videotapes produced by others. Other sources they recommend are interviews and correspondence with museums, libraries, historical societies, and colleges and universities for help in finding sources on the individual.

The McKissacks advise, too, that research on the historical time period of the subject is necessary. In the writing, they strongly suggest that notes be taken carefully and kept in order, that at least three reference sources be checked if there is disagreement with certain facts, and that all disagreements be noted and cited in the writing.

To add color to the life of the subject, they suggest that general reference materials such as atlases, dictionaries, almanacs, historical timelines, and other sources be consulted and relevant information be incorporated into the narrative as appropriate. Finally they caution the young writer to be objective about the subject's life and offer a balanced view of the person, noting strengths and weaknesses, successes as well as failures. Be honest, they say.

Other helpful resources that provide avenues into biography instruction and use include resources such as the *School Library Activities Media Monthly* (www.schoollibrarymedia.com); Scholastic Books teacher guides such as the McKissacks' guide; books published by Libraries Unlimited and their Teacher Ideas Press (www.teacherideaspress.com), Highsmith Press publications (www.highsmith.com), and Linworth Publishing (www.linworth.com), as well as others.

Examples of lesson plans that rely on biography and that can be well supported through the school library media center and taught by the school library media specialists include the following located at the Educator Reference Desk^{SM} website (www.eduref.org/index.shtml):

- "The Fiction of Franz Kafka" (David W. Nicholson, 1999), www.eduref.org/cgi-bin/printlessons.cgi/Virtual/Lessons/Language_ Arts/Literature/LIT0028.html
- "Genealogy Research" (Nelda Helt, 1994), www.eduref.org/cgi-bin/ printlessons.cgi/Virtual/Lessons/Social_Studies/History/HIS0005.html
- "Women in American History" (Kristine A. McIntosh, 2000), www.eduref. org/cgi-bin/printlessons.cgi/Virtual/Lessons/Social_Studies/US_ History/USH0046.html
- "Interviewing of Historical Figures" (Judy Ross, 1994), www.eduref.org/ Virtual/Lessons/Social_Studies/History/HIS0009.html

Although these plans were all developed by classroom teachers and teachers-in-training, they incorporate standard library resources, and their designs suggest that they could be taught by the school library media center specialists with appropriate modifications and/or taught in collaboration.

CONCLUSION

Biography performs many roles in society. It is a central player in forming a sense of national character and identity. Biography exerts a social control role in that it communicates and defines in exact ways national values, expectations, and rationalizations for citizenship and citizen behavior. Through biography, cultural values are reinforced. Political biography has always played a significant role in society. It helps define and reinforce government principles whether they are democratic or totalitarian, and it can, if used in positive ways, promote social dialogue between competing and even conflicting ideologies at work in society. In recent years biography has been used to help redefine the positive roles and places in society of various groups that have been previously marginalized.

The abundance of biographical communication in society and the importance of celebrities in modern popular culture and youth society have increased the power of biography to influence attitudes and behaviors of both children and young adults. Biography now must be considered one of the major means of influencing behaviors and values of the young. As the twenty-first century unfolds biography must be seen and used as both a powerful positive cultural and social force and as an effective means for the education of our youth.

NOTES

1. *Oxford Dictionary of National Biography*, http://www.oup.com/oxforddnb/info (accessed Sept. 1, 2004).

2. *Dictionary of American Biography*, http://www.gale.com/servlet/BrowseSeries Servlet?region=9&imprint=144&titleCode=S25&edition=1 (accessed Sept. 1, 2004).

3. Ilana Pardes, *The Biography of Ancient Israel: National Narratives in the Bible* (Berkeley: University of California Press, 2002).

4. Pardes.

5. Anne Scott MacLeod, *A Moral Tale: Children's Fiction and American Culture, 1820–1860* (Hamden, Conn.: Archon Books, 1975), 93–117.

6. MacLeod, 104.

7. MacLeod, 106.

8. MacLeod, 106.

9. Barbara Chatton, "Biography," in *The Continuum Encyclopedia of Children's Literature*, ed. Bernice E. Cullinan and Diane G. Person (New York: Continuum, 2001), 84–86.

10. Parson Weems Publishing Service, "Who Are We," http://www.parsonweems.com/ whoweare.asp (accessed Sept. 9, 2004).

11. Jean Webb, "Walking into the Sky: Englishness, Heroism, and Cultural Identity: A Nineteenth- and Twentieth-Century Perspective," in *Children's Literature and the Fin de Siècle*, ed. Roderick McGillis (Westport, Conn.: Praeger, 2003), 51–57.

12. Webb, 51.

13. "History and Biography," in *Oxford Companion to Children's Literature*, ed. Humphrey Carpenter and Mari Prichard (Oxford: Oxford University Press, 1984), 252–53.

14. Matthew Schneirov, *The Dream of a New Social Order: Popular Magazines in America, 1893–1914* (New York: Columbia University Press, 1994), 2–4.

15. Schneirov, 191.

16. Schneirov, 155–56.

17. Schneirov, 192–93.

18. Sybil Oldfield, "Women's Biographies," in *Encyclopedia of Life Writing: Autobiographical and Biographical Forms*, vol. 2, ed. Margaretta Jolly (London: Fitzroy Dearborn, 2001), 948–50.

19. Lou Cannon, *Reagan* (New York: Putnam, 1982), 19, citing Jerry Griswold, "Young Reagan's Reading," *New York Times Book Review*, Aug. 30, 1981, from a letter from Reagan to O. Dallas Baillio, Director of the Mobile Public Library, 1977.

20. Pat Pflieger, "Nineteenth-Century American Children & What They Read: Some of Their Magazines," http://www.merrycoz.org/MAGS.HTM (accessed Oct. 18, 2004).

21. Lorinda Beth Cohoon, "Serializing Boyhoods: Periodicals, Books, and American Boys, 1840–1911" (dissertation, University of Southern Mississippi, 2001), abstracted in *Dissertation Abstracts International* 62-A (Jan. 2002): 2420.

22. "Buffalo Bill," in *The Oxford Companion to Children's Literature*, ed. Humphrey Carpenter and Mari Prichard (New York: Oxford University Press, 1998), 87.

23. Fred Raymond Erisman, "There Was a Child Went Forth: A Study of *St. Nicholas Magazine* and Selected Authors, 1890–1915" (dissertation, University of Minnesota, 1966), abstracted in *Dissertation Abstracts International* 27-A (Dec. 1966): 1818.

24. Schneirov.

25. Mary F. Brewer, "Politics and Life Writing," in *Encyclopedia of Life Writing: Autobiographical and Biographical Forms*, vol. 2, ed. M. Jolly, 721–22.

26. Barrey Gewen, "Forget the Founding Fathers," *New York Times Book Review*, June 5, 2005, 30–31.

27. Gewen, 32.

28. Gewen, 32–33.

29. Gewen, 33.

30. Gewen.

31. Gewen.

32. Gewen.

33. Donna E. Norton and others, *Through the Eyes of a Child: An Introduction to Children's Literature*, 6th ed. (Upper Saddle River, N.J.: Merrill Prentice-Hall, 2003), 530–47.

34. Carl Rollyson, "Biography and Fiction," in *Encyclopedia of Life Writing: Autobiographical and Biographical Forms*, vol. 1, ed. M. Jolly, 22–13.

35. Steve Weinberg, *Telling the Untold Story: How Investigative Reporters Are Changing the Craft of Biography* (Columbia: University of Missouri Press, 1992), 1–2.

36. Weinberg, 19–35.

37. Wendy Everett, "Film," in *Encyclopedia of Life Writing: Autobiographical and Biographical Forms*, vol. 1, ed. M. Jolly, 323–24.

38. "Worth It, But Flawed," review by a reader of *Peekaboo*, by Jeff Lenburg, http://www.amazon.com (accessed Oct. 12, 2004).

39. Paul Saettler, *The Evolution of American Educational Technology* (Englewood, Colo.: Libraries Unlimited, 1990), 184–94. See also his *The Evolution of American Educational Technology*, 3rd ed. (Mahwah, N.J.: L. Erlbaum Associates, 2005).

40. National Education Association of the United States, Department of Elementary and Secondary Schools, Committee on Library Organization and Equipment, *Standards Library Organization and Equipment for Secondary Schools of Different Sizes*, C. C. Certain, chairman (Chicago: American Library Association, 1925).

41. "Critical Thinking across the Curriculum Project—Critical Thinking Core Concepts," Longview Community College, Lee's Summit, Missouri, http://www.kcmetro.cc.mo.us/longview/ctac/corenotes.htm (accessed Oct. 8, 2004).

42. "Critical Thinking across the Curriculum Project."

43. "Critical Thinking across the Curriculum Project."

44. "Critical Thinking across the Curriculum Project."

45. Louise M. Rosenblatt, *Literature as Exploration*, 5th ed. (New York: Modern Language Association of America, 1995).

46. Rosenblatt.

8

BIOGRAPHY IN ART

INTRODUCTION

Biography as presented in art tells us much about culture and society. Portraits give life to historical persons and groups. We can learn about persons and groups and the societies and culture that produced and influenced them through styles and symbols used by artists. Portraits present social realities and, as such, they act as an interface between art and social life. Because of this they easily reflect the norms of conformity, acceptable social presentations, and the prejudices that exist in society and culture. These attributes reflect how class, race, age, gender, physical beauty, occupation, and social and civic standings are presented within their historical settings and therefore provide insight to us as we seek to better understand the contexts of their times.[1]

Understanding art and how it interacts with society aids us in expanding the power of biography to inform and instruct youth. Art history and the sociology of art are important aids in this endeavor. Art history helps us see how various eras of culture have influenced artistic values and interpretations. The sociology of art can help us better determine the function of art in society and to locate patterns of artistic expression that can inform about and correlate with social structure.[2] For this discussion I will consider the sociology of art in terms of how it helps us better understand the dynamics of social life and customs, and how these dynamics influence the production of biographical art and the symbols used to convey biographical information. When applied to biographical art, the sociology of art requires astute observations and critical analyses.

Following this directive, this chapter will define visual literacy and will attempt to show how visual literacy skills can ensure a more critical use of art as biography, history, and social observation. This chapter will consider how art depicts individuals, classes of people, gender roles, and other important social interactions. It also will consider how art has been institutionalized and nationalized according to values given to it by society, culture, and time. The chapter concludes with suggestions of how art can be used in libraries and classrooms to enhance youths' understanding of the human experience.

VISUAL LITERACY AND BIOGRAPHICAL ART

Visual literacy is used in many disciplines ranging from art to history, including school library media and information work. In general, visual literacy means to have the ability to understand visual messages and to express oneself with at least one visual discipline. For the purpose of biographical information used in the context of this discussion, visual literacy means to:

- Understand the subject matter and meaning within the context of the culture that produced the work
- Analyze the syntax—compositional and stylistic principles of the work
- Evaluate the disciplinary and aesthetic merits of the work
- Intuitively grasp the gist, the interactive and synergistic quality of the work[3]

Although visual literacy includes many applications, this discussion will focus primarily on visual analogies and imagery, visual organizers, and visual mapping.

In biographical art, visual analogies and imagery offer understanding of how the painter or photographer selected and used images as analogical statements suggestive of time, place, political power, class and social position, gender roles, respect for authority, religion and spirituality, and honor and shame. Although social and cultural symbols and references are abundantly available in art, using visual literacy principles, students will often need to be guided in how to see and learn from biographical information expressed as art.

HOW ART CONVEYS BIOGRAPHICAL AND HISTORICAL INFORMATION

A look at some of the great paintings from the past provides abundant information about many, if not all, of the issues of human life. Early Paleolithic stone and wall paintings provide information not so much about individuals, but about the social lives of these early people. We learn from their art how they respected the power and danger of powerful animals that they encountered in their daily lives, and how often they depicted humans as small and insignificant in comparison to the animals on which they depended for food and clothing.[4] Stone paintings of this period also show the importance of social organization, management, cooperation, and the hierarchical structure of the communal hunt necessary for the killing of animals for food and group survival.

Patricia Lauber's *Painters of the Caves* (National Geographical Society, 1998) provides information for young readers on the people and the social fabric of several societies that produced early European cave drawings. Another informative book of this type for children is Brad Burnham's *Cave of Lascaux: The Cave of Prehistoric Wall Paintings* (Rosen Publishing, PowerKid Press, 2003). Mario Ruspoli's *Cave of Lascaux* (Harry N. Abrams, 1997), written for a general adult audience, also describes the civilization that produced the Lascaux paintings. Jean Clotte and Paul G. Bahn provide a more advanced archaeological analysis, with colored photographs of the Chauvet Cave discovered in 1994, in their *Chauvet Cave: The Art of Earliest Time* (University of Utah Press, 2004).

Ancient Egyptian art likewise provides us with biographical and cultural information. The ancient Egyptians lived in a society that was "death-driven," not because they did not enjoy life as they lived it, but because they enjoyed it so much that they wanted it to continue after death. They institutionalized death in their society to the point that it became one of the driving forces of their culture. Egyptians were ruled by god-kings who were assured of an enjoyable and abundant life after death. It is from this death-driven culture that we learn much about the lives of these god-kings. Egyptian religion of the time required that at least the images of powerful rulers be preserved after death so the soul could join it again after death and continue to receive the blessings of the good life. As time passed, this privilege was given to those of lesser stature in society. From the art left by the Egyptians as they celebrated life and anticipated death, we know much about the biography of their rulers and even about persons of lower stature. Because of the need for the body to be reunited with the soul, figures of persons must be recognizable, thus giving us a good idea about how the ancient Egyptians actually looked.

From this art, we also gain a perspective on everyday life in ancient Egypt. Symbols used in their art tell us about gender. For example, women were painted in lighter colors than men, and assumed subservient roles, although women were often recognized for their wisdom and leadership. Art was likewise used to show social ranking, with larger figures indicating higher stature. Rituals such as mourning and marriage customs were important to the Egyptians and are well described in their art. Similarly, symbols used to indicate royal and religious authority were extremely important, and we see this reflected in the art of their rulers and their entourages.

The importance given to family and social life is also reflected. For example, we have images that suggest the affection in family life and family relationships. This art also shows us the importance that the ancient Egyptians placed on their environment with many of their art symbols reflecting their association with nature, especially animals.[5, 6]

Susie Hodge's *Ancient Egyptian Art* (Heinemann Library, 1998) provides an interesting analysis for children ages 9–12 in her depictions of culture, religion, and science. Other books that provide information about life in ancient Egypt include *In the Daily Life of the Ancient Egyptians*, by Henrietta McCall (School Specialty Children's Publishing, 2001), *Life in an Egyptian Workers Village*, by Jane Shuter (Heinemann Library, 2004), and *Daily Life of the Egyptian Gods*, by Dimitre Meeks and his colleagues (Cornell University Press, 1996). The famous queen Cleopatra receives special attention in Andrew Langley's *Cleopatra and the Egyptians* (Scholastic Library Publishing/Franklin Watts, 1986) and in *Cleopatra: The Life of an Egyptian Queen*, by Gary Jeffrey and Anita Ganeri (Rosen Publishing Group, 2005). Another famous queen, Nefertiti, is presented in *Queen Nefertiti*, written by the Bellereophon staff (Bellereophon Books, 1992).

Biographical coverage of ancient rulers is found in almost all of the major encyclopedias and some specialized biographical reference sources such as the *Abridged Encyclopedia of World Biography* (Gale Group/Gale Research International, Ltd., 1999). Even more comprehensive coverage is found in its parent set, *Encyclopedia of World Biography*, 2nd ed. (1997).

Most of the ancient cultures of the world integrated biography into art through religion, government, and other important aspects of life. Sculpture was used in the ancient Near East (i.e., Sumaria, Babylonia) in such places as Isin, Larsa, Eshnunna, Asur, and Mari. Often these sculptured portraits were idealized representations of rulers showing fine bodies draped in dress and surrounded by symbols of their stature and authority.

For example, Hammurabi (1792–1750 BCE), the sixth king of the First Dynasty of Babylon, who introduced one of the first law codes (known as the Code of Hammurabi), is well represented in this art. In a relief held in the Louvre in Paris we see him as a seated king. Another granite head found at Susa and also held at the Louvre represents this king or one of his predecessors, wearing the royal hat, showing an idealized face depicting his role as king and royal legislator. Another figure held in the Louvre, a small bronze, shows a figure, most likely Hammurabi, kneeling on one knee in prayer, wearing the royal hat symbolizing kingship and authority.[7]

Elaine Landau's *The Babylonians* (Milbrook Press, 1997) records the history of this ancient people and describes their contributions to civilization, including Hammurabi's code of law. Using a broader approach, Elena Gambino writes about the Mesopotamians by integrating their history, culture, and mythology into her accounts (*Ancient Mesopotamians* [School Specialist Children's Books/Pert Bedrick Books, 2000]).

The ancient Chinese likewise used idealized portraits for social information. Their portraits depicted individuals who exemplified moral and political values considered worthy of inspiration and emulation. For example, funerary banners and wall paintings in tombs often depicted officials dressed in ways that symbolized governmental ranking, social organization, and personal status. Chinese portraits also developed to the point of emphasizing inner qualities such as temperament, manner, style, and behaviors of the subjects.

Historical portraits were important in Chinese art. Chinese portraits depicting historical events were complex in terms of presenting narrations of events, situations, and relationships. They often served as vignettes, showing actions of important persons, and could have been used as much for entertainment as for celebrating the life of an individual. Aside from funeral banners, portraits of individual monks, nuns, teachers, and other devoted followers were often hung in temples as memorials. From a biographical perspective and for identification, Buddhist painters paid attention to details of furniture, costume, color, light, and shadow to highlight distinctive appearances and temperaments of their Buddhist subjects.[8]

For the most part, early Japanese portrait art was religious and didactic in approach. Early portraits (produced before the twelfth century CE) were generally created well after the subjects' deaths. Generally these were of emperors and aristocrats. Portraits of Buddhist monks and nuns, warriors, and devoted laymen and women were also hung in residential chapels, Buddhist temples, and Shinto shrines. Here they played a role in memorial ceremonies and in remembering the dead. Portraits of Confucius and his followers and other Chinese sages also hung in the Japanese Imperial Palace.[9]

Another Japanese art movement of the twelfth century was the representation of living aristocrats involved in court activities. These paintings often showed faces clearly drawn and recognizable. As time passed, formal memorial portraits of persons not closely associated with religion became increasingly common as ruling families commissioned portraits for their family temples. Such demands encouraged the development of more realism in portrait art and influenced the growth of fine portrait art of the fourteenth and later centuries.[10]

Jan Stuart's *Worshiping the Ancestors: Chinese Commemorative Portraits* (Stanford University Press, 2001), written for a general adult audience but suitable for young adults, provides information on the Ming and Qing portraits and explores the artistic, historical, and religious significance of these paintings. Stuart also places these in context with other types of commemorative portraiture. Kamini Khanduri's *Japanese Art and Culture* (Raintree, 2003) provides a general overview of Japanese art for children with illustrations, including temple art and portrait prints to promote Kabuki actors and opera singers and, beginning in the seventeenth century, the widespread use of woodblocks.

Ancient African art had similar qualities as those of other ancient cultures. African portraits pictured important individuals, and the art was closely related to ancestor cults, political organizations, and ritual activity. Memorial portraits of specific ancestors were common. Ancestors had a vital role to play in that they protected the living from harm, ensured their comfort, and helped them with everyday problems. African memorial portraits honored heads of households, heads of state, women of strength and courage, priests, and ritual actors. Their portrait images were presented as social icons rather than specific personalities, and they were used to illustrate important social and cultural values and behaviors, reflective of what a good person within the culture should emulate.

Because of the stylized approaches and symbolism used in African portrait art and its cultural differences from Western styles and symbols, it is difficult to identify many of the individuals in these portraits. Identity symbols varied throughout the various African societies and included attributes signifying high rank, clan totems, lineage headdresses, positions in the family order, gender identifications, scarification marks, and clothing. Generally these portraits were idealized and emblematic in showing respect.[11] *African Art and Culture*, by Jane Bingham (Steck-Vaughn/Raintree, 2003), and *African Art*, by William Rae (Facts on File, 1996), address in general terms some of the characteristics of African art, including portraits.

Middle Eastern art after the introduction of Islam was heavily influenced by theological considerations and prohibitions that often limited the portrayal of living persons. Nevertheless an Islamic portrait art did arise. Because the prophet Muhammad was not considered divine by his followers, as was Christ by Christians, there are few Islamic traditions focusing on his birth. *The Birth of the Prophet Muhammad,* from Rashib al-Din's *Universal History*, as copied at Tabiz in 1315 (now in University Library, Ebinburgh), seems to borrow much from Christian art in depicting Muhammad's birth. In this portrait we see that Muhammad's mother replaces Mary, the prophet's uncle takes the place of Joseph, and three women at the left stand for the Magi. As with Christ, angels from heaven also attend the birth.[12]

The prophet's cloak also appears in many accounts and has important theological interpretations. For example, Shiites base their claim that descendants of the prophet's family have the right to lead the Muslim community through their historical loyalty to the prophet's grandson Hasan and because of the prophet's words as he placed his family under his cloak saying, "People of the House, God only desires to put away from you abominations and to cleanse you" (Koran 33:32). The cloak has also been associated with the miracle cure of the poet al-Busiri. The cloak is pictured in *Muhammad Placing the Black Stone in His Cloak,* from Rashid al-Din's *Universal History.* A 1315 copy of this is now located in the University Library, Edinburgh.[13] Muhammad's rise into heaven is presented in *Ascension of the Prophet Muhammad,* copied from Nazmi's *Khamsa* (1540), now in the British Library, London. In this painting Muhammad is dressed in green and veiled in white. He is encased in a blazing halo against a blue sky filled with stars. He is led into the presence of God by the Angel Gabriel on Buraq, the human-headed steed.[14]

Islamic art produced portraits of important secular figures as well, including political and literary personalities. These include *Jahangir Presenting a Book to a Sufi* (India, 1615–1620), now in the Freer Gallery of Art,

Washington, D.C.; *Portrait of Fath Ali Shah* (Iran, 1813), in the Negarostam Museum, Tehran; and *Sultan-Muhammad, The Court of Gayumars*, in the private collection of Prince Sadrydduib Aga Khan, Geneva.

Important Greek personalities and scholars are also found in this art, but dressed in the Muslim style. The Greek physician Dioskorides is pictured in *Dioskorides and a Student*, from a manuscript of the Arabic translation of Dioskorides's *De Materia Medica*, copied in 1229 and now located in the Topkapi Palace Library, Istanbul. Dioskorides is seated on a low stool with his pupil kneeling on a pillow before him. Both men wear turbans and robes with decorated arm bands. In some art of this period, these arm bands provided information about the textiles found in the portraits, and the artist who created the art and his patron.[15]

Of all the artistic cultures that have arisen throughout history, Greek and Roman art has influenced Western art the most. We see this influence in almost all the major capitals of the Western world. The Greeks and Romans, like those before them, used portrait art to influence and control society. Both the Greeks and Romans employed statues of athletes to commemorate victories, votive statues in worship of the gods, funerary sculpture devoted to the memory of loved ones, and public statues to honor those in power and influence to establish governing authority. In ancient Greece, aside from grave memorials of individuals, portraits were largely commemorative or honorary and were given to celebrate powerful persons such as statesmen, poets, orators, rulers, and philosophers. Often Greek sculpture allowed identification of the subject primarily through inscriptions and depiction of specific characterizations, but by the fifth century BCE, physical appearances began to take on importance.[16]

The Romans produced a great variety of portraits of men, women, and children both in groups and individually. Portraits followed a given typology emphasizing the heads, thereby allowing for other social attributes to be added that reflected one's position in Roman society. Subjects included priests, commanders, statesmen, consuls, intellectuals, successful plebeians, soldiers, and husbands and wives—all encoded with socially recognizable symbols of stature and position in society.[17]

For the more mature reader, Mark D. Fullerton's *Greek Art* (Cambridge University Press, 2000) provides an overview of the political, social, and religious functions of Greek art. He gives particular attention to Greek artistic styles that provided cultural meanings as well as constructed personal and communal identities. For younger readers, *Ancient Roman Art*, by Susie Hodge (Heinemann Library, 2003), provides information on painting, mosaic, pottery, architecture, and Roman portraiture sculpture.

Later imperial art, after the Christian conversion of Rome, shows Roman leaders less as individuals and more as men of strength who considered themselves to be God's representatives or deputies on Earth. Men of lesser stature emulated the emperors in that they too are shown in portraits dressed in fine clothes of power and authority. The imagery of the emperor as teacher was also used as an important social message.

Early Christian art adopted Roman imperial art characteristics as well. This art depicted Christ and his immediate followers and saints of the Church as both teachers and leaders. As did the Greeks and Romans, early Christian portrait art used many of the same types of symbols to show authority and leadership such as clothing, positions, and surroundings. Christian art was more didactic in that it sought to convert and to move people away from sin. Figures were presented in dramatic actions and struggles, nature and still-life celebrated God's gifts to humanity, and biblical stories were selected to emphasize humankind's fall from grace in the Garden of Eden and the Church's plan for salvation in terms of what was important to the evolving Christian faith. As the Roman Empire fell, these characteristics became the dominant theme in medieval art.[18]

Byzantine art of the early Christian era presents the authority and power of the new Church and the people who ruled it in "restrained elegance, emotional austerity, and frozen authoritative solemnity." *Justinian and His Attendance*, from the church of San Vitale, Ravenna (526–547), shows these characteristics. This work presents the Emperor Justinian as lordly, slender, imperious, remote, and exalted. Surrounded by his bishops, clergy, and members of his army, Justinian presents an image that forcefully combines the might of the Church and the state.[19] This relationship of church and state power and the conflicts that often arose from this combination came to play a powerful, if not dominant role in European church-and-state relationships, history, and biography for hundred of years.

Religious icons of early medieval periods give us insight both into biographical concepts that were deemed important to those in authority, and they lend understanding to important religious notions. These icons, often of the Virgin Mary, Christ, and the saints, show power, purity, vision, and, in the case of Mary, maternity. Christ is generally depicted as authoritative and ruler of the universe.[20]

Later in medieval times, alongside medieval religious portraits and icons, we find painted portraits of medieval rulers such as the French king Francis I, painted by Limousin. The medals and coins of the period showing profiles of rulers also offer biographical information in that they present simplified likenesses of rulers.

Profile portraits of high-ranking individuals became more common with the passing of medieval time. In style, individuals of high rank were often presented in devotional composition.[21] Secular individuals also appear in religious settings such as in cathedrals for which they had some significant relationships, such as being major contributors or founders.

From a biographical perspective we see that more realism and personal identity were becoming increasingly prevalent and that realistic gestures, expressions, and human conditions were coming into play.[22] With the progression of time, from a social perspective, we can observe in these paintings both persons of the Church as well as kings, princes, and wealthy patrons dressed richly and offering elaborate gifts to the Church, perhaps suggesting that in their minds richness and wealth in and of itself might offer or even ensure a means to heaven.[23]

Wendy Beckett's *The Duke and the Peasant: Life in the Middle Ages* (Prestel Publishing, 1997) presents a comfortable interpretation of medieval life through art by the Limbourg brothers. In this work, based on the Duc de Berry's *Book of Hours*, we view peasants living and working in harmony and serving the duke and other richly dressed aristocrats who dwell in magnificent castles.

PORTRAIT ART AS BIOGRAPHICAL INTERPRETATIONS

Although the concept of portraits has existed in some form or another throughout history and in most cultures, the modern concepts with its reliance on personality, stature, and identity did not arise in strong measure until the seventeenth and eighteenth centuries and was certainly influenced by social, psychological, and literary developments. Since the Renaissance, ideas supporting individuality and the uniqueness of the individual rather than group identity had enjoyed widespread social and cultural acceptance in the West. In nineteenth-century Europe psychological concepts regarding personality were forcefully developed and stated by academics, and accepted by educated persons. As noted in chapter 1, beginning in the 1600s and 1700s biographical writing was starting to establish itself as a legitimate literary genre.

Influenced by the many social and cultural trends of their times, portrait artists grew more comfortable in using their artistic talents to reflect the personality, psychology, and sociology of their subjects. This new freedom allowed them to more completely emphasize the individuality, class, gender, occupations, and social statures of those they painted.[24]

Class and Social Positions in Art

How class is used in art is best understood through external signs such as physical appearances, positioning of subjects in portraits in relation to others, dress, deportment and conduct, and physical objects of stature and power. For example, artists painting portraits of eighteenth-century European aristocrats might picture them surrounded by settings and trappings suggesting classic Roman times and decor. The subjects might be placed near objects that reflect their refined and/or socially approved interests in science, philosophy, or religion. Body positions of these subjects might reflect gentle politeness or political power and dominance. Symbols of social status became common in such portraits, such as the picturing of hunting dogs for aristocratic gentlemen and jewels and fine gowns for aristocratic ladies.

Royalty were generally presented with symbols of their royal bearings such as crowns and other symbols of office and family—coats of arms, royal robes, thrones, scepters, medallions. (See Figure 8.1.) Such symbolism is

Figure 8.1
Queen Victoria in her younger
years, commanding and regal.
Statue located on the grounds of
the Legislative Building, Victoria,
British Columbia. Drawing by
Richard H. Hendler, based on his
photography.

well illustrated in Jean-Augusta-Dominique Ingres' painting *Napoleon I on His Imperial Throne* (1806).[25]

Anthony Van Dyck's *Queen Henrietta Maria with Sir Jeffrey Hudson* (1633) is another good example of how royalty was expected to be portrayed. Henerietta Maria was the Catholic wife of Charles I of England. Van Dyck painted her dressed to go hunting wearing a broad-brimmed black hat and a shimmering blue satin dress trimmed in gold. Although the composition of the painting suggested a relaxed, informal atmosphere for the time, symbols of the queen's rank and personality are placed throughout the painting. Her royal crown is at her right, and in the background we see an orange tree suggesting the queen's purity and perhaps her devotion to the Virgin Mary. Van Dyck used vertical columns and drapes to enhance the queen's royal stature and magnificence. The painting shows a beautiful, tall, slender young queen when, in reality, she was not an attractive women. Charles' nieces said of her: "so beautiful in her picture, [but in reality] a little women with long lean arms, crooked shoulders, and teeth protruding from her mouth like guns from a fort."[26] Official portraits often show a ruler as he or she wants to be seen by their publics.

Artwork commissioned for public celebrations and recognition of nobility also illustrates this concept of using symbols to enhance stature and respect.

Figure 8.2
Commemorative card honoring
Czar Nicholas I of Russia.
Published by permission of Scott
Tambert, Alexander Media.

Commemorative pieces come in many forms, such as medallions, cards, stamps, special minted coins, and porcelain and fine dinnerware. Figure 8.2 above is a commemorative card in honor of Czar Nicholas I of Russia.

In countries where official noble titles were not recognized, such as the United States, artists who painted persons of wealth and social standing used similar objects. Gilbert Stuart's 1796 (Lansdowne) portrait of George Washington shows the first American president surrounded by symbols of American democracy and nationhood.[27] The United States, as well as most other countries, has used postage stamps to honor persons of national significance. Collectively these stamps both celebrate the nation and support a national biographical tradition.

John Jay, the first chief justice of the Supreme Court of the United States, is presented in a 1789 painting (Figure 8.4) in a manner similar to how Washington and most famous figures of the day were painted. He is seated, wearing the robes of his high office, with his hand securely on what appears to be a scholarly law book.

American aristocratic women of the eighteenth century are painted with delicate feminine features, clothed in elegant dresses and holding their bodies rigidly, indicating high social status. European family origins and traditions for Americans might be indicated with symbols from England or other European settings. For example, Ralph Earl's painting of Mrs. Timothy Conklin (1791) shows in the background a village parish church, indicating refined English country origins. Men of political importance such as James

Figure 8.3
Collage of famous
Americans suggested by U.S.
postage stamps. Likenesses
include Francis Parkman,
Oliver Wendell Holmes,
Martha Washington, and Jack
London. Drawing by Richard
H. Hendler.

Figure 8.4
John Jay, first chief justice
of the United States
Supreme Court. Painted in
1789 wearing robes suggesting high status and official
office. The National Archives.
ARC identifier 532926.

K. Polk and Henry Clay were often given power in portraits by emphasizing
a strong physical presence. Their political importance was indicated through
the display of symbols such as the American flag and documents important to
their careers and political lives.[28]

As the middle class rose in power and wealth in both Europe and other countries, persons of lower classes soon became subjects of portraits. These included merchants, landowners, lawyers, and skilled craftsmen and craftswomen. Sometimes portraits of favored servants of both the aristocracy as well as prosperous middle-class households were painted. For portraits of persons of the professional and merchant classes, symbols of occupations such as account books, work tools, and clothing were used. More natural and realistic body positions and social settings, such as middle-class homes and workplaces, were likewise employed. From a historical perspective, it is worth noting that much of the contemporaneous criticisms leveled at these paintings were not so much at the art, but echoed the opinion that these portraits served no social use and were simply works created to satisfy the vanities of the growing middle class.

Gender in Art

The portraits of male and female subjects generally depict them in the context and social roles of their time. For example, in the 1920s in Germany, the fashion was for the artist to be a detached observer. Following this reasoning, women were pictured in the androgynous style of the 1920s.

For the most part, in the history of portrait painting, individual women have been pictured in terms of their beauty and allegorically in that they were often viewed as goddesses, muses, or historical religious figures. In terms of beauty, early portraits were designed to depict what was considered ideal beauty and not so much to represent the actual individual. These formulistic presentations of beauty were found not only in portraits, but in literary expression as well. Together literature and portrait art influenced how women were romanticized well into the nineteenth century. These characteristics are very much suggested in the paintings of American aristocratic women of the nineteenth century. Here we find beauty laced with rank and trappings of privilege and sexuality.

Males were also idealized and romanticized within the context of their times. Males were portrayed in their professional, social, political, and other leadership roles more so than women. They were shown within the context of these various settings, with dress appropriate to their status and with symbols of rank and achievement. These various symbols suggested masculinity and male values, and they reflect what was valued within time periods and social classes by the subjects and painters. For example, middle- and lower-class values and behavior expectations might indeed vary from those of the nobility and aristocracy, and such differences would be reflected in portrait art. On the whole, as mentioned previously, portraits of male leaders generally exhibited power symbols such as placement and body stance, displays of military symbols and political achievements, and other signs of authority.

On the other hand, courtly manners of the same period might require that men of noble and aristocratic rank be presented with grace, elegance, and emotions, while men of lower status might be pictured showing more realistic and robust behaviors.[29, 30]

PHOTOGRAPHY AND BIOGRAPHY

Photography is very much a part of portrait making. Photography as an invention is generally dated from the 1820s when it was developed as a means of mechanically reproducing images. Photography played an important role in the further development of portraits. Its primary advantage for portraits was its ability to reproduce exact likenesses. Photography both challenged and enhanced portrait painting in that it offered new business avenues for artists, and it increased the artistic venues open to them.

Photography was affordable, relatively inexpensive, and quick. It offered persons and families who previously could not afford to commission a painted portrait the opportunity to have their own likenesses reproduced. It also introduced new social customs, such as the calling card with one's likeness embedded (the *carte-de-visite*), the keeping of photographs as mementoes, and billboard advertising such as promoting the performances of actors and musicians. Along with this came the marketing of products using photography and identification of public figures with products. Photography also helped create the celebrity culture in the nineteenth century and fueled the demand for biographical information,[31] a legacy that continues today.

In terms of style and approach, early portrait photography used the same conventions that painted portraits employed. The photographer used painted backgrounds of courtly garden scenes and/or stately columns, prompts, sitting positions and stances, family and relationship groupings, and other appropriate status symbols.[32] Strategies for marketing photographic services soon developed whereby traveling photographers visited homes in both cities and the country photographing families and individuals, often with their valued belongings such as livestock. To accommodate less affluent customers, the well-prepared photographer sometimes maintained wardrobes of clothes to show clients at their best.

Both painted and photographic portraits offer a sense of biography in two ways. As has been noted, portraits offer an abundance of biographic and social information. A series of portraits over the course of a person's life reflects the stages of life that a person experiences. We see this in the collective portraits of the famous as well as the lesser known. Consider portraits such as those of Queens Elizabeth I and II, King Henry VIII, presidents of the United States, prime ministers of Great Britain, and other world and historic figures, and see how each set of portraits of these individuals offers differing and progressive reflections of their lives as they mature in life.[33]

Russell Freeman's contributions to our appreciation of biography through both painting and photography cannot be overlooked. His Newbery Medal–winning book, *Lincoln: A Photobiography* (Houghton Mifflin, 1989), is an outstanding example of how portrait art can be used to tell the life of a person. This unromanticized look at Lincoln reveals his boyhood, marriage, professional life before the presidency, views on the Civil War, and death and burial ceremonies. Other similar books by Freeman using art and/or photography include *Eleanor Roosevelt: A Life of Discovery* (Houghton Mifflin, 1997), *In the Days of the Vaqueros: America's First True Cowboys* (Houghton Mifflin, 2001), and *Children of the Wild West* (Houghton Mifflin, 1990).

Other books that help young people better understand the power of photography as biography and social history include *Restless Spirit: The Life and Work of Dorothea Lange*, by Elizabeth Partridge (Penguin Group/Viking Juvenile, 1999). Partridge relates how Lange's images of migrant workers, Japanese American internees, and rural poverty influenced the shaping of important social reforms in the United States. Another important name in photography is Edward S. Curtis. Laurie Lawlor's *Shadow Catcher: The Life and Work of Edward S. Curtis* (Walker & Co., 1994) tells how Curtis's photographic documentation of Native American culture, now over one hundred years old, continues to offer the world one of the most extensive and informative collections in the world. A similar work, *Photographing Montana, 1894–1928: The Life and Work of Evelyn Cameron*, by Donna M. Lucey (Mountain Press Publishing, 2000), reveals how Cameron, through photographs, letters, and diaries, documented life in nineteenth- and early twentieth-century rural Montana.

A variety of topics of both people and social and cultural issues use photographs to enhance biographical information. Among others, these include profiles of Canadian women athletes in *Amazing Women Athletes*, by Jill Bryant (Second Story Press, 2001), *We Were There Too! Young People in U.S History*, by Phillip M. Hoose (Farrar, Straus and Giroux, 2001), and *Into a New Century: Women of the West*, by Liza Ketchum (Little, Brown, 2000). William L. Katz has used photographs well in many of his books of history and biography including *Black Women of the Old West* (Simon & Schuster Children's Publishing/Atheneum, 1995), *Black Indians: A Hidden Heritage* (Simon & Schuster Children's Publishing/Simon Pulse, 1997), and *Black Pioneers: An Untold Story* (Simon & Schuster Children's Publishing/Atheneum, 1999). *The Saga of Lewis and Clark: Into the Uncharted West*, by Thomas and Jeremy Schmidt, with photographs by Wayne Mumford, is a richly illustrated account of the famous expedition (Dorling Kindersley, Ltd., 1999)

ARTISTS AS BIOGRAPHERS

Artists become biographers in several important ways. Through self-portraits and the interpretations they give to portraits of others, they provide us with biographical information about themselves, their society, and the interplay of human relationship, social status, and cultural roles.

Art scholar Shearer West tells us that for various reasons artists did not paint self-portraits until the Renaissance. Before that time social norms considered the painter to be a craftsperson, and his or her craft was simply mechanical. Before and early in the Renaissance, artists would often place themselves in paintings of historical or religious events, making the suggestion that they were witnesses to these great events.

Along with other humanistic themes, the Renaissance introduced a more focused awareness of self-identity, and artists responded to that in several ways. From a literary and social perspective, and encouraged by self-identify concepts, the Renaissance also helped support the development of autobiography and "self-narratives" as literary expression,[34] a movement that undoubtedly influenced artists.

During the Renaissance the status of the artist began to move from craftsperson to artisan, supported by the development of art as an academic discipline and the development and teaching of art theory. Practical reasons also promoted the growth of artists' self-portraits. Painters did not want to remain anonymous as was often the role demanded of them. They wanted to be identified with and celebrated for their work. They also wanted to experiment with new styles and techniques, and they needed to advertise their work for the sake of commissions and to gain patronage from the wealthy and powerful. Often an artist would send his or her self-portrait to a potential client as an example of his or her work.[35]

Self-perception, social status and class, and gender also influenced the development of self-portraits of artists. In their attempts to gain the support and patronage of influential persons in society, artists often used self-portraits as a way of presenting themselves to possible patrons both as a personality as well as a skilled artist.[36]

In an attempt to raise the status of the artist from that of craftsperson to one of high social class, male artists particularly began to paint themselves as members of these higher social classes and ranks with all the trappings of such status. In many of their self-portraits male artists relied less and less on picturing the tools of their trade (i.e., paint brush and easel). Instead they turned to painting themselves encased with symbols of high status—dress, pose, attitude. Women artists in their self-portraits continued to associate themselves more with the artist as craftsperson and typically surrounded themselves with artist's tools and studio environments. Nevertheless, they also often painted themselves dressed as aristocratic women. This characteristic of women being associated with tools of their trade continued well into modern times, apparently with society demanding that women prove that they indeed had the artistic skills and techniques worthy of an artist.[37]

As the role of the artist became more established in society and less dependent on royal, religious, or wealthy patronages, many male artists considered themselves free spirits and eagerly challenged the norms of society, especially those of middle-class culture. For example, in the early twentieth century, many well-known male artists expressed their sexual freedom though self-portraits. Such attitudes and behaviors undoubtedly encouraged the development of the modern stereotype of the male artist as both sexual and creative.[38] Apparently female artists never assumed this level of social protest.

Although artists' self-portraits are not completely life-story narratives, they do hold elements of autobiography. In fact, artists' self-portraits rose along with the growth of autobiography as a literary form in the late sixteenth century.

Both Catholic and Protestant theologies encouraged self-examination and contemplation, and artists often used this to reflect on issues and struggles in their own lives. With the growing acceptance of psychoanalysis, artists in the nineteenth and twentieth centuries also turned to self-portraits as a means of self-exploration and psychoanalysis.[39]

Self-portraits and artists' portraits of others come in many styles and presentations, allowing us to see both the art and the artist as well as the society in which both the artist and his or her subjects lived.[40] This is one of their strongest contributions to biographical narratives.

Numerous books about artists, both fiction and nonfiction, are available. In the Newbery Medal novel *I, Juan de Pareja*, by Elizabeth de Trevino (Farrar, Straus and Giroux, 1984), we learn much about the character of artist Diego Velásquez through the eyes of his slave Juan de Pareja, who became a celebrated artist in his own right. Story has it that de Pareja learned to paint in secret with no help from Velásquez and, upon a visit by the Spanish king to Velásquez's studio, de Pareja threw himself on the mercy of the king. Once the king had seen de Pareja's work, he is said to have said, "Any man who has this skill cannot be a slave." Velásquez was then forced to free de Pareja. Another story has it that Velásquez freed him because of de Pareja's personal loyalty during Velásquez's wife's illness.[41]

Often books on artists are published as parts of series. Some examples include "The Primary Source Library of Famous Artists" (PowerKids Press) and "Artists in Their Time" (Scholastic Library Publishing). Other useful biographical resources include *100 Artists Who Shaped World History* (Sagebrush Education Resources, 1997) and, of particular interest in terms of self-portraits, *Look at Me: Self-Portraits*, by Ruth Thompson (Smart Apple Media, 2005). In terms of reference materials, Thomson Gale offers *Authors and Artists for Young Adults: A Biographical Guide to Novelists, Poets, Playwrights, Screenwriters, Lyricists, Illustrators, Cartoonists, Animators, & Other Creative Artists*. This multivolume set discusses the lives and works of authors and artists of particular interest to young adults. Omnigraphics's Biography Today Library is an extensive source of biographical information. The company advertises that for "more than 12 years Biography Today has provided collective biographies that speak directly to young readers ages 9

Figure 8.5
A Painter's Studio, by Louis
Léopold Boilly; suggests high
status and expanding gender
roles of artists. Chester Dale
Collection, Image © 2005 Board
of Trustees, National Gallery of
Art, Washington, D.C. Published
with permission.

and up." Of interest to us here is that contemporary artists are now covered in
their "Biography Today Subject Series."[42]

BIOGRAPHICAL ART, NATIONALISM, AND MODERN HISTORY

Biography, art, and nationalism have played important roles in human history,
including the establishment of modern national states. This is certainly true of
national art from the United States, Great Britain, France, Germany, and almost
all modern states. Nationalism in Europe became a powerful political force in the
nineteenth century and was influenced by romantic-age ideas endorsing emotions, identity, and the belief that for a nation to be legitimate, it must be based
on the will of the people rather than on kingship, empire, or religion.

Nationalism is defined in several ways including civic nationalism (acceptance of and loyalty to the state), ethnicity (identity and loyalty to race, language, and family origins), and religion (acceptance and loyalty to a religion
and its expansion). By its very nature nationalism requires that boundaries be
established and exclusion be defined or that some code of beliefs and values
be accepted and followed.[43]

Other definitions of nationalism that are reflected in biographical art
include cultural nationalism, which aspires to give positive identification to
citizens and the enlightened and/or superior culture that citizenship affords;
liberal nationalism, espousing liberal democracy; and triumphal nationalism,
offering claims to superiority.[44] Artwork based on nationalism, and even the

struggle against it, offers us much in the way of biographical information and insight.

Although nationalistic art has existed in various forms for centuries, art produced by changing and emerging nations since the 1700s offers us telling examples of how painting, photography, and film have promoted national identity, military might, and political control and ascendancy. We find this in many countries including England, France, Germany, Canada, and the United States. Biography plays a significant role in this art. The July Revolution of 1830 in France provides examples of art depicting the revolt against the rule of restored Bourbon king Charles X to the French throne. Perhaps the most famous of this art is *Liberty Leading the People*, painted by Eugène Delacroix, now exhibited in the Louvre. Joseph-Désiré Court's *The King Distributing Battalion Standards to the National Guard* shows the new king, Louis-Philippe, in an official ceremony, standing under a canopy in front of the Ecole Militaire, dressed in courtly attire, posing on a dais and surrounded on each side by officers of the National Guard, with the duc d'Orleans and the prince de Joinville standing next to the king. This painting and its symbols emphasize protection provided by the citizen's militia. The Ecole Militaire attests to the institutional legitimacy of the regime, as does the presence of nobility, with the ragtag crowd that supported the July 1830 revolution now transformed into an official retinue, carrying the colors of the revolution and offering order as demanded by the bourgeoisie.[45]

Artist interpretation of nationalism and the rise of popular government also are seen in Paul Delanche's *Cromwell Opening the Coffin of Charles I*, painted in 1831 and now at the Musée des Beaux-Arts, Nimes, France. Cromwell, the victor, looks into the coffin and at the body of the dead king, whom he has just executed. Cromwell is attired in simple dress with gloved fingers spread in a V-shape as he raises the lid of the coffin and looks with both curiosity and vindictiveness at the body. This painting reflects the nationalistic spirit of the era in which it was painted. In dramatic narration, the painting suggests a victory against an unjust ruler and monarch.[46]

Arrival of Friedrich II of Prussia in the Elysium, by artist G. W. Hoffman in 1788, now in the German National Museum, Berlin, is an example of German nationalism as represented by the power of monarchy and its legitimate control of the nation state. This engraving, completed shortly after Friedrich's death, shows the king as he arrives in paradise, surrounded and greeted by his ancestors and other well-known figures from history including Alexander the Great, Julius Caesar, and Plato. No women appear to be there to greet him after his death. Is this absence a biographical statement of Friedrich's life—that of a homosexual who preferred to have little association with women during his lifetime?[47]

Another example of later German nationalism is *The Frankfurt National Assembly*, painted in 1848 by Paul Bürde, also in the German National

Museum. In this painting the artist brings together well-known members of this popularly elected parliament (elected by direct manhood suffrage), including Jacob Grimm.[48]

Political art in the United States mirrors some of the same elements as those just presented. The art in the U.S. Capitol building in Washington offers some excellent examples of nineteenth-century American nationalism. Huge paintings of important events in American history circle the entire wall of the rotunda, with each making a biographical and/or historical statement. Among others, these include *Embarkation of the Pilgrims*, *Surrender of Lord Cornwallis*, *Surrender of General Burgoyne*, *Baptism of Pocahontas*, and *General George Washington Resigning His Commission* (Figure 8.6).[49, 50] This last work was painted by John Trumbull around 1817. Washington is shown giving up his role as commander in chief of the army. He is surrounded by important political figures of the time including Thomas Jefferson, James Monroe, and James Madison. Martha Washington and her grandchildren are also pictured watching from the gallery, but she was not actually at the ceremony. The important symbolism here is that with Washington giving up his

Figure 8.6
***General George Washington Resigning His Commission*, by John Trumbull; symbolizes American civilian government.** Rotunda of the U.S. Capitol, Washington, D.C. Courtesy of the Office of the Architect of the Capitol.

command, the republic was now in the hands of civilian authority and was not likely to become a military dictatorship.[51]

The Apotheosis of Washington, a fresco painted by Constantino Brumidi in 1865, is suspended above the Capitol's rotunda. A section of this is *George Washington Rising to the Heavens* (Figure 8.7), where Washington is shown "rising to the heavens in glory, flaked by female figures representing Liberty and Victory/Fame." Washington is also surrounded by thirteen maidens symbolizing the original states of the union. *Apotheosis* means the rising of a person to the rank of a god or the glorification of a person as an ideal. The use of this term offers insight into American nationalism of the time as well as the role that religion played in American life.[52] It also reflects the esteem given to Washington by Americans at the time. For example:

After his death, the moral educators of the early 19th century crowned Washington as the ultimate symbol of virtue: an honest mortal worthy of imitation. Once defined as the embodiment of virtue, Washington was able

Figure 8.7
***George Washington Rising to the Heavens*, by Constantino Brumidi; a glorification of the first American president.** Rotunda of the U.S. Capitol, Washington, D.C. Courtesy of the Office of the Architect of the Capitol.

to be appropriated by groups of all stripes. He could be an icon of domestic perfection and almost-aristocratic refinement or the ultimate symbol of the selfless citizen soldier. Politically, socially—and of course, commercially—Washington's image has become an easily-recognized and powerful tool.[53]

This power in terms of how it is used in conjunction with other national heroes to define the character of an American national biography cannot be overlooked today.

This veneration is further reflected in numerous paintings and sculptures of Washington throughout the capital city.

Figure 8.8 below suggest a young man contemporaneous of Washington's time pictured in a Roman toga. This drawing reflects Romanized imagery commonly used during the eighteenth and early nineteenth centuries. We see this Roman influence strongly reflected in portraits and sculptures of Washington by such artists as William Satchwell Leney (1769–1831), Joseph Wood (1778–1830), and Jean Antoine Houdon, (1741–1828).[54] The acceptance by artists of the eighteenth and nineteenth centuries of this Roman style

Figure 8.8
Young man in Roman costume-dress equates prominence with great and noble persons of antiquity. Drawing by Richard H. Hendler.

illustrates how ingrained and influential this form of artistic interpretation and adoration was among artists and their publics during those eras in celebrating the lives of persons of rank and station.

The sculpture *Washington in Roman Costume*, by Horatio Greenough, was completed in 1840. Modeled after a stature of Zeus, it shows Washington seated, naked to the waist, and holding a lighted torch. At one time the statue was housed in the rotunda of the U.S. Capitol, then it was moved onto the capitol grounds. In 1908 it was sent to the Smithsonian and is now on display at the National Museum of American History. Despite its patriotic and nationalistic intent, it was always controversial.[55] A statue of Washington in Roman dress also stands in the North Carolina Capitol building.

A traditional painting of Washington not in Roman style is *The Washington Family*, painted by Edward Savage in 1796. In this painting George and Martha Washington are seated at a table. At Washington's side is one of his stepsons. The Washingtons' older child stands behind the table. The overall approach reflects an English courtly style. Savage suggests that "Washington's uniform and the papers beneath his hand allude to his 'Military Character' and 'Presidentship.'" On the table in front of Martha is a map of the newly formed District of Columbia, and she is pointing her finger at Pennsylvania Avenue, the grand avenue where the White House will stand. In the background Savage has added imagined details of Mt. Vernon such as marble columns and a faceless black man dressed as a livery servant. A world globe also stands by the child at Washington's side, perhaps suggesting the rise of the United States as a world power.[56]

Art was also used in the early days of the American republic to endorse or reflect national sentiment and policies. Artist George Bingham is a good example of this. Bingham, through his art, celebrated common people, democracy, and regionalism. He, like other artists of the time, departed from classical, European taste. Because this type of art was commercialized and could only be bought by the well-to-do, it often reflected the prejudices of the cultural elite and social control exerted by them. Bingham's art reflects the national conflictive feelings about the place of Native Americans in national life and the geographic needs of an expanding nation. His best-known painting is *Daniel Boone Escorting Settlers through the Cumberland Gap*, painted between 1851 and 1852. In this he endorses the national policy of westward expansion by whites and the displacement of native populations. In the painting we see Boone and white settlers bringing civilization and order to the dark and forbidding wilderness filled with hostile forces. Although Boone himself was a slaveholder and had slaves with him on his travels into wilderness country, Bingham ignores their presence in this painting.[57] Enrico Causici's *Conflict of Daniel Boone and the Indians, 1773* (Figure 8.9), a sandstone relief created between 1826 and 1927 and now placed above an entry door of the rotunda of the U.S. Capitol, reflects the same sentiments of conflict and suppression.[58]

Numerous resources are available concerning the art of the U.S. Capitol and the city of Washington. Bruce E. Smith's *Art and History of Washington, D.C.* (Bonechi, 2004) provides many well-selected and informative images of biographical art located throughout the city. The United States Capitol Historical Society also provides publications and educational resources relating to the U.S. Capitol building and its art. These resources are described on their website (www.uschs.org/03_education/

Figure 8.9
Conflict of Daniel Boone and the Indians, 1773, **sandstone by Enrico Causici; contemporary view, celebrating the conquest of the wilderness frontier.** Rotunda of the U.S. Capitol, Washington, D.C. Courtesy of the Office of the Architect of the Capitol.

03.html). A book that encourages active artwork by children is *How to Draw Washington's Sights and Symbols*, by A. Weintraub (Rosen Publishing Group/PowerKids Press, 2002). This is one title in their "A Kids Guide to Drawing America" series.

ART AS NATIONAL POLICY: NAZISM AND SOVIET COMMUNISM

Probably the two most vivid and recent examples of countries using art to promote nationalism and a national ideology are Nazi Germany and the former Soviet Union. According to many historians, anti-Jewish sentiments were used by the Nazis to ensure that Hitler's programs would gain popularity among the masses. Historians note that anti-Semitic prejudice was widespread among the mass population in the Germanic world of the time and that this needed to be, and could be, incorporated into the Nazis' ideology, along with the resentment of Germans regarding terms forced on Germany after World War I. In addition to this, Nazis' values grew out of an irrational view of traditions coming from the Romantic Movement of the early nineteenth century. These included adherence to passion, lack of hypocrisy, traditional family values, and devotion to community. This was an ideology that appealed greatly to the German working class.[59]

One of the first aims of the National Socialist Society for Germany was to address the "corruption of art" and reeducate the population concerning the powerful relationship between race and art. Under this ideology, all modern art was termed "Jewish," "Degenerate," and "Bolshevik," and a program of destruction and removal from public view began.[60] For its reeducation purposes, Nazism preferred that art be expressed on a gigantic scale through sculpture, architecture, and film. The Nazis' concept of the ideal body could be expressed well through sculpture. Sculpture was well suited to proclaim nationalistic and state-approved values like loyalty, work, family, and the "German Spirit and its divine destiny." In biographical terms, Hitler was a central figure in much of this sculpture. Hitler favored architecture and the Olympic stadium was built not only to celebrate the games, but to highlight the achievements of Nazism. The stadium, which still stands in Berlin today, not only served the Olympic Games, but was constructed to "hold hundreds of thousands of people to celebrate Nazi rituals."[61]

The Nazis used films well in their goals of promoting nationalism. *Triumph of the Will* is perhaps the most famous of all these films. Made for a German audience, it was produced on a grand scale and written and directed by Leni Riefenstahl. It celebrates the 1934 Nazi Party Rally at Nuremberg. Its use of nationalistic symbols is outstanding. Hitler is associated with military might and the history of the Germanic peoples. As the film opens, Hitler is seen arriving magnificently by air, flying in over medieval Nuremberg. As he arrives, crowds march in formation to meet him, and crowds line the route to his hotel. Crowds cheer along the route, and in one scene a "woman with a child is allowed to step out of the crowd to shake hands with the Fuehrer." At his hotel Hitler waves to the crowd below him from his balcony near a lighted sign reading *"Heil Hitler."* Throughout the film the audience sees German military and Nazi symbols and popular support for Hitler. Swastikas and eagles, uniforms, helmets, flags, cheering crowds, and marching military and civilian units are cleverly positioned for effect. The film goes on to record the ceremonial parade that includes workers and laborers who march and shout, *"Ein Volk, ein Führer, ein Reich!"* (One people, one Leader, one Empire!). Also included in this gigantic parade are the *Hitlerjugend* (Hitler Youth) and military units such as the artillery and cavalry. In the evening the audience sees the end of the ceremony with its torchlight ceremony involving thousands and its continued display of party insignia, reminding the audience of the power of Hitler and his party.[62]

Numerous biographical reflections based on art materials have come out of the Nazi experience. Significant personalities involved in Nazi art have been written about and discussed widely. These include Joseph Thork, Hitler's favorite sculptor, and Albert Speer, his favored architect and designer of Hitler's new Reich chancellery and his stunningly grandiose office complex. Speer's life and accomplishments are discussed in Fred Ramen's *Albert Speer: Hitler's Architect* (Rosen Publishing Group, 2001) and at the website "The Architect of the 20th Century" (www.dataphone.se/~ms/speer/welcom.htm).

Film producer Leni Riefenstahl is particularly interesting in biographical terms because of her influence on advancing the cause of Nazism and Aryan superiority through her innovative films. Her story is told in the film *The Wonderful, Horrible Life of Leni Riefenstahl* (Image Entertainment, 2003; www.image-entertainment.com) and on the web at "Leni Riefenstahl" (www.dataphone.se/~ms/speer/welcom.htm). Her landmark film, *Triumph of the Will*, produced in 1934, was released in DVD format in 2001 by Synapse Films of Novi, Michigan (www.synapse-films.com).

Books for older youth and mature younger children helpful in the study of this art movement include Gerald Green's *The Artists of Terezín* (Holmes & Meier, 1983), Berthold Hinz's *Art in the Third Reich* (Random House, 1979), Henry Grosshans' *Hitler and the Artist* (Holmes & Meier, 1983), Margot Stern Strom and others' *Seeing through Paradise: Artists and the Terezín Concentration Camp* (Massachusetts College of Art, 1991), Hana Volavkova's *I Never Saw Another Butterfly: Children's Drawings and Poems from Terezín Concentration Camp, 1942–1944* (Schocken Books, 1993), and James E. Young's *Holocaust Memorials in History: Art of Memory* (Prestel-Verlag, 1994).

After the German occupation of France, well-known artist Tomi Ungerer was forced into the Hitler Youth during his childhood. During the five years of occupation of France, Ungerer drew and recorded some of his experiences of Nazi indoctrination. These wonderful documents are presented in his memoir, *Tomi: A Childhood under the Nazis* (Roberts Rinehart, 1998).

In the former Soviet Union, Stalinist art followed some of the same principles as the Nazis and reinforces the ideas of how art and biography found in art advances nationalism. Alexander Jartsev writes that political artist experimentation came to an end when the Soviet Union entered into the "Great Patriotic War" (i.e., German invasion of Russia as part of World War II). Public art became the only possible way to express art, and conformity was demanded. Artists had no artistic freedom outside the dictates of Stalinist ideology. The regime expected clarity and unambiguousness from all artists. In its struggle against its enemies, the Stalinists considered art a weapon in war. Examples of this include F. A. Kaurtsev's *Honor to the Heroes from the Transpolar Flyover* (1939), and Aleksandr Deyneka's *Shot Down Pilot* (1943) and *The Defense of Sevastopol* (1942).

Art was to act as a means of identity for soldiers and as a way of educating the public about their roles in Soviet society. Even apart from the war effort, images and symbols in art were to convince the population that the Soviet system offered salvation from lives of oppression. Not only was art to act as a motivation to fight in war and to bring victory to the country, but it was to show that joy and happiness was the reward for all those who toiled for the system under the fatherly guidance of Stalin.

Examples of this genre that exalted Stalin include *Praised Be the Great Stalin!*, by Yuri Kugach (1950) and *Our Wise Leader and Dear Teacher (Stalin among the People at the Kremlin)*, by Boris Joganson (1952). In this art ordinary people and workers are pictured as contented and happy, and willing to carry on the great proletarian struggle. Fyodor Bogorodsky's *Youth Tranquil* shows youth happy and content, and Aleksandr Laktionov's *Letter from the Front* (1962) reinforces the idea of civilian support and admiration for those who serve in the military. The porcelain set *Metal* (1930), by Mikhail Mokh, encourages workers to be engaged in helping to make the Soviet Union a great industrial and military power.[63]

Dream Factory Communism: The Visual Culture of the Stalin Period, by Max Hollein (Hatje Cantz Verlag GMbH & Co KB, 2004), offers the mature reader an analysis of the philosophical base for Stalinist art. Biographies of Stalin such as *Joseph Stalin: From Peasant to Premier*, by Nancy Whitelaw (Dillon, 1992), *The U.S.S.R. under Stalin*, by Stewart Ross (Franklin Watts, 2000), and *Stalin: Russia's Man of Steel*, by Albert Marrin (Penguin Books, Canada, 1993) also provide insight into the man and his vision of an artistically and nationalistically correct Soviet Union.

USING BIOGRAPHICAL ART IN LIBRARIES AND CLASSROOMS

Biography in art can be used in many ways in both library programming and in classroom instruction. As with any library and instructional unit or program, all presentations must be based on sound educational and instructional theories and practices. Some of the best sources for these concepts are

national, state, provincial, and local school curriculum guidelines and directives. Professional associations and organizations such as museums and
national libraries also offer suggestions for teaching together with teacher
resources. Common themes run through these various guides as listed below:

Art at National, State, and Provincial Levels

The American National Standards for Arts Education reads:

> The arts have been an inseparable part of the human journey; indeed, we
> depend on the arts to carry us toward the fullness of our humanity. We value
> them for themselves, and because we do, we believe knowing and practic-
> ing them is fundamental to the healthy development of our children's minds
> and spirits. That is why in any civilization—ours included—the arts are
> inseparable from the meaning of the term "education." We know from *long
> experience that no one can claim to be truly educated who lacks basic
> knowledge and skills in the arts.*[64]

The British National Curriculum Programmes of Study outline these
instructional objectives for visual art study:

• Explore and develop ideas
• Investigate and make art, crafts, designs
• Evaluate and develop art
• Acquire knowledge and understanding
• Increase breadth of knowledge

The Ministry of Education for Ontario provides these guidelines:

• Understanding art concepts
• Critical analysis and application
• Performance and creative work
• Communication

> Communication concepts include: how to communicate ideas, thoughts,
> feelings, and experiences; how to use elements of design such as line,
> shape, form, and space; how to respond to works of art; and how to describe
> ideas found in art, and how to use art vocabulary correctly.

The Texas Essential Knowledge and Skills (TEKS) requirements for art as
administered by the Texas Education Agency under Title 19, Chapter 74 of
the Texas State Administrative Code state that in order for students to be successful in the TEKS examinations, all Texas schools' art departments must

ensure that art programs be based on: artistic perception, creative expression and performance, foundations in historical and cultural heritage, and response to and evaluation of art. Specifically, schools must plan a curriculum that will promote development of:

• Thinking and problem-solving skills
• Art concepts and skills
• Creative skills
• Initiative, self-confidence, imagination, and originality

Art at Local Levels

North East Independent School District in San Antonio, Texas, based on Texas Education Agency directives, offers these principles for their art programs:

• Develop and organize ideas from the environment
• Express ideas through original artwork, using a variety of media with appropriate skill
• Demonstrate an understanding for art history and culture as records of human achievement
• Make informed judgments about personal artwork and the artwork of others

At basic levels most art programs concentrate on teaching color, shape, forms, lines, how to recognize art in everyday environments, and how to create simple art. Picture books for younger children offer excellent resources for the early development of art awareness. *Art through Children's Literature: Creative Art Lessons for Caldecott Books*, by Debi Englebaugh (Greenwood Publishing Group, 1994), offers examples of suitable books of a biographical nature to use with younger children. *Children of Promise: African-American Literature and Art for Young People*, by Charles Sullivan (Harry N. Abrams, 1991), also provides biographical information, much of which is in art formats.

Children at several age levels can use biographies of artists to understand art styles and concepts, and to illustrate how artists create and use style in innovative and unique ways to express their ideas and personalities. *Van Gogh: The Touch of Yellow*, by Jacqueline Loumaye (Chelsea House Publishers, 1994), is a good example of this type of resource. In this book, two children discover the art of Van Gogh and learn about his tragic life.

Craft and art activities can also be used to bring biography and art together. Young children can be introduced to the concept of commemorative coins and/or postage stamps and be encouraged to create a commemorative piece in honor of an admired personality. For older youth, political, social, and cultural symbols as well as gender references used in paintings during various historical periods can be used to foster critical thinking and evaluative skills as well as increasing cultural knowledge. *Art—Images and Ideas*, Bk. 8, by Laura H. Chapman, part of the publisher's "Discovering Art" series (Davis Publications, 1992), can be used to good effect here. Books in the "Key to Art" series, published by Lerner Publishing Group (e.g., *The Key to Renaissance Art*, by Jose F. Arenas [1990]), although not necessarily biographical in purpose, offer biographical insights through the many illustrations and solid information concerning various types of art and styles produced during the various periods covered by the series.

Suggestions for instructional units and curriculum guides are available from several free sources including ERIC's "The Educator's Reference Desk^SM" (www.eduref.org/Virtual/Lessons/index.shtm), the Library of Congress' "The Learning Page—Lesson Plans" (http://memory.loc.gov/learn/lessons/index.html), the "Awesome Library" (www.awesomelibrary.org/Classroom/Arts/Arts_and_Crafts/Arts_and_Crafts.html), and "Knowledge Network Explorer" (www.kn.pacbell.com/wired/bluewebn). In terms of planning general information literacy programs, Ruth Small's *Designing Digital Literacy Programs with IM-PACT: Information Motivation, Purpose, Audience, Content, and Technique* (Neal-Schuman Publishers, 2004) will be useful. Books concerning artists and their works offer avenues for good book-talks and discussions.

CONCLUSION

As with most subject areas an understanding of the biography of individuals who have influenced the discipline is fundamental. This is especially true in the area of art, which has been used throughout human history to influence and control society and its institutions. We see this in ancient societies, in current totalitarian society, and even in democratic societies in the modern world. Art also has a vital role to play in modern democratic society. A study of art and the interplay of symbols used in art to express the roles of persons of great status and importance as well as ordinary people who exist in society is necessary to bring about a richer and more critical look at human culture. A study of biography as it is reflected in art can help satisfy that need. School library media specialists and writers for youth, as well as producers and publishers, play an important role in seeing that such issues are better addressed in the future.

NOTES

1. Richard Brilliant, *Portraiture* (London: Reaktion Books, 1991), 7–20, 35–37.
2. Malcolm Bull, "Sociology of Art," in *Grove Art Online*, Oxford University Press, http://www.groveart.com.content.lib.utexas.edu:2048 (accessed Oct. 27, 2004).

3. "Visual Literacy," http://staff.ed.uiuc.edu/esecaras/ES/draft9_1/vis_lit.html (accessed Oct. 27, 2004).

4. Wendy Beckett, *The Story of Painting*, 1st American ed. (New York: Dorling Kindersley, 1994), 10–11.

5. Howard Hibbard, *The Metropolitan Museum of Art* (New York: Harrison House, 1980), 28–49.

6. Beckett, 12–13.

7. Pierre Amiet, "Mesopotamia," in *Grove Art Online*, Oxford University Press, http://www.groveart.com.content.lib.utexas.edu:2048 (accessed Dec. 12, 2004).

8. Jessica Harrison-Hall, "China—Portrait Painting," in *Grove Art Online*, Oxford University Press, http://www.groveart.com.content.lib.utexas.edu:2048 (accessed Dec. 12, 2004).

9. "Japan—Portraiture," in *Grove Art Online*, Oxford University Press, http://www.groveart.com.content.lib.utexas.edu:2048 (accessed Dec. 12, 2004).

10. "Japan—Portraiture."

11. "Africa. Imagery and Iconography: Portraiture," in *Grove Art Online*, Oxford University Press, http://www.groveart.com.content.lib.utexas.edu:2048 (accessed Dec. 12, 2004).

12. Jonathan Bloom and Sheila Blair, *Islamic Arts* (London: Phaidon Press, 1997), 201–2.

13. Bloom and Blair, 84–86.

14. Bloom and Blair, 342.

15. Bloom and Blair, 225–26, 288–89, 330, 340–41.

16. Andreas Beyer, *Portraits: A History* (New York: Harry N. Abrams, 2003), 8–21.

17. Beyer.

18. Beyer, 14–15.

19. Beckett, 24–26.

20. Beckett, 26–27.

21. "Portraiture: The Evolution of Portrait Painting," in *Encyclopedia.Com*, http://encyclopedia.com/html/section/portrait_theevolutionofportraitpainting.asp (accessed Nov. 10, 2005).

22. Kathleen Lane, "Monumental Sculpture to c. 1300," in *The Oxford History of Western Art*, ed. Martin Kemp (Oxford: Oxford University Press, 2000), 101.

23. Martin Kemp, "Church and State: The Establishing of European Visual Culture 410–1527," in *The Oxford History of Western Art,* ed. Martin Kemp (Oxford: Oxford University Press, 2000), 68.

24. Shearer West, *Portraiture* (Oxford: Oxford University Press, 2004), 16–17.

25. West, 70.

26. John Oliver Hand, *National Gallery of Art: Master Paintings from the Collection* (Washington, D.C.: National Gallery of Art in association with Harry N. Abrams, 2004), 174–75.

27. Hand, 75.

28. Lisa Reitzes and others, *A National Image: The American Painting and Sculpture Collection in the San Antonio Museum of Art* (San Antonio, Tex.: San Antonio Museum of Art, 2003), 22–23, 28–29, 51–52.

29. West, 145–61.

30. Reitzes, 19–63.

31. West, 188–91.

32. West.

33. Brilliant, 132–40.

34. West, 163–85.

35. West.

36. West, 165–69.

37. West, 167–73.

38. West, 169.

39. West, 180–84.

40. Brilliant, 141–74.

41. "Juan de Pareja [Spanish Baroque Era Painter, ca. 1610–1670]," in ArtCyclopedia, http://www.artcyclopedia.com/artists/juan_de_pareja.html (accessed Nov. 27, 2004).

42. Omnigraphics, "Biography Today Library," http://www.omnigraphics.com/category_view.php?ID = 2 and http://www.omnigraphics.com/product_view.php?ID = 274 (accessed Nov. 27, 2004).

43. "The Internet Modern History Sourcebook: Nationalism," http://www.fordham.edu/halsall/mod/modsbook17.html#Nationalism (accessed Nov. 4, 2004).

44. "The Internet Modern History Sourcebook."

45. Albert Boime, *Art in an Age of Counterrevolution, 1815–1848* (Chicago: University of Chicago, 2004), 252.

46. Boime, 338.

47. "Frederick the Great (1712–1786)," in *GLBTQ: An Encyclopedia of Gay, Lesbian, Bisexual, Transgender & Queer Culture*, http://www.glbtq.com/social-sciences/frederick_great,2.html (accessed Dec. 15, 2004).

48. "Collection Graphic Arts," German National Museum, http://www.dhm.de/ENGLISH/sammlungen/grafik (accessed Nov. 5, 2005).

49. United States Capitol Historical Society, *We, the People: The Story of the United States Capitol, Its Past and Its Promise* (Washington, D.C.: United States Capitol Historical Society, 2004), 80–81.

50. United States Capitol Historical Society, "History and Exhibits—*Baptism of Pocahontas*," http://www.aoc.gov/cc/art/rotunda/baptism_pocahontas.cfm (accessed Nov. 5, 2005).

51. "Works of Art in the Capitol Complex—United States Capitol—*General George Washington Resigning His Commission*," http://www.aoc.gov/cc/art/rotunda/washington_resigning.cfm (accessed Nov. 5, 2005).

52. "Works of Art in the Capitol Complex—United States Capitol—*The Apotheosis of Washington*, the Rotunda Canopy Fresco," http://www.aoc.gov/cc/art/rotunda/apotheosis/apotheosis.htm (accessed Nov. 16, 2004).

53. "*Apotheosis of George Washington*: Brumidi's Fresco & Beyond," Initial Construction: Laura Dove and Lisa Guernsey, spring 1995 (first extension: Scott Atkins, spring 1996; second extension: Adriana Rissetto, spring 1997), http://xroads.virginia.edu/~CAP/gw/gwmain.html (accessed Dec. 7, 2005).

54. Thomas Addis Emmet, collector, New York Public Library, Emmet Collection, "The Pictorial Field-Book of the Revolution," vol. 2 (Chapters 9–11) [graphics]. ca. 1727–1890. Also cited as "Emmet Collection of Manuscripts Etc. Relating to American History. The Book of the Revolution," vol. 2 (Chapters 9–11).

55. Smithsonian Institution, "Legacies: Collecting America's History at the Smithsonian," http://www.smithsonianlegacies.si.edu/objectdescription.cfm?ID = 66 (accessed Dec. 10, 2004).

56. National Gallery of Art Collection, "Edward Savage, American 1761–1817, *The Washington Family*," http://www.nga.gov/collection/gallery/gg62/gg62-564.0.html (accessed Dec. 10, 2004).

57. Boime, 545–50.

58. "Works of Art in the Capitol Complex—United States Capitol—*Conflict of Daniel Boone and the Indians*," http://www.aoc.gov/cc/art/rotunda/reliefs/conflict.cfm (accessed Nov. 5, 2005).

59. "Nazism," in *The Free Dictionary by Farlex*, http://encyclopedia.thefreedictionary.com/nazismv (accessed Nov. 5, 2005).

60. History Online, "Nazism: Degenerate Art," http://mithec.prohosting.com/history/content/nazi%20art.html#degenerate%20art (accessed Nov. 23, 2004).

61. History Online, "Nazism: Architecture," http://mithec.prohosting.com/history/content/nazism.html#architecture (accessed Nov. 23, 2004).

62. Curriculum Online, "Media Study—Nazism in Feature Films," National Curriculum (GCSE) [for England and Wales], http://www.eriding.net/amoore/gcsemedia/nazis.htm (accessed Nov. 23, 2004).

63. Alexander Jartsev, "The Didactic Landscape: A Stalinist Dream of Art," http://art-bin.com/art/asovietarteng.html (accessed Nov. 26, 2004).

64. National Arts Education Associations, "The National Standards for Arts Education," developed by the Consortium of National Arts Education Associations (under the guidance of the National Committee for Standards in the Arts), 1994, http://artsedge.kennedy-center.org/teach/standards/overview.cfm (accessed Feb. 6, 2006).

9

REFLECTIONS

INTRODUCTION

Without question, biography influences societal dialogue. This is especially true in terms of how biography and biographical concepts impact youth and affect the cultural and social perceptions of youth. For this reason, if no other, we must be concerned with how biography is used in our modern world, and we all must be aware of current issues and trends in biography in our society that affect us personally.

ISSUES AND TRENDS

Influences of Biography on Behaviors, Learning, and Attitudes

Research from various fields such as psychology and sociology has indicated that biography plays a powerful role in the sociological and psychological well-being of youth. Biography for youth today presents role models and helps define acceptable behavior, social expectations, and values. It also shows youth what is rewarded in society and what is less valued. Nevertheless, more research is needed in terms of how to better determine the effects of biography on youth as they encounter biography in the school library media center and youth programs in public libraries. Most of the research on how literature affects youth has focused on fiction. Because of the wide influence of biography in society, now is the time to better understand its lasting effects through good research.

Learning and behavioral theories (e.g., Albert Bandura, see chapter 4) have given us new insights into how biography can be used effectively in everyday instructional situations. By understanding these theories, school library media specialists and teachers can use biography to influence learning, critical thinking, and the development of better information seeking skills for students of all ages. Social and cultural theories (e.g., Urie Bronfenbrenner and Lev Vygotsky, see chapter 4) can influence how professionals of all kinds who serve youth can better view their roles as important change agents in the lives of youth and how they can help youth be successful in the complex societies of today. Again, more research is needed to confirm these theories and their use within the everyday world of school library media specialists and public youth librarians.

Interests: Old and New

A great deal of research concerning the interest of youth, including reading interests, has been conducted over the years, and this research is revealing in several ways.[1, 2, 3, 4, 5, 6, 7, 8, 9, 10] From these we know that reading is influenced by a number of sociocultural and personal factors. For example, gender is a powerful predictor of reading interest (e.g., girls read more than boys; girls prefer fiction while boys prefer nonfiction; boys read more newspapers than girls, etc.). Boys are seemingly more interested in reading biography than girls.

Interest in reading and the types of materials read are influenced by geographic location, the home environment, peers, and important authority figures such as parents, teachers, and school library media specialists. Institutional factors such as libraries and the availability of books also play a role in reading interests. These institutional symbols give permission to youth to enjoy reading, and they offer rewards for reading in various ways. The ability to go to a public library or the school library media center and select and check out a book or other items and the ability to walk into a bookstore and select and buy a book both offer the rewards of ownership, personal control, and personal responsibility.

The development of interests, including reading interests, serves the psychological needs of individual youth. Psychological needs are unique to individuals, and they are serious and deeply held. Generally one's interests must be satisfied for contented living. Because interests are based on social and individual psychological needs, they are so serious and so embedded in personality that they can direct one's life in either positive or negative ways.[11]

Reading interests are social, cultural, and psychological, and they are time- and place-based. Research has demonstrated that certain interests (including reading interests) are prevalent over time. In general, youth seem to show an interest in money, personal attractiveness, and various forms of fun and recreation. New interests develop with changing times and changes in culture and cultural behavior. For example, since the 1960s reading interests have expanded to include health, sexuality, the environment, family life, social issues, gender relationships, and ecology. Although reading interests still largely reflect traditional gender designations, recent societal and cultural changes have also provided opportunities for both males and females to move beyond these limitations.

Positive role models can demonstrate that reading is rewarding and important in the lives of youth. The American Library Association's (ALA) public relations ad campaigns and "Read" posters using well-known public figures and celebrities to promote reading are excellent examples of this concept. Beyond celebrities, positive role models such as teachers, parents, and school library media specialists can reinforce the idea that reading is fun and important, and they can help youth broaden their reading interests, including the reading of biography.

Behavior of School Library Media Specialists

As mentioned in chapter 3, Mark Dressman, in his ethnographic study of the school library culture, contended that school media specialists (he used the term *school librarians*) are very much conditioned by a sociocultural frame of reference that is feminized to favor fiction. He contends that novel writing as it developed in the seventeenth century was seen as women's work, and fiction writing gave women a way out of the home and into the world of power and influence.

When public libraries developed (followed by school libraries), the work with children was largely in the hands of women who saw the development of literacy and improvement of literary taste as two of their primary goals. To Dressman, female librarians of the late nineteenth and early twentieth centuries believed that providing the best in fine literary fiction was the most effective means available to them to promote these goals. Most of these women came from the middle classes, were well educated for the time, and had a missionary zeal for improving the masses, especially the lower classes. Even today we recognize this period as the "golden age of children's literature" because it produced some of the lasting classics of American and British youth literature.

Dressman feels that this allegiance to fiction still remains strong within the culture of school library media specialists. He presents as evidence what he sees as the predominance of fiction in award books, in recommended-reading lists, and in writings appearing in major professional journals. His contentions may or may not be correct, but what it says to school library media specialists today is to look closely at our own beliefs about reading and genre, and to evaluate carefully our behaviors and values as we promote both fiction and nonfiction, including biography, to youth.[12]

Reader-Response Theory and Bibliotherapy

Research and the study of how readers respond to what they read have been left largely in the hands of educators, reading specialists, and communication specialists. Nevertheless, how readers respond to what they read is one of the underlying questions that school library media specialists and public librarians ponder. We assume that youth respond to what they read and what is read to them. But how do they respond? The two major views are that readers bring a lot of their culture, society, and personal experiences to what they read, and they use those experiences to make sense of their reading (the political or ideological approach). The other view (the phenomenological approach) is that they are in an interactive exchange with the text. In other words, readers both share and interact with what is written, creating an interactive dialogue between reader and text. From a practical point of view, and based on what school library media specialists and youth librarians in public libraries know and observe, both theories probably contribute to how youth experience reading. More research on reader response, based on the perspective of school library media programs and programming offered in public libraries, is needed to help us better understand this interactive process.

Bibliotherapy is certainly responding to what is read, but it is focused on changing behavior in a more planned and coordinated way than is reader-response theory. Developmental bibliotherapy is the usual form used when bibliotherapy is undertaken by school library media specialists and youth librarians. It is designed to help youth improve in expected and successful ways in meeting their social and psychological developmental needs.

As society becomes more complex and public institutions such as schools and public libraries are increasingly faced with more diversified populations and behaviors in youth, developmental bibliotherapy undoubtedly will be used more in schools and public libraries. With this in mind, more research is needed to help us understand the effectiveness of biography in developmental bibliotherapy. Accessible training in developmental bibliotherapy is also needed. Although much has been written about bibliotherapy in the professional literature, it appears to be self-taught by those who have practiced it in school library media centers and public library settings. Systematic training for those who want to develop this expertise is not widely available.

At-Risk Youth and Biography

One of the most pressing problems we face today is how to meet the social and educational needs of at-risk youth. Greg Druian and Jocelyn A. Butler, in their review of research on at-risk youth, noted that the research shows that at-risk youth are subject to negative demographics, socioeconomic conditions, and institutional characteristics. These include:

• Living in high-growth states
• Living in unstable school districts
• Being a member of low-income families

- Having low academic skills (though not necessarily low intelligence)
- Having parents who are not high school graduates
- Speaking English as a second language
- Being single-parent children
- Having negative self-perceptions; being bored or alienated; having low self-esteem
- Pursuing alternatives [to school] (Males tend to seek paid work as an alternative; females may leave to have children or get married.)[13]

Effective school programs for at-risk youth appear to have several characteristics in common. They tend to:

- Separate dropouts from other students
- Have strong vocational components
- Utilize out-of-classroom learning
- Be intensive—small, individualized with low student-teacher ratio—and offer more counseling than the regular school curriculum[14]

Biography can work well within such programs. Biographies of individuals from various types of work situations can be used effectively with at-risk students. The problem is that not many biographies dealing with nonprofessional workers have been written. Although this is changing, those that are available often focus on other aspects of life such as racial and gender discrimination rather that how average people go about working, solving life's problems, and leading satisfying lives.

Biography can also be used in counseling programs where discussions about various options concerning work, school, and responsibilities can be considered under expert guidance. Although not about specific people, a number of books for younger readers that are useful for this purpose include *Day with a Mechanic*, by Joanne Winne (Scholastic, 2000), and *Jobs People Do: A Day in the Life of a Firefighter*, by Linda Hayword (DK Publishing, 2001). The "I Want to Be" series, published by Firefly Books, with many volumes written by Dan Liebman, provides insight into occupations such as police officer and mechanic. Books for older youth that single out occupations and focus on the lives of individuals who work in those occupations are not easily found. As stated previously, when such biographies are published they tend to concentrate on other aspects of life rather than the characteristics of the job and what those jobs mean to people. Nevertheless, some useful titles conducive to discussion include *The Ditchdigger's Daughters: A Black Family's Astonishing Success Story*, by Yvonne Thornton, as told to Jo Coudert (Carol Publishing Group, 1995), and *Leon's Story*, by Leon Walter

Tillage (Farrar, Straus and Giroux, 2000). Another book having discussion potential is *Working: People Talk about What They Do All Day and How They Feel About What They Do*, by Studs Terkel (New Press, 1997). This easy-to-read book written by one of America's better known populist social critics offers insights into the lives of real people who share their work lives with readers.

The Place of Biography in Society and Communication Patterns

Biography has power, but that power is influenced by how it is used and presented within the context of society. We see this in the influence of celebrity biographies and how media showcases and promotes personalities and biographical information about them. Within the last few decades, cable television has intensified this by bringing into play what might be called "ordinary citizens" and culling from them news events. A case in point is the attention given to the Laci Peterson murder case in California from 2003 to 2005. This murder, the search for the killer, the trail of her husband Scott, his conviction, and his sentence of death occupied cable television for at least three years. Analysis of this case indicates that a strong psychological need for identification was present within the audience as well as the economic need for commercial television (especially cable television) to create and sustain an audience. The criticism is also raised that much of this type of coverage is based on race and class. That is, white, middle-class, affluent person-alities caught up in such circumstances are favored over lower-class individuals, many of whom often come from minority cultures.

Apparently, through the interest given to the Peterson case by commercial television, the general public was encouraged to identify with this young, attractive, middle-class family who seemed to be living the American dream.

Murders from earlier times, such as the case of Lizzy Borden being accused then acquitted of murdering her upper-class parents in 1892, also appear to engender similar reactions. Today Lizzy Borden has her own web-site, DVDs, discussion forum, books written about her, music lyrics singing her deeds, and even an opera detailing her psychological frame of mind. Costumes, ghost stories, and a rock band named in her memory also celebrate her existence. The house in which she lived and in which the murders were committed is now a well-known and highly sought after bed-and-breakfast.

A look at popular culture, teen magazines, and Internet web pages that are widely available to the public today further illustrates this search for identifi-cation. Similarly, print mass media carefully selects entertainment personali-ties for coverage and presents them embedded with information calculated to satisfy the identification needs of the readership. Why else would we need to know so much about Brad Pitt, Uma Thurman, and Matt Damon—all high-lighted in the April 4, 2005, issue of *Us Weekly*?

Anna Marcia Swenson-Davis studied how Marilyn Monroe became a symbol of identification; in Monroe's case, that symbol became one of the failure of the American dream.[15] Benson Fraser and William J. Brown looked at the strong identification influence that Elvis Presley had and continues to have on his fans. They suggest that this identification with Presley comes from selected media images that satisfy the personal psychological needs of fans. They also consider how the influence of media-controlled celebrity images might influence society.[16] From his research, Lynn McCutcheon noted too that the celebrity system is very much a part of contemporary society. McCutcheon's research with college students, based on standardized psychological and sociological measurements, indicated that those who felt the world was "just and fair" tended to be more involved with celebrity worship than students who were suspect of society's fairness.[17] He and his colleagues—John Maltby, James Houran, and Diane Ashe—offer further understanding of modern society's obsession with celebrity worship in their book *Celebrity Worshippers: Inside the Minds of Stargazers* (PublishAmerica, 2004).

Important sports figures are also included in this type of coverage in much the same way as entertainment personalities. As discussed in chapter 6, Gill Lines notes that the press and media have tremendous influence on how the images of sports figures are presented to the public. Traditionally the male sports figure was seen as presenting the best in the way of social ideals and masculinity, virtues that were learned on the playing fields but were transferred easily into everyday life. He contends that this has changed with the growth and intrusion of media into sports, and society as a whole. This intrusion has changed the traditional images from models of upright behavior and good sportsmanship to that of the "wounded hero," marred with drunkenness, domestic abuse and violence, and references to secret gay relationships. The female hero, in his view, has been marginalized, trivialized, and objectified so much that she is basically invisible and even questionable as a role model for young women.[18] If the celebrity system is as flawed as much of the research indicates, might not these findings alone suggest the need for better information literacy education in schools and public libraries?

Biography has always played an important role in defining national identity. Most nations have embraced this through the selection of national heroes that promote nationalism and patriotism. The use of biography in school curricula has traditionally favored this kind of biography. Recent trends in publication and use indicates that this has broadened to include an expanded variety of personalities that help define a nation.

Closely related to this is the development of the investigative biography. Such biographies are often political in nature in that they report on personalities who hold or who have held political power. For example, Robert A. Caro is interested in understanding political power and how that power controls our lives. His research on President Lyndon Baines Jonhson illustrates his approach to understanding power and its use. Similarly Kitty Kelley says that she writes only about persons who have influence on our lives. She has been criticized for her interpretations of the private lives of the famous, but her defense is that their private lives play too important a role in our own lives to be ignored. She recognizes that the families of those about whom she writes are often hurt by what she reports, but she claims that she is an investigative biographer and that these families are really victims of men and women who seek power at the cost of family.[19]

Sometimes well-known writers such as Agatha Christie take a more personal view of their craft and write about their own families and experiences. In the first of her three autobiographies, *Agatha Christie: An Autobiography* (Berkley Publishing, 1996), Christie writes about how she became a writer, her financial problems, and difficulties in her first marriage. Roald Dahl's *Boy: Tales of Childhood* is a bittersweet account of the famous author's childhood (Farrar, Straus, and Giroux, 1984; Penguin Books, 1992).

Unusual experiences such as survival of life-threatening situations or overcoming great odds often encourage others to write about experiences. Pan-Mei Natasha Chang's narrative *Bound Feet & Western Dress* (Anchor, 1997) recounts the conflicts that her great aunt Chang Yu-I experienced in China as she dealt with the demands of tradition and modern life, and her rise to prominence as a woman of accomplishment. *Left for Dead: My Journey Home from Everest*, by Beck Weathers, M.D., with Stephen G. Michaud (Villard Books, 2000), recounts how Weathers survived his ordeal of being lost and nearly frozen to death on Mount Everest. *Finding Fish: A Memoir*, by Antwone Fisher (Perennial, 2001), is the personal account of a not so ordinary man. Fisher is deserted by his mother early in his life, is taken into foster care by a cruel caregiver, and suffers abuse at her hand, yet he maintains his humanity and dignity.

Publishers in the youth market, being very much aware that celebrities as well as political and issue-oriented personalities have an impact on society, have attempted to meet that challenge with biographies that seek to satisfy the curiosity of youth as well as to provide good, well-researched, and well-written biographies for youth. This type of publishing is likely to continue as school library center specialists and public youth librarians recognize the appeal of these biographies to youth along with their apparent effectiveness in instructional settings.

Publishers and writers have also recognized the power of visualization to inform and entertain. The graphic novel has become extremely popular with youth, and libraries appear eager to meet this interest and to provide graphic novels and other formats to their readers. We also see this trend in biography where illustrations are used as they are in the graphic novel to convey information and emotional impact. Examples of this include *Maus*, by Art

Spiegelman (Pantheon Books, 1986), and *Persepolis: The Story of a Childhood* (Pantheon, 2003) and *Persepolis 2: The Story of a Return*, by Marjane Satrapi (Random House, 2004).

Series books, whether fiction or nonfiction, appeal to almost all levels of readers. Numerous publishers have recognized this and have responded with an abundance of well-written biographical series on a variety of individuals from numerous fields. In order to ensure that they have an active line of biographies available for the market, publishers actively seek writers that can write according to the series guidelines, as well as authors who are versed in understanding the curricula and instructional needs of schools and who can propose ideas for publication, research those ideas, and write for a school audience.

Fictionalized biography has also been rather controversial with both school library media specialists and literacy critics. The major argument against it is that it is not authentic. Those who support it say that it is one way of interesting very young children in biography. By using fiction based on historical evidence, both information and personality of the subject can be presented at a level that young children can appreciate. The Library of Congress cataloging procedures have caused problems in that their rules require that if fiction is a part of the narrative, then it must be classified as fiction, with appropriate subject headings labeling the work as fiction. This has become more of a problem in recent decades as more and more school library media centers and public libraries use Library of Congress–based cataloging. Nevertheless, it seems apparent that publishers will continue to seek and publish fictionalized biography and that it will be used by those who work with young children.

Presenting Biographies to Youth

As youth mature and gather insights about the workings of society, school library media specialists and youth librarians in public libraries, teachers, and parents can help them develop critical thinking and information literacy skills that will help them place biographies into a framework helpful to them in understanding the world.

Professional writings and publications by school library media specialists and others have certainly addressed this need through their ideas and suggesting how biographies can be used by school library media specialists and others. These suggestions are numerous and include ideas on instructional units, booktalks, bookwalks, book fairs where biographical materials are available, story hours, use of creative dramatics, and other forms of presentations such as news and current event coverage. Although obviously effective in programming, what appears to be lacking is testing through research for the effectiveness of these suggestions on behavior, attitudes, and skills of youth.

Biographies for the Young

Very young children have a need and interest in biography (see chapter 3), but because of their limited life-experiences and their developmental lack of time sense, they are not prepared to face some of the complexities that biography presents. Authors of biographies for young children must recognize this and construct their biographies accordingly. One of the primary obligations of authors, as well as those who use biographies with young children, is a responsibility to help children make sense out of the information that is presented. Presentations of biographical materials must be carefully scripted both in their narration and in their delivery so that sense-making is enhanced.

Art in picture biography provides more than illustrations. For young children, art provides important information clues to help them understand and remember specific as well as broader concepts. Teachers, school library media specialists, and youth librarians in public libraries can further aid in children's understanding, sense-making, and appreciation of biography by providing carefully constructed learning and reading experiences based on developmental needs that are both age- and learning-appropriate.

Changing Population Patterns

Population trends in most Western countries—the United States, Canada, and most western European countries—are changing. In the United States, youth minority populations are expected to outstrip those of the now majority population. By 2050, the largest youth population in the United States will be minority youth.[20] In some of the American southwestern states such as Texas, by 2020, if not sooner, the majority population is expected to be composed of non-Anglo ethnic groups.[21] Standard reading interest studies have shown that minorities like to read about persons of their own ethnic backgrounds. This reading preference does not mean that minority youth read only about their own groups, but these collective population trends and reading interests in Western countries suggest that they will affect the types and amounts of biographies published and the types of programs presented in schools and libraries during the next several decades.

Selection and Collection Management

Like any other type of materials collected in a school library media center and public library, selection of biographies must be based on a collection development plan that offers guidance and direction as to how the biographies are to be acquired over an extended period of time. This plan must be well integrated into the overall materials selection policy, but the plan will give special guidance about types of materials to be acquired and the level to which they are to be acquired. How extensive will the selection program be: exhaustive, representative of the publication output in the subject area, or highly selective based on well-established criteria such as demands of the curriculum and interests of students and other users?

Weeding procedures must also be considered. Biographies date quickly. What is popular and desired one year may be forgotten by the next. This is especially true of entertainment and sport personalities. Weeding must also consider the physical condition of the materials and its overall attractiveness. From a marketing point of view, worn out, unattractive books and items that will not be read or circulated should be removed from the collection and replaced with newer copies, new editions, or other types of biographies appropriate for the collection. The Texas State Library and Archives Commission provides a guide to weeding called the CREW method.[22] This, as well as other methods, should help in weeding decisions.

An analysis of circulation figures over a selected period of time should also help to determine what should be replaced, what is popular, and what is missing from the collection in terms of current needs. Interviews, surveys, and structured observations of users should also provide helpful information. Standard biographies that may not receive much popular attention should nevertheless be acquired and retained in a collection. Historic personalities such as George Washington, Abraham Lincoln, and Queen Victoria as well as others need to be available to youth to support their need for cultural information as well as the curriculum needs of the school.

For older youth in secondary schools, selected standard definitive biographies written for adults should be systematically acquired. Reference materials, both electronic and print, also must be an integral part of the collection development.

Major selection aids useful for biography include *Booklist*, *School Library Journal*, the *Horn Book* magazine, the *Children's Catalog*, *Middle and Junior High School Library Catalog*, *Senior High School Catalog*, *Public Library Catalog* (all part of the H. W. Wilson Company's "The Wilson Standard Catalog" series), and the major award lists. Professional and curriculum subject area periodicals published by national associations such as the National Council of Teachers of English (www.ncte.org/pubs/journals), the National Council for the Social Studies (www.socialstudies.org/publications), and the National Science Teachers Association (www.nsta.org/nstapubs) offer selection guidance (e.g., reviews and annual lists of outstanding trade books). Well-known selection periodicals include *Voice of Youth Advocates (VOYA)*, *Booklist*, *Book Links*, *Language Arts*, *English Journal*, and *Social Education*. All of these should be routinely checked for useful titles. Together with these, commercial vendors such as Follett Library Resources (www.flr.follett.com/intro/keepyou.html) offer online selection services.

Marketing and Display of Biography

Biography is exciting reading, but it often needs to be marketed or promoted in schools and libraries. There are several ways of doing this. Traditionally bulletin boards and exhibits have been used to promote biography. This type of promotion lends itself to official holidays honoring well-known and famous individuals. Birthdays of the well known, persons of local significance such as founders of the town, cultural and civil leaders, and others also make good exhibit and bulletin board displays. Bulletin boards and displays can also be designed to coordinate with movies and dramas that might be playing in the community. As noted previously, the ALA offers numerous posters of well-known individuals who promote reading. These posters can be integrated into biographies of these individuals as well as persons involved in similar work.

Visit classrooms where short promotional talks about biography can be presented to classes. Booktalks can also be used as marketing tools both in classrooms and in libraries. For younger children, story hours can promote interests in biography.

Bibliographies and finding guides to biographies in the collection as well as in other local libraries are also effective marketing strategies. School library media centers have computer links to local library collections, and guidance is often needed to help students use those collections. Finding guides help in promoting biography as aids to research, and well-designed reading lists can be used to whet interest in biography for both recreational as well as informational reading.

Shelving and arrangement of biographies on shelves and in other display areas are also marketing devices. Taking cues from bookstore displays, libraries are now displaying books as they would offer merchandise for sale, with front covers prominently displayed.[23] Advertisers realize that they must capture a potential customer's attention—often with five seconds—convince that customer that the product is needed, and persuade that customer to buy. Advertisers generally have a target market in mind and design a marketing strategy fitting that well-defined market segment.[24] In the small library media center libraries, the target audience for a particular type of biography might be a club, those who attend certain events, teacher groups, or classes.

Social Marketing

Nonprofit organizations often base their marketing strategies around a "social marketing" philosophy. Basically, nonprofit organizations offer services to the public that are designed to help advance and improve society. This may be in health, literacy, and better use of resources. School library media specialists and public librarians serving youth do this on a continuous basis.

Social marketing strategies provide well-developed theoretical and practical help and approaches for marketing biography within school library media centers and public libraries.[25]

Role of Parents and Other Caregivers

Parents and other caregivers play an important role in helping youth relate to and understand biography. Parents can play a role in creating a family literacy program that not only includes fiction and nonfiction, but ensures that biography is included in the family program. Gloria DeGaetano and Kathleen Bander, in their book *Screen Smarts: A Family Guide to Media Literacy* (Houghton Mifflin, 1996), offer suggestions for television viewing that can be adapted for biography.

Based on their suggestions, young children can be taken to a story hour in the public library and parents can ask that biography be included in the presentations. Parents can also direct their children to biography sections in public libraries and bookstores and engage their children in conversations about their favorite people who might have biographies written about them. In the bookstore and library, they can point out biographies of some of the favorite people as they are found on the shelves. Of course, seeing a parent buy biographies or checking out biographies from a library can serve as a good influence on a child. Home activities can include reading biographies to children and talking to children about their favorite celebrities and why they admire them. Another approach is to ask children what kinds of biographies they would write if they could write a biography about their favorite person. Parents can also encourage children at home to develop a "circle of friends" consisting of their favorite famous persons and have them seek out information about them in reference books, at school library media collections, at the public library, at bookstores, and on the Internet.

Parents can encourage older youth to discover new interests and activities through biography. Encourage older youth to become newspaper readers, paying attention to biographical information provided there. Parents can encourage their children to seek out further information about the same subject in other sources. Parents can also encourage children to be critical observers of biographical information presented through the mass media, especially television.

With a family literacy program in mind, parents can visit their children's school library media center and help their young children select biographies. School library media specialists and public librarians can help parents and other caregivers in this task by helping them become aware of the vast amount of biographical materials available to youth today, and by providing some direction and guidance in how to engage children and older youth in biography.

AREAS OF CONCERN

Cultural Values and Conflicts

In many Western countries, cultural values have changed over the decades, and are continuing to change. Along with values, these changes involve the role of public institutions in public life such as schools and libraries. In the United States public education is under attack by some not only because of its perceived inability to educate children effectively, but because of its failure or refusal to inculcate patriotic values, acceptable social behavior, and respect for authority and traditional values.

Changing values and conflicts are also seen in the so-called decline of traditional Christianity in western Europe and the rise of Christian fundamentalism in the United States. Scholar George Weigel, writing in *The Cube and the Cathedral: Europe, America, and Politics without God* (Basic Books, 2005), sees the decline of Christianity in Europe beginning in the nineteenth century with atheistic humanism and materialistic philosophies that lead to fascism and communism. According to Weigel, Marx's materialism and Auguste Comte's positivism attempted to exclude "transcendent reference points from cultural, social, and political life." In Weigel's view, this introduced spiritual boredom, hyperindividualism, and a lack of confidence in the future, leading to the decline of the family in western Europe. Mark Lilla notes that the decline of Christianity in Europe grew out of World War I and the failure of liberal religion of the time to address significant human problems. He adds to this that after World War II, many Europeans rejected organized religion due to its perceived failures.[26]

The breakdown of traditional hierarchies and the growing affluence of the population also influenced the decline of European Christianity. The need for workers as replacements for both the declining birthrate of Europeans and the loss of life during World War II introduced minority populations from non-Christian cultures that held different cultural and religious views and values. Scholar Bernard Lewis as well as others predict that Europe will be Islamic by the end of the twentieth-first century.

An article in a May 20, 2005, issue of the *New York Times* reported on the rise of Christian fundamentalism and evangelism on Ivy League college campuses in the northeast United States. Leaders in this movement believe American leadership has traditionally come from these colleges and that leadership must be converted to Christian fundamentalism. Matt Bennett, a leader in this movement and a member of one of America's wealthiest families (his father founded the Holiday Inn chain) states that "if you are going to change the world, we have got, by God's power, to see these campuses radically changed."

How do these views and changing population characteristics affect biography for youth? We can test this by simply asking the question: Are biographies that cover personalities who are leading and very much involved in these changes available to children and young adults? What type of coverage do mainline publishers offer in the area of non-Christian leaders in major religious movements? What types of coverage do they offer concerning fundamentalist Christian leaders? The complaint is often made that popular libraries only reflect mainline, liberal thought and that a wide array of human life and experiences are simply not available in the popular library because mainline national, cultural, social, and political orthodoxy is endorsed and maintained by libraries.

Points of View and Variety of Personalities

Methods for presenting points of view in biographies for youth are crucial. For the most part popular libraries, especially school library media centers, have attempted to present well-written and balanced biographies reflective of cultures and societies. For that reason biographies that have dogmatic interpretations of values and beliefs have been avoided in favor of biographies that present personalities reflecting their influences on society and culture. Biographies of Martin Luther King Jr., Gandhi, Mother Teresa as well as the prophet Mohammad, Buddha, Lenin, Stalin, and Hitler fall into this category. Lives of Christian saints and personalities from the Bible are included in this group as well.

For school library media centers, and public libraries to some extent, problems arise with biographies that might seem too ideological, politically and religiously focused, and condemning of others who may not follow a particular point of view, theology, and ideology. Mainline publishers may have overlooked subjects that need attention. For example, Christian hymnists Philip Bliss, Fanny Crosby, Charles Wesley, and Ira Sankey may be worthy of interpretative coverage as are religious fundamentalists Pat Robinson, Jerry Falwell, and self-identified fundamentalist Osama bin Laden. Major review sources mentioned earlier offer reviews and suggestions for coverage of these sensitive topics. Well-developed collection management policies will help in making decisions about biographies and their appropriateness for individual collections.

Censorship

Just like other materials, biographical information is subject to censorship. This censorship is based on conflicts arising from concepts and values and the perceived need to control access to ideas and information to protect youth from harm and hurtful ideas. The reasons for censorship of biography are many, ranging from rejection of personalities because they are not seen as suitable role models for youth to dislike of political and social ideas held by individuals. Along with these concerns come objections related to lifestyle, religion, class conflicts, and racism. Censors have attacked such biographies and personal narratives as *The Autobiography of Benjamin Franklin* (Dover Publications, 1996), *Black Like Me*, by John Howard Griffin (Signet, 35th ed.), and *Black Boy*, by Richard Wright (Perennial, 1998).

In legal terms censorship is when materials are removed from a collection or prevented from being published or disseminated based on government orders. In general, we tend to think of censorship in much broader terms. The ALA has identified a number of actions that, while not official censorship, tend to influence and often inhibit access to information. These include: **inquiry,** when someone asks why a certain title is in the collection; **expression of concern,** when an inquiry conveys a judgmental tone, often embedded with concerns about values; **complaint**, when an oral objection is made about an item being in the collection; **challenge,** when a formal complaint is filed against an item in the collection; **attack**, when a publicly worded statement is published and/or discussed in the media; and, finally, **censorship**, when an item is ordered removed from the collection under government order (e.g., court directive, administrative action).[27]

The First Amendment of the United States Constitution protects freedom of speech and academic freedom in the United States. The Constitution is a rigid document that cannot be changed easily. Because of this and the open language of the amendment, the interpretation of First Amendment rights has largely fallen into the hands of American courts. There are two important U.S. Supreme Court rulings that affect censorship rulings today. The first is *Miller v. California* (1973), which established obscenity standards in the United States.[28] The second is *Board of Education, Island Trees, New York v. Pico* (1982), which placed some limitations on what a school board can censor in a school media library collection. *Island Trees v. Pico* does provide some level of protection against school board censorship as it states that materials in a school media library collection cannot be removed based solely on the dislikes of a board. Materials can be removed only for sound educational reasons.[29] The question is often asked as to how this can be determined. The government's motives are generally interpreted by the courts based on evidence (documents, statements, court testimonies) that reveals the behavior and intent of the government's decision to censor.[30] In recent years principles established in *Pico* have been used by courts in censorship cases not related to school library media centers and collections, but that involve government control of access to information.[31]

Censorship in other countries, such as the United Kingdom, Canada, Australia, and New Zealand, is similar in that legislative laws define what can be censored. As in the United States, the interpretations of these laws are often left to the courts, which follow principles based on constitutional mandates, common law, and well-established legal precedents. In these various countries laws and interpretations of them vary from the very open to a more restrictive view of what is permissible within a particular country.

A well-developed collection plan and an official materials selection policy can help in preventing legal censorship. Once a plan and selection policies are in place, they must be followed exactly and records kept of selection decisions. Such records can include invoices, order forms, MARC records with review sources noted, requests for information, requests for acquisition of certain types of materials, and professional reviews published in well-established professional review sources (for materials considered for purchase as well as those actually acquired). This documentation will be helpful if there is ever a challenge made to an item in the collection. The documents will offer evidence that the item was thoroughly considered and selected within the official guidelines of the materials selection policy. Well-documented selection procedures and documents can also be used in courts of law in support of selection decisions.

ACCESS TO BIOGRAPHICAL INFORMATION

Mass Media

The mass media have always provided an abundance of biographical information to the public and will continue to do so. This is assured by the growth and availability of communication technology. These venues include commercial television, cable television, radio, various print media, and, of course, the Internet.

The mass media have generally been seen as adversaries to information literacy and educational attainment, but Steven Johnson, in *Everything Bad Is Good for You: How Today's Popular Culture Is Actually Making Us Smarter* (Riverhead Books, 2005), defends television media. Johnson is concerned not about the moral values presented in the media, but with its ability to engage the audience in advanced levels of cognitive reasoning and development involving complex thought and analysis.

Much of his argument reflects information literacy skills and literacy analysis. He asserts that the complicated plot lines in historically popular television shows such as *Hill Street Blues* and currently popular *The Simpsons* help with learning. Laying aside some theories, such as those presented by Kohlberg that children proceed along age-specific stages of cognitive development, Johnson argues that such programs require a wide array of knowledge found outside the shows to understand their social and relationship nuances. "Electronic media such as television, DVDs, and videogames force youth to think as adults, analyzing complex social networks, managing resources, tracing subtle narrative intertwining, [and] recognizing long-term patterns."[32]

School media specialists and others who teach youngsters will not find this completely new, but such recognition by Johnson may help the public understand some of the teaching and programming that school library media specialists and teachers continually develop to help youth become better critical thinkers and more discriminating users of information.

Small, Single Issue, and Local Biography Publishers

The publishing industry grew from newspapers. The general practice in the seventeenth and early eighteenth centuries was for newspapers to also publish books and other items in addition to their broadsides, newspapers, and journals. Benjamin Franklin's printing shop is a good example of this. Large publishing companies in the United States and other English-speaking countries arose around the early and mid-1800s, largely as the result of the improvements in print technologies, communication systems (mail delivery and transportation systems), improvement in literacy rates, and public demand for reading materials.[33, 34]

Similarly, many modern small and local presses have developed in recent times because of improvement in print technologies (e.g., computer printing technology) and the need to satisfy demands for specialized information. From a biographical point of view the need for biographical information is wide-ranging. To meet this need, small, special-interest publishers have arisen, and they can easily concentrate their efforts on reaching clearly identified audiences and markets. These include local (state, province, and district) publishers of genealogy and biography; religious publishers whose publications address specific theological tenets and ideas; and publishers that cater to certain lifestyles such as gay, lesbian, and transgender people or certain hobbies and interests, such as sports. As mentioned throughout this book, school library media specialists and youth librarians can learn about these often elusive publishers through their advertisements, the Internet, and their presence at trade shows and conferences. Figure 9.1 is a catalog of Morgan Reynolds Publishing, one of several companies that specialize in publishing biographies for youth.

Reference Materials

Biographical reference resources are perhaps some of the most requested materials in the school library media center as well as public libraries. Requests for biographical references and materials are far-reaching and encompass many of the issues raised in this book. Print-based reference materials will always be in demand, and we see the publishing of these materials increasing with each passing decade. Electronic biographical resources are

**Figure 9.1
Catalog cover of Morgan
Reynolds Publishing.
"A Company Offering Well
Researched Nonfiction
Biography for Youth."
[Publisher's statement.]**
[Published with permission and
courtesy of Morgan Reynolds
Publishing.]

now required to support a modern library media center and public library reference collection for youth. Examples of these include Grolier Online® *Facts on File*, and Thomson Gale. Grolier Online® offers extensive reference resources including biographical materials. It describes its service as follows (boldface highlights suggesting biographical resources are the author's):

1. The core of Grolier Online is its encyclopedias.
2. The next level is the information available in related articles. Our encyclopedias contain over 583,000 article-to-article links that take you directly to other resources within Grolier Online.
3. The third level is access to print resources represented by Grolier Online's 34,000 bibliographies, containing over 100,000 citations to individual works.
4. The fourth level is access to magazine and periodical articles that match research topics. **Grolier Online's links to periodicals from 750 journals**.

5. The fifth level is the **Grolier's Internet Index, our collection of more than 320,000 links to over 40,000 sites on the World Wide Web**.

6. The sixth level is an unparalleled assemblage of materials that supports our core reference collection:

   - **Teacher Resources**
   - **Research Starters**
   - **Homework Help**
   - **Current Events and News**
   - The Grolier Online Atlas
   - Age-specific Dictionaries
   - Timelines
   - Projects and Activities
   - **Biographies**
   - Literary Selections
   - Educational Games
   - And so much more!

Facts on File is another fine biographical resource. *Facts on File* began as a print-based current events news source in the 1940s, and because of this history, it is now able to offer extensive online coverage of biographical materials. *Facts on File* states:

> [Our] Reference Databases are interdisciplinary, interactive databases on a wide range of subjects, such as American history, science, multicultural studies, women's studies, geography, and careers. Our Curriculum Resource Center gives librarians, teachers, students, and researchers fast, instant access to the binder content they've come to rely on. (www.factsonfile.com)

Because this resource is so wide-ranging, it is an excellent tool for biographical materials, since biographies comprise major sections of most of these databases. Both Grolier Online® and *Facts on File* base their costs on several factors that are collated with enrollment and budget characteristics of individual schools, districts, and regional centers.

CONCLUSION

Interest in biography will not wane. Interest and interactions with other people is a part of the human experience. Technology has always played a role in recording and in accessing biography, ranging from clay tablets to computers. Information technology will continue to play this role. If we can reasonably predict the near future, we are likely to see more print and online resources develop, driven both by genuine educational needs as well as by contrived market forces. The mass media will continue to provide biographies for entertainment as well as information. Small presses and publishers representative of special interests and needs will continue to develop.

Debates about how to present biography to youth will continue and will be better focused as we come to more fully understand how children and adolescents learn and process information. Debates will continue on the forms of biography appropriate for young children (fictionalized biography, mass media presentations, etc.); but these debates are good and necessary for both practical and theoretical development of the field.

School media centers and public libraries will undoubtedly play a larger role in all types of educational endeavors. Not only will they continue to offer print and electronic resources, but their expertise in helping students and children learn will be recognized and expected as demands from the public increase for the better integration of youth into civil society and improved academic achievement of students.

Research has not been conducted systematically in terms of how biography is used in school library media settings or in the public library. This research is essential. We must continually seek to better understand biography's impact on learning, and the behaviors and attitudes of both individuals and groups.

As we study ways to better use biography with youth, we should always keep in mind that it is a part of traditional education that has always placed great emphasis on history, literature, philosophy, political science, foreign language, and the classics. Columnist and professor Thomas G. Palaima reminds us that the study of biography along with and included in history, languages, art, literature, and philosophy develops empathy and perception. Biography, in alliance with these traditional subjects as well as with science and technology, "takes us beyond ourselves and our own narrow pursuits and desires and helps us understand others."[35] School library media specialists and youth librarians have an important role to play in that undertaking.

NOTES

1. W. Bernard Lukenbill, "The Reading Interests of Adolescents," in *Reaching Young People through Media*, ed. Nancy Bach Pillon (Littleton, Colo.: Libraries Unlimited, 1983), 15–34. The bibliography of this article cites reading interest studies back to 1889.

2. Alan C. Purves and Richard Beach, *Literature and the Reader: Research in Response to Literature, Reading Interests, and the Teaching of Literature* (Urbana, Ill.: National Council of Teachers of English, 1972).

3. George W. Norvell, *The Reading Interests of Young People*, rev. ed. (East Lansing: Michigan State University Press, 1973).

4. Donna McCoy, "Surveys of Independent Reading: Pinpointing the Problems, Seeking the Solutions" (research paper, Murray State University, 1991), ERIC document no. ED 341 021.

5. Constance Schultheis, "A Study of the Relationship between Gender and Reading Preferences of Adolescents" (research paper, Kent State University, 1990), ERIC document no. ED 367 376.

6. Leena M. Snellman, "Sixth Grade Reading Interests: A Survey" (research report, University of Virginia, 1993), ERIC document no. ED 358 415.

7. Charlotte S. Huck and others, *Children's Literature in the Elementary School*, 6th ed. (Madison, Wis.: Brown & Benchmark, 1997), 40–43.

8. Doreen O. Bardsley, "Boys and Reading: What Reading Fiction Means to Sixth Grade Boys" (dissertation, Arizona State University, 1999), abstracted in *Dissertation Abstracts International* 60-A (Sept. 1999): 653.

9. Magaretha M. Joubert, "The Reading Interests and Reading Habits of Afrikaans-Speaking Teenagers in Pretoria" (master's thesis, University of South Africa, 2002), abstracted in *Masters Abstracts International* 42 (Aug. 2004): 1114.

10. Brian W. Sturm, "Dogs and Dinosaurs, Hobbies and Horses: Age-Related Changes in Children's Information and Reading Preferences," *Children and Libraries* 1 (Winter 2003): 39–51.

11. James B. Dusek, "The Hierarchy of Adolescent Interests: A Social-Cognitive Approach," *Genetic Psychology Monographs* 100 (Aug. 1979): 41–72.

12. Mark Dressman, *Literacy in the Library: Negotiating the Spaces between Order and Desire* (Westport, Conn.: Bergin & Garvey, 1997), 165–66.

13. Greg Druian and Jocelyn A. Butler, *Effective Schooling Practices and At-Risk Youth: What the Research Shows* (Portland, Ore.: Northwest Regional Educational Laboratory, 1987), 4–5. ERIC document no. ED 291 146.

14. Druian and Butler, 7.

15. Anna Marcia Swenson-Davis, "From Sex Queen to Cultural Symbol: An Interpretation of the Image of 'Marilyn Monroe'" (dissertation, University of Michigan, 1980), abstracted in *Dissertation Abstracts International* 41-A (Oct. 1980): 1676.

16. Benson P. Fraser and William J. Brown, "Media, Celebrities, and Social Influence: Identification with Elvis Presley," *Mass Communication & Society* 5 (May 2002): 183–206.

17. Lynn E. McCutcheon, "Machiavellianism, Belief in a Just World, and the Tendency to Worship Celebrities," *Current Research in Social Psychology* 8 (Jan. 2003): 131–39. Also available at http://www.uiowa.edu/~grpproc/crisp/crisp.8.9.html (accessed May 30, 2005).

18. Gill Lines, "Villains, Fools or Heroes? Sports Stars as Role Models for Young People," *Leisure Studies* 20 (Oct. 2001): 285–303.

19. "*Texas Monthly* Talks with Evan Smith," television programs viewed on KLRU, Austin, Texas, May 2005. Excerpts from Caro interview available at http://www.klru.org/texasmonthlytalks/archives/robert_caro/robert_caro.asp (accessed Sept. 23, 2005). Excerpts from Kelley interview available http://www.klru.org/texasmonthlytalks/archives/kelley/kitty_kelley.asp (accessed Sept. 23, 2005).

20. U.S. Department of Commerce, the Minority Business Development Agency (MBDA), *Dynamic Diversity: Projected Changes in the U.S. Race and Ethnic Composition 1995 to 2050* (Washington, D.C.: U.S. Census Bureau, 1999).

21. Texas Agricultural and Natural Resources Summit Initiative, *The Population of Texas*, http://agsummit.tamu.edu/Publications/9611/poplong.htm (accessed May 24, 2005).

22. *The CREW Method: Expanded Guidelines for Collection Evaluation and Weeding for Small and Medium-Sized Public Libraries*, revised and updated by Belinda Boon (Austin: Texas State Library and Archives Commission, 1995).

23. Mary Ann Nichols, *Merchandising Library Materials to Young Adults* (Greenwood Village, Colo.: Libraries Unlimited, 2002).

24. Gilbert A. Churchill and J. Paul Peter, *Marketing: Creating Value for Customers* (Burr Ridge, Ill.: Irwin, 1995).

25. Philip Kotler and others, *Social Marketing: Improving the Quality of Life*, 2nd ed. (Thousand Oaks, Calif.: Sage Publications, 2002).

26. Jay Tolson, "European, Not Christian," *U.S. News & World Report*, May 20, 2005 (citing unreferenced commentary by Mark Lilla).

27. American Library Association, "Support for Dealing with or Reporting Challenges to Library Materials: Definitions," http://www.ala.org/ala/oif/challengesupport/ challengesupport.htm (accessed May 24, 2005).

28. W. Bernard Lukenbill, *Collection Development for a New Century in the School Library Media Center* (Westport, Conn.: Greenwood Press, 2002), 74–76.

29. Lukenbill, 77–80.

30. Lukenbill, 79–80.

31. Lukenbill, 80.

32. James Poniewozik, "Children, Eat Your Trash!" review of *Everything Bad Is Good for You: How Today's Popular Culture Is Actually Making Us Smarter*, by Steven Johnson (Riverhead Books, 2005), *Time*, May 9, 2005, 67.

33. "History of Publishing Website Main Contents," http://apm.brookes.ac.uk/publishing/ contexts/main/mainmenu.htm (accessed May 24, 2005).

34. "The Reader's Companion to American History: Publishing," http://college. hmco.com/history/readerscomp/rcah/html/ah_072200_publishing.htm (accessed May 24, 2005).

35. Thomas G. Palaima, "At UT, an Education That Leaves Out Essentials," citing an undated Christopher Ricks interview, *Austin American Statesman*, May 21, 2005.

BASIC SELECTION AND ACCESS AIDS FOR BIOGRAPHY

INTRODUCTION

Below is a basic and highly listed assortment of selection and access aids that will help in building collections and making biographical materials available to both children and young adults. These items have been chosen because they offer access to biography as well as to other types of materials that are needed within a collection striving to meet the educational, cultural, and social needs of youth as highlighted in this book as well as in other discussions. Most of the titles listed date from 2000, but several older aids have been included because they offer needed retrospective coverage of biographical items still available in print and/or available in library collections.

SELECTION AIDS AND SOURCES OFFERING ACCESS TO BIOGRAPHICAL INFORMATION

ALA's Guide to the Best Reading in 2005: ALSC, Booklist, RUSA, YALSA. Plastic holder with inserts. Chicago: American Library Association, 2005. Includes books listed in *Notable Children's Books*, *Notable Books*, *Editor's Choice*, and *Best Books for Young Adults*. Includes the best in fiction, nonfiction, and poetry for all ages.

ALAN Review. Periodical. Published three times a year, *ALAN* offers reviews of fiction and nonfiction books of interest to young adults. It is published through the auspices of the National Council of Teachers of English with the interests of English and literature teachers and their students in mind. (www.english.byu.edu/resources/alan)

Association for Library Service to Children. *Notable Books for Children.* Chicago: Association for Library Service to Children, annual. An annual list of books considered by a committee of professionals to be the best published during the preceding year. Listing includes fiction and nonfiction, with generous attention to biography. The association also publishes annually its "Notable Films and Videos for Children." (www.ala.org/alsc). See also Young Adult Library Services Association, listed below.

Barancik, Sue. *Guide to Collective Biographies for Children and Young Adults.* Lanham, Md.: Scarecrow Press, 2005. Provides access to biographies contained in some 700 collections suitable for children and young adults.

Barr, Catherine, ed. *From Biography to History: Best Books for Children's Entertainment and Education.* New Providence, N.J.: R. R. Bowker, 1998. Although becoming dated, this is an excellent source for connecting history and biography. It includes the best biographies of some 300 individuals, ranging from Pocahontas to Jane Goodall.

Barr, Catherine, and John T. Gillespic. *Best Books for Children: Preschool through Grade 6.* 8th ed. Westport, Conn.: Libraries Unlimited, 2005. Includes more than 25,000 in-print titles for children in grades K–6. Arranged by themes, the concise annotations provide bibliographic information and review citations.

Beers, Kylene, and Teri Lesesne. *Books for You: An Annotated Booklist for Senior High.* 14th ed. Urbana, Ill.: National Council of Teachers of English, 2001. Presented here is a thematic listing of more than 1,000 books for high school students. Arranged by themes, readers (teachers, librarians, students, and parents) are encouraged to explore many areas including biography. Award-winning books are highlighted in an appendix.

Booklist. Periodical. Presents reviews of recommended books, nonprint items, and computer programs for use in school library media centers and public libraries. Essays and reviews cover special topics such as easy-to-read and foreign-language materials. Through its Booklist Publications imprint, it issues bibliographies, lists, and special monographs designed to help in the selection of materials. (www.ala.org/booklist)

The Book Report. Periodical. A review source for print and multimedia material, including online resources, software, and hardware. It considers the needs of curriculum development and highlights social themes and issues that have curriculum and information appeal. In addition to reviews it offers advice about how to integrate books into curriculum and instruction. (www.linworth.com/bookreport.html)

Book Review Digest. Periodical. First published by the H. W. Wilson Company in 1905, it is designed to provide bibliographic citations and digests of reviews of books as they appear in the professional and literary press. Includes children and young adults reviews along with bibliographic and acquisition information. Its electronic format is *Book Review Digest Plus*, with links to reviews it sites. (www.hwwilson. com/databases/brdig.htm)

Books in Print. Periodical. First published by the R. R. Bowker Company in 1948, *Subject Guide to Children's Books in Print* followed in 1970. These sources were not originally considered selection aids, but rather acquisition aids, providing school library media center specialists and public youth librarians with convenient access to information on the availability of books within the book trade market. In recent years *Books in Print* has become more useful as a selection aid through its publishing of abstracts of reviews of selected items. It electronic version, *Books in Print Plus*, has expanded this to include reviews of children and young adult books as well as special services such as award books and guides to materials according to grade, reading, and special interests. (www.bowker.com)

Brown, Jean E., and Elaine C. Stephens. *Your Reading: An Annotated Booklist for Middle School and Junior High.* 11th ed. Urbana, Ill.: National Council of Teachers of English, 2003. Intended to be used by teachers, students, and parents in selecting good and interesting books to read, this source offers a variety of books, fiction and nonfiction, for the middle-school and junior high child.

Bulletin for the Center for Children's Books. Periodical. Offers reviews of children's books and books for adolescents. Review are brief, but rating scales offer recommendation suggestions as well as suggested audience and uses (e.g., R means "recommended," NC means "not recommended," SPC indicates subject matter or treatment will tend to limit the book to specialized collections). Reading levels for each book are also provided. (http://bccb.lis.uiuc.edu)

Carter, Betty B., and others. *Best Books for Young Adults.* 2nd ed. Chicago: American Library Association, 2000. A compiling of book selections appearing on YALSA's "Best Books for Young Adults" list.

Elementary School Library Collection. Published by the Brodart Company, it is similar in format to the "Wilson Standard Catalog" series. It includes recommendations for books and audiovisual materials such as computer software. It is available in both CD format and print. (www.brodart.com)

Facts on File, Inc. *Facts on File's Reference Databases.* Electronic resource. Contained in these various databases are "interdisciplinary, interactive databases on a wide range of subjects." The coverage includes American history, science, multicultural studies, women's studies, geography, and careers. The Curriculum Resource Center provides librarians, teachers, students, and researchers with "fast and instant access" to information. (www.factsonfile.com/newfacts/Factsonline.asp?PageValue=Online)

Grolier, Inc. *Grolier Online.* Electronic resource. Biographical coverage in this online system is constructed around the company's existing seven encyclopedia databases, containing huge amounts of "age-appropriate" biographical information ranging from media photos to current events. (http://auth.grolier.com/features/overview.html?user=librarian; http://auth.grolier.com/cgi-in/updatelist?templateName=/marketing/teacher.html)

Guide to the Best Reading in 2004: ALSC, Booklist, RUSA, YALSA. Chicago: American Library Association, 2004. A guide to the major books appearing on such lists as "Notable Children's Books," "Notable Books," "Editor's Choice," "Best Books for Young Adults," and "Outstanding Books for the College Bound."

The Horn Book Guide to Children's and Young Adult Books. Periodical. Attempts to list and comment on all children's and young adult books published in the United States. Although comments are brief, the guide provides a rating scale indicating the quality of the book and includes a guide to genre and subject areas. (www.hb.com/guide)

The Horn Book *Magazine: About Books for Children and Young Adults.* Periodical. A fine literary review and discussion journal devoted to promoting reading and culture through the reviews and critical analysis of books for children and young adults. Various sections or departments include reviews of newly published books, recommended paperbacks, new editions and reissues, and science books. Special columns are devoted to discussing young adult books, re-reviewing older books, and reviewing Canadian books. It also publishes *The Horn Book Guide to Children's and Young Adult Books*, which is a rather complete listing with annotations and brief reviews of children's and young adult books published in the United States. See also description above. (www.hbook.com)

H. W. Wilson Co. *Biography Index.* Periodical and electronic resource. Published first in 1946, this is an index to biographical materials appearing both in periodicals and in monographs. The monographs listed can serve as suggestions for purchase, and the periodical citations will help broaden a library's access to biography through its detailed indexing. *Biography Index* is now available in electronic format. (www.hwwilson.com/Databases/bioind.htm). See references to other biographical references produced by the H. W. Wilson Co. listed below.

————. "Standard Library Catalog" Series. Offers several basic guides to collection development. These include *Children's Catalog* (1909); *Standard Catalog for High School Libraries* (1928), which also covers books suitable for junior high schools; *Junior High School Library Catalog* (1965); and *Middle and Junior High School Library Catalog* (1995). Guides in this series present "standard" collections of titles based on expert recommendations for elementary, middle, junior high, and senior high school library media centers. In keeping with the company's philosophy of service, all recommendations made by this series are based on professional, expert opinion. Yearly supplements are published for each title in the series listing new materials as well as newer editions of older works. In 2000 all titles in the "Standard Library Catalog" series became available in electronic format.

————. *Wilson Biography Databases*. Electronic resource. These resources offer both reference and selection aid information. The coverage is extensive and international and spans all times from antiquity to the present. Search engines provide numerous ways to access information that is continually updated. Full descriptions are available online. (www.infohio.org/ERPreview2005/wilson2005.html)

Internet Sources, Commercial. Electronic resources. Sources such as the Biography Channel (www.biography.com), the BBC (www.bbc.co.uk), the Disney Channel (www.disney.go.com/disneychannel), A&E (www.aetv.com), the Discovery Channel (www.discovery.com), and the History Channel (www.historychannel.com) offer avenues to a wide variety of easily accessed biographical materials. See chapter 6 for more information about these and others.

Karsten, Eileen. *From Real Life to Reel Life: A Filmography of Biographical Films* Lanham, Md.: Scarecrow Press, 1993. Lists all important biographical film shown in the United States since the beginning of sound films. Included in the list are *The Private Lives of Elizabeth and Essex*, *The Babe Ruth Story*, *Patton*, *Sophia Loren: Her Own Story*, *The Eddy Duchin Story*, *Words and Music*, *Pride of the Yankees*, *Born Free*, *The Lion in Winter*, *Magnificent Doll*, *Deep in My Heart*, and *A Man for All Seasons*. Most of these films are now in video or DVD formats, making them widely available.

Kirkus Reviews. Periodical. Offers long and detailed reviews of both fiction and nonfiction books for adults, adolescents, and children. Reviews are intended for booksellers and librarians and appear before the books are published, allowing librarians and bookstores to stock in anticipation of demand. The children's section, which must be subscribed to apart from the basic subscription, offers special lists such as holiday books. (www.kirkusreviews.com)

Klatt. Periodical. Publishes reviews of paperback books, young adult hardcover fiction, audio books, and educational software appropriate for young adults in classrooms and libraries. Reviews include most fields of interest—fiction, literature and language arts, biography and personal narratives, education and guidance, social studies, history and geography, sciences, the arts, and recreation. Newsletter supplements are provided. (www.hometown.aol.com/kliatt)

Lima, Carolyn W., and John A. Lima. *A to Zoo: Subject Access to Children's Picture Book*. 7th ed. Westport, Conn.: Libraries Unlimited, 2005. This has become a standard reference resource for collection development and reader's advisement that includes over 4,000 titles published since 2001. It includes current, up-to-date information on fiction and nonfiction picture books for children. Subject and bibliographic guides are provided along with title and illustrator indexes.

Matthew, Kathryn I., and Joy L. Lowe. *Neal-Schuman Guide to Recommended Children's Books and Media for Use in Every Elementary Subject*. New York: Neal-Schuman, 2001. With a focus on literacy development and literature appreciation in children, this guide offers an extensive listing of books and media that will be used and enjoyed by both teachers and students in all subject areas.

McClure, Amy A., and Janice V. Kristo. *Adventuring with Books: A Booklist for Pre-K–Grade 6*. 13th ed. Urbana, Ill.: National Council of Teachers of English, 2002. A long-time favorite, it lists more than 850 books published between 1999 and 2001 suitable for children for research, learning, and pleasure reading.

National Portrait Galleries. Many nations maintain national portrait galleries. These galleries select and display portraits of men and women who have made significant contributions to a nation's history, culture, and art. Most of these galleries offer a variety of materials for sale. Among these are: Australia, Canada, Great Britain, New Zealand, the United States (Smithsonian), and Scotland.

New York Public Library. Office of Young Adult Services. *Books for the Teen Age*. New York: New York Public Library, annual. Published yearly since 1929 and written especially to encourage teenagers to read, this lists good quality books in all areas, including biography.

Parents' Choice Features. Electronic resource. An online newsletter of review and discussion intended for parents and educators, including librarians. It provides written reviews in all areas of children's media including books, television, home video, recordings, toys, music, and computer software. The organization also offers an extensive list of awards. (www.parents-choice.org)

Publishers Weekly: The Book Industry Journal. Periodical. A trade journal that offers broad coverage of events in the book trade, including children's and young adult publishing. Reviews are offered for current books just released by various publishers. (http://publishersweekly.reviewsnews.com)

School Library Journal. Periodical. Serves children's, young adult, and school library media specialist as a dependable review source. It contains review sections on computer software, audiovisual media, and fiction and nonfiction books. Reviews are written by professionals knowledgeable about the needs of youth and their education. (http://slj.reviewsnews.com)

Science Books and Films. Periodical. Published by the American Association for the Advancement of Science in six print issues per year, it reviews print, film, and software materials in all areas of the sciences for all ages. Reviews are directed at all types of librarians and educators. *Science Books and Films Online* is its companion that is included in a subscription to *SB&F*. (http://www.sbfonline.com/)

Smith, Henrietta M., and others, eds. *Coretta Scott King Awards: 1970–2004*. Chicago: American Library Association, 2004. Includes information on African American winners of the Coretta Scott King Award, all of whom write and/or illustrate outstanding books for children and young adults.

Teacher Librarian: The Journal for School Library Professionals. Periodical. An independent library journal that addresses the needs of professionals who work with children and young adults. In addition to reviews of books and nonprint media, it features articles on current issues and trends. Reviews covers of children's and young adult books, new nonfiction, best sellers, video materials, computer software, and Internet resources. It also profiles authors and illustrators. *Teacher Librarian* is a continuation of *Emergency Librarian*, published from 1973 to 1998. (www.teacherlibrarian.com)

Thompson, Sally Anne, comp. *60 Years of Notable Children's Books*. Chicago: American Library Association, 2004. List 1,500 books appearing on the *Notable Children's Books* from 1940 through 1999.

Thomson Gale. *Biography Resource Center*. Electronic resource. This is a huge biographical online reference database including a large variety of subject areas having biographical interest and focus such as science, multicultural studies, business, politics, government, history, entertainment, sports, the arts, and literature. It includes almost 414,000 biographies collected from a variety of well-known biographical resources. Full-text articles are provided along with useful search mechanisms. (http://www.gale.com/BiographyRC/index.htm)

Van Orden, Phyllis. *Selecting Books for the Elementary School Library Media Center: A Complete Guide*. New York: Neal-Schuman, 2000. This title presents a comprehensive guide to fiction and nonfiction materials for children. Coverage ranges from picture books to government resources.

Veccia, Susan H. *Uncovering Our History: Teaching with Primary Sources*. Chicago: American Library Association, 2003. Highlights the sources available through the Library of Congress's American Memory website and how they can be used to encourage an interest in history. Describes over 100 digitized collections available through the Library of Congress, many of which are biographical.

Voice of Youth Advocates (VOYA). Periodical. A hard-hitting review and discussion journal intended to help librarians who work with adolescents. It reviews films, video games, and fiction of all kinds, including adventure, occult, science fiction, and general fiction. Generous space is given to the review of nonfiction. Pamphlets, professional reading, reference books, and reprints are also reviewed. For books intended for the young adult, a rating system denotes books according to literary quality as well as their likely popularity. (http://www.voya.com)

Wood, Irene. *Culturally Diverse Videos, Audios, and CD-ROMs for Children and Young Adults*. New York: Neal-Schuman, 1999. Now dated, this source still offers guidance in the selection of biographies reflective of such groups as African Americans, Latinos, Native Americans, Asians, Arabs, Jews, Cajuns, and various European American groups. A companion volume is *Culturally Diverse Library Collections for Youth*, by Herman L. Totten and others (Neal-Schuman, 1996).

Young Adult Library Services Association (YALSA). *Best Books for Young Adults*. Chicago: Young Adult Library Services Association, annual. This annual list issued by YALSA of the American Library Association offers a well-developed selection of titles including both fiction and nonfiction and an abundant selection of fine biographies. The association also issues "Best Films and Videos for Young Adults" annually. Other titles published by YALSA include *Outstanding Books for the College Bound*, *More Outstanding Books for the College Bound* (2005), *Best Books for the Young Adult* (2000), *Popular Paperbacks for Young Adults*, *Selected Audiobooks for Young Adults*, and *Selected DVDs & Videos for Young Adults*. See also entries above for Carter and the Association for Library Service to Children.

SELECTED BIBLIOGRAPHY

Amabile, Teresa M. *Creativity in Context: Update to the Social Psychology of Creativity.* Boulder, Colo.: Westview Press, 1996.

American Association of School Librarians and Association for Educational Communications and Technology. *Information Power: Building Partnerships for Learning.* Chicago: American Library Association, 1998.

Aust, Patricia H. "Using the Life Story Book in Treatment of Children in Placement." *Child Welfare* 60 (Sept.–Oct. 1981): 535–36, 553–60.

Avery, Gillian. *Beyond the Child: American Children and Their Books, 1621–1922.* Baltimore, Md.: Johns Hopkins University Press, 1995.

Baker, Kimberly Middleton. "Adolescents and the Meanings They Make from Television." Dissertation, New York University, 2000. Abstracted in *Dissertation Abstracts International* 61-B (Jan. 2001): 3876.

Bardsley, Doreen O. "Boys and Reading: What Reading Fiction Means to Sixth-Grade Boys." Dissertation, Arizona State University, 1999. Abstracted in *Dissertation Abstracts International* 60-A (Sept. 1999): 653.

Batchelor, John, ed. *The Art of Literary Biography.* New York: Oxford University Press, 1995.

Becker, Carl. *The Subversive Imagination: The Artist, Society, and Social Responsibility.* New York: Routledge, 1994.

Beyer, Andreas. *Portraits: A History.* New York: Harry N. Abrams, 2003.

"Biography." In *Columbia Encyclopedia.* 6th ed. New York: Columbia University Press, 2001–2004. http://www.bartleby.com/65.

Biography Today: Profiles of People of Interest to Young Readers: Author Series. Detroit, Mich.: Omnigraphics, Inc., 2003.

Biography Today: Profiles of People of Interest to Young Readers: General Series. Detroit, Mich.: Omnigraphics, Inc., 2002.

Black, Ann N. *Born Storytellers: Readers Theatre Celebrates the Lives and Literature of Classic Authors.* Westport, Conn.: Libraries Unlimited, 2005.

Blanchard, Margaret, ed. *History of the Mass Media in the United States: An Encyclopedia.* Chicago: Fitzroy Dearborn, 1998.

Blass, Rosanne J. *Booktalks, Bookwalks, and Read-Alouds: Promoting the Best New Children's Literature across the Elementary Curriculum.* Westport, Conn.: Libraries Unlimited, 2002.

Bleich, David. *Readings and Feelings: An Introduction to Subjective Criticism.* Urbana, Ill.: National Council of Teachers of English, 1975.

Bloom, Jonathan, and Sheila Blair. *Islamic Arts.* London: Phaidon Press, 1997.

Blowers, Helene, and Robin Bryan. *Weaving a Library Web: A Guide to Developing Children's Websites.* Chicago: American Library Association, 2004.

Boime, Albert. *Art in an Age of Counterrevolution, 1815–1848.* Chicago: University of Chicago, 2004.

Booker, M. Keith. *A Practical Introduction to Literary Theory and Criticism.* White Plains, N.Y.: Longman, 1995.

Boon, Belinda. *The CREW Method: Expanded Guidelines for Collection Evaluation and Weeding for Small and Medium-Sized Public Libraries.* Revised and updated by Belinda Boon. Austin: Texas State Library and Archives Commission, 1995.

Breitbart, Andrew, and Mark Edner. *Hollywood Interrupted: Insanity Chic in Babylon—The Case against Celebrity.* New York: Wiley, 2004.

Bressler, Charles E. *Literary Criticism: An Introduction to Theory and Practice.* 3rd ed. Upper Saddle River, N.J.: Prentice Hall, 2002.

Brilliant, Richard. *Portraiture.* London: Reaktion Books, 1991.

Browne, Ray B., ed. *Popular Culture across the Curriculum: Essays for Educators.* Jefferson, N.C.: McFarland, 2004.

Bruner, Jerome S. *Toward a Theory of Instruction.* Cambridge, Mass.: Harvard University Press, 1966.

Burgin, Robert L., ed. *Nonfiction Readers: Advisory.* Westport, Conn.: Libraries Unlimited, 2004.

Burke, Eileen M. *Literature for the Young Child.* Boston: Allyn & Bacon, 1989.

Burke, Eileen M., and Susan Mandel Glazer. *Using Nonfiction in the Classroom.* New York: Scholastic, 1994.

Butzow, Carol M., and John W. Butzow. *The American Hero in Children's Literature: A Standards-Based Approach.* Westport, Conn.: Teacher Ideas Press, 2005.

Carpenter, Humphrey, and Mari Prichard, eds. *Oxford Companion to Children's Literature.* Oxford: Oxford University Press, 1984.

Carter, Betty. "Reviewing Biography." *The Horn Book* 79 (March/April 2003): 165–75.

Churchill, Gilbert A., and J. Peter Paul. *Marketing: Creating Value for Customers.* Burr Ridge, Ill.: Irwin, 1995.

Cohoon, Lorinda Beth. "Serializing Boyhoods: Periodicals, Books, and American Boys, 1840–1911." Dissertation, University of Southern Mississippi, 2001. Abstracted in *Dissertation Abstracts International* 62-A (Jan. 2002): 2420.

Combs, James. "Television Aesthetics and the Depiction of Heroism: The Case of the TV Historical Biography." *Journal of Popular Film and Television* 8 (Summer 1980): 9–18.

Conteh-Morgan, Miriam E. *The Undergraduate's Companion to African Writers and Their Web Sites.* Westport, Conn.: Libraries Unlimited, 2005.

Cullinan, Bernice E., and Diane G. Person, eds. *The Continuum Encyclopedia of Children's Literature.* New York: Continuum, 2001.

Currie, Dawn. *Girl Talk: Adolescent Magazines and Their Readers.* Toronto: University of Toronto Press, 1999.

Day, Terry V. "Television and the Identity of African American Male Adolescents." Dissertation, The Wright Institute, 2000. Abstracted in *Dissertation Abstracts International* 61-B (March 2001): 4977.

Donelson, Kenneth L., and Alleen Pace Nilsen. *Literature for Today's Young Adults.* 7th ed. Boston: Allyn & Bacon, 2004.

Donham, Jean, Kay Bishop, Carol Collier Kuhlthau, and Dianne Oberg. *Inquiry-Based Learning: Lessons from Library Power.* Worthington, Ohio: Linworth, 2001.

Dressman, Mark. *Literacy in the Library: Negotiating the Spaces between Order and Desire.* Westport, Conn.: Bergin & Garvey, 1997.

Drew, Bernard A. *100 Most Popular Genre Fiction Authors: Biographical Sketches and Bibliographies.* Westport, Conn.: Libraries Unlimited, 2005.

Dunaway, David King. "Sketches from Life: Radio and Biography." *Biography: An Interdisciplinary Quarterly* 20 (Fall 1997): 462–71.

Dusek, James B. "The Hierarchy of Adolescent Interests: A Social-Cognitive Approach." *Genetic Psychology Monographs* 100 (Aug. 1979): 41–72.

Duthie, Christine. " 'It's Just Plain Real!' Introducing Young Children to Biography and Autobiography." *New Advocate* 11 (Summer 1998): 219–27.

Eagleton, Terry. *Literary Theory: An Introduction.* Minneapolis: University of Minnesota Press, 1996.

Earles, K. A., R. Alexander, M. Johnson, J. Liverpool, and M. McGhee. "Media Influences on Children and Adolescents: Violence and Sex." *Journal of the National Medical Association* 94 (Sept. 2002): 797–801.

Edelstein, Alan. *Everybody Is Sitting on the Curb: How and Why America's Heroes Disappeared.* Westport, Conn.: Praeger Publishers, 1996.

Elliott, Joan B., and Mary M. Dupuis, eds. *Young Adult Literature in the Classroom: Reading It, Teaching It, Loving It.* Newark, Del.: International Reading Association, 2002.

Erisman, Fred Raymond. "There Was a Child Went Forth: A Study of *St. Nicholas Magazine* and Selected Children's Authors, 1890–1915." Dissertation, University of Minnesota, 1966. Abstracted in *Dissertation Abstracts International* 27-A (Dec. 1966): 1818.

Flood, Elizabeth Clair. *Cowgirls: Women of the Wild West.* Santa Fe, N. Mex.: Zon International Publishing Co., 2000.

Fraser, Benson P., and William J. Brown. "Media, Celebrities, and Social Influence: Identification with Elvis Presley." *Mass Communication & Society* 5 (May 2002): 183–206.

Freeman, Evelyn B., and Barbara A. Lehman. *Global Perspectives in Children's Literature.* Boston: Allyn & Bacon, 2001.

Frenken, Ralph. "The History of German Childhood through Autobiographies." *Journal of Psychohistory* 24 (Spring 1997): 390–402.

Freund, Elizabeth. *The Return of the Reader: Reader-Response Criticism.* London: Methuen, 1987.

Gamson, Joshua. "The Assembly Line of Greatness: Celebrity in Twentieth-Century America." *Critical Studies in Mass Communication* 9 (March 1992): 1–24.

———. *Claims to Fame: Celebrity in Contemporary America.* Berkeley: University of California Press, 1994.

Glasgow, Jacqueline. *Using Young Adult Literature: Thematic Activities Based on Gardner's Multiple Intelligences.* Norwood, Mass.: Christopher-Gordon, 2002.

Gould, Madelyn, Patrick Jamieson, and Daniel Romer. "Media Contagion and Suicide among the Young." *American Behavioral Scientists* 46 (May 2003): 1269–84.

Gowen, L. Kris, and Molly McKenna. *Image and Identity: Becoming the Person You Are.* Lanham, Md.: Scarecrow Press, 2005.

Green, Dewayne Arden. "A Study of the Impact of Bibliotherapy on the Self-Concept of Mexican-American Children Ten and Eleven Years of Age." Dissertation, University of Northern Colorado, 1988. Abstracted in *Dissertation Abstracts International* 50-A (Nov. 1989): 1252.

Greene, Ellin. *Books, Babies, and Libraries: Serving Infants, Toddlers, Their Parents and Caregivers.* Chicago: American Library Association, 1991.

Groff, Patrick. "Biography: A Tool for Bibliotherapy?" *Top of the News* 36 (Spring 1980): 269–73.

———. "How Do Children Read Biography about Adults?" *Reading Teacher* 24 (April 1971): 609–15.

Grossberg, Lawrence, Cary Nelson, and Paula A. Treichler, eds. *Cultural Studies.* New York: Routledge, 1992.

Grove Art Online. Oxford: Oxford University Press, 2005. http://www.groveart.com.

Gruber, Diane. "Much of Their Tuition: The Historical Matrix of Youth, Consumerism, and Mass Culture as Illustrated in the Pages of the *Youth's Companion,* 1827–1929." Dissertation, Purdue University, 2002. Abstracted in *Dissertation Abstracts International* 64-A (Jan. 2004): 2533.

Gurian, Michael. *The Good Son: Shaping the Moral Development of Our Boys and Young Men.* New York: Jeremy P. Tarcher, 1999.

———. *What Stories Does My Son Need? A Guide to Books and Movies That Build Character in Boys.* New York: Jeremy P. Tarcher, 2000.

———. *The Wonder of Girls: Understanding the Hidden Nature of Our Daughters.* New York: Atria, 2002.

Gurian, Michael, and Arlette C. Ballew. *The Boys and Girls Learn Differently: Action Guide for Teachers.* San Francisco: Jossey-Bass, 2003.

Gustafson, Chris. *Acting Out: Reader's Theater across the Curriculum.* Worthington, Ohio: Linworth, 2002.

Hand, John Oliver. *National Gallery of Art: Master Paintings from the Collection.* Washington, D.C.: National Gallery of Art in association with Harry N. Abrams, 2004.

Hannabuss, Stuart, and Rita Marcella, eds. *Biography and Children: A Study of Biography for Children and Childhood in Biography.* London: Library Association Publishing, 1993.

Hassell, Hughes, and Jacqueline C. Mancall. *Collection Management for Youth: Responding to the Needs of Learners.* Chicago: American Library Association, 2005.

Hayes, Nicky. *Teach Yourself: Psychology.* New York: Contemporary Books, 1994.

Herald, Diana Tixier, and Wayne A. Wiegand. *Genreflecting: A Guide to Popular Reading Interests.* 6th ed. Westport, Conn.: Libraries Unlimited, 2005.

Huck, Charlotte S., with Janet Hickman and Susan Ingrid Hepler. *Children's Literature in the Elementary School.* 6th ed. Madison, Wis.: Brown & Benchmark, 1997.

Hujala, Eeva. "The Curriculum for Early Learning in the Context of Society." *International Journal of Early Years Education* 10 (June 2002): 95–104.

Humphrey, Mary. *Living the Hero's Quest: Character Building through Action Research.* Westport, Conn.: Libraries Unlimited, 2005.

Hurst, Carol Otis, Lynn Palmer, Vaughn Churchill, Margaret Ahearn, and Bernard
   McMahon. *Curriculum Connections: Picture Books in Grade 3 and Up.*
   Worthington, Ohio: Linworth, 1999.

Jeffries-Fox, Suzanne Kuulei. "Television's Contribution to Young People's Concepts
   about Occupations." Dissertation, University of Pennsylvania, 1979. Abstracted
   in *Dissertation Abstracts International* 39-A (April 1979): 5784.

Johnson, Steven. *Everything Bad Is Good for You: How Today's Popular Culture Is
   Actually Making Us Smarter.* New York: Riverhead Books, 2005.

Jolly, Margaretta, ed. *Encyclopedia of Life Writing: Autobiographical and Biographical
   Forms.* Vols. 1 and 2. London: Fitzroy Dearborn, 2001.

Joubert, Magaretha M. "The Reading Interests and Reading Habits of Afrikaans-
   Speaking Teenagers in Pretoria." Master of Information thesis, University of South
   Africa, 2002. Abstracted in *Masters Abstracts International* 42 (Aug. 2004): 1114.

Karolides, Nicholas J., Margaret Bald, and Dawn B. Sova. *100 Banned Books:
   Censorship Histories of World Literature.* New York: Checkmark Books, 1999.

Kemp, Martin, ed. *The Oxford History of Western Art.* Oxford: Oxford University Press,
   2000.

Knowles, Elizabeth, and Martha Smith. *Boys and Literacy: Practical Strategies for
   Librarians, Teachers, and Parents.* Westport, Conn.: Libraries Unlimited, 2005.

Kotler, Philip, Ned Roberto, and Nancy Lee. *Social Marketing: Improving the Quality of
   Life.* 2nd ed. Thousand Oaks, Calif.: Sage Publications, 2002.

Krashen, Stephen D. *The Power of Reading: Insights from the Research.* 2nd ed.
   Westport, Conn.: Libraries Unlimited, 2004.

Kundanis, Rose M. *Children, Teens, Families, and Mass Media: The Millennial
   Generation.* Mahwah, N.J.: Lawrence Erlbaum Associates, 2003.

Kwon, Kyoon. "A Study of Values and Children's Biographies." Dissertation, University
   of Tennessee, 1984. Abstracted in *Dissertation Abstracts International* 45-A
   (Dec. 1984): 1578.

Les Brown's Encyclopedia of Television. 3rd ed. Detroit: Visible Ink Press, 1992.

Lewis, Cynthia. *Literary Practices as Social Acts: Power, Status, and Cultural Norms in
   the Classroom.* Mahwah, N.J.: Lawrence Erlbaum Associates, 2001.

Lines, Gill. "Villains, Fools or Heroes? Sports Stars as Role Models for Young People."
   Leisure Studies 20 (Oct. 2001): 285–303.

Logan, Debra Kay. *Biography across the Curriculum: Language Arts, Grades 4–6.*
   Worthington, Ohio: Linworth, 2003.

Long, Jeffrey E. *Remembered Childhoods: A Reading Guide of Autobiographies and
   Memoirs of Childhood and Youth.* Westport, Conn.: Libraries Unlimited, 2005.

Lukenbill, W. Bernard. *Collection Development for a New Century in the School Library
   Media Center.* Westport, Conn.: Greenwood Press, 2002.

———. *Community Resources in the School Library Media Center: Concepts and
   Methods.* Westport, Conn.: Libraries Unlimited, 2004.

———. "The Reading Interests of Adolescents." In Nancy Bach Pillon, ed., *Reaching
   Young People through Media,* 15–34. Littleton, Colo.: Libraries Unlimited, 1983.

Lukens, Rebecca J. *A Critical Handbook of Children's Literature.* 7th ed. Boston: Allyn
   & Bacon, 2003.

Lundin, Anne, and Wayne A. Wiegand, eds. *Defining Print Culture for Youth: The Culture
   Work of Children's Literature.* Westport, Conn.: Libraries Unlimited, 2003.

Lunine, Brij David. "Creativity and Constraint: The Role of Television and
   Popular Culture in the Lives of Adolescents." Dissertation, University of

New Mexico, 2004. Abstracted in *Dissertation Abstracts International* 65-A (Oct. 2004): 1420.

Lyga, Allyson A. W., and Barry Lyga. *Graphic Novels in Your Media Center: A Definitive Guide*. Westport, Conn.: Libraries Unlimited, 2004.

MacLeod, Ann Scott. *A Moral Tale: Children's Fiction and American Culture, 1820–1860*. Hamden, Conn.: Archon, 1975.

Mallon, Gerald P., ed. *Social Services with Transgendered Youth*. New York: Harrington Park Press, 1999.

Marcus, Laura. *Auto-Biographical Discourses: Theory, Criticism, Practice*. Manchester, UK: Manchester University Press, 1994.

McCoy, Donna. "Surveys of Independent Reading: Pinpointing the Problems, Seeking the Solutions." Research paper, Murray State University, 1991. ERIC document no. ED 341 021.

McCutcheon, Lynn E. "Machiavellianism, Belief in a Just World, and the Tendency to Worship Celebrities." *Current Research in Social Psychology* 8 (Jan. 2003): 131–39.

McDonough, Sharon Kowalski. "The View Up Close: Creative Writing in a Juvenile Correctional Facility." Dissertation, Auburn University, 2002. Abstracted in *Dissertation Abstracts International* 63-A (Aug. 2002): 498.

McElmeel, Sharron L. *Children's Authors and Illustrators Too Good to Miss: Biographical Sketches and Bibliographies*. Westport, Conn.: Libraries Unlimited, 2004.

McGillis, Roderick, ed. *Children's Literature and the Fin de Siècle*. Westport, Conn.: Praeger, 2003.

Milkie, Melissa A. "The Social Psychological Impact of Gender Images in Media: A Multi-Level Analysis of Girls, Peers Networks, and Media Organizations." Dissertation, Indiana University, 1995. Abstracted in *Dissertation Abstracts International* 56-A (May 1996): 4560.

Miller, Frank. "Buddy: Interviewing Each Other." *Social Studies and the Young Learner* 12 (Jan.–Feb. 2000): 13–14.

Moore, John Noell. *Interpreting Young Adult Literature: Literary Theory in the Secondary Classroom*. Portsmouth, N.H.: Boynton/Cook, 1997.

Morin, JoyAnn Hauge. *Social Studies Instruction Incorporating the Language Arts*. Boston: Allyn & Bacon, 2003.

Newcomb, Horace, ed. *Museum of Broadcasting Communications Encyclopedia of Television*. 3 vols. 2nd ed. New York: Fitzroy Dearborn, 1997.

Nichols, Mary Ann. *Merchandising Library Materials to Young Adults*. Greenwood Village, Colo.: Libraries Unlimited, 2002.

Nikolajeva, Maria. *Aesthetic Approaches to Children's Literature: An Introduction*. Lanham, Md.: Scarecrow Press, 2005.

Norton, Donna E. *Multicultural Children's Literature: Through the Eyes of Many Children*. 2nd ed. Upper Saddle River, N.J.: Pearson/Merrill Prentice-Hall, 2005.

Norvell, George W. *The Reading Interests of Young People*. Rev. ed. East Lansing: Michigan State University Press, 1973.

Nuccio, Lena Marie. "The Effects of Bibliotherapy on the Self-Esteem and Teacher-Rated Classroom Behavior on Third-Grade Children of Divorce." Dissertation, University of Southern Mississippi, 1997. Abstracted in *Dissertation Abstracts International* 59-A (Aug. 1998): 409.

Olson, Joan Blodgett Peterson. "An Interpretive History of the *Horn Book* Magazine, 1924–1973." Dissertation, Stanford University, 1976. Abstracted in *Dissertation Abstracts International* 37-A (Nov. 1976): 2875.

Orth, Maureen. *The Importance of Being Famous: Behind the Scenes of the Celebrity-Industrial Complex*. New York: Henry Holt, 2004.

Pardes, Ilana. *The Biography of Ancient Israel: National Narratives in the Bible*. Berkeley: University of California Press, 2002.

Partridge, Elizabeth. "The Creative Life." *School Library Journal* 48 (Oct. 2002): 42–43.

Petri, Gail G. *The American Memory Collections from A–Z: Primary Resource Guide and Reproducible Activities across the Curriculum: Grades 4–6*. Worthington, Ohio: Linworth, 2003.

——— *The American Memory Collections from A–Z: Primary Resource Guide and Reproducible Activities across the Curriculum: Grades 7–9*. Worthington, Ohio: Linworth, 2003.

Purves, Alan C., and Richard Beach. *Literature and the Reader: Research in Response to Literature, Reading Interests, and the Teaching of Literature*. Urbana, Ill.: National Council of Teachers of English, 1972.

Reinhartz, Judy, and Don M. Beach. *Teaching and Learning in the Elementary School: Focus on Curriculum*. Upper Saddle River, N.J.: Merrill, 1997.

Reviving Ophelia: Saving the Selves of Adolescent Girls. Written by Mary Pipher (VHS, DVD). Northampton, Mass.: Media Education Foundation, 1998.

Roberts, Patricia L. *Family Values through Children's Literature and Activities, Grades 4–6*. Lanham, Md.: Scarecrow Press, 2005.

Rodgers, Adrian, and Emily M. Rodgers, eds. *Scaffolding Literacy Instruction: Strategies for K–4 Classrooms*. Portsmouth, N.H.: Heinemann, 2004.

Rosenbaum, David. "In Times of Trouble, the Founding Fathers Sell Well." *New York Times*, July 4, 2004.

Rosenblatt, Louise M. *Literature as Exploration*. 5th ed. New York: Modern Language Association of America, 1995.

Ross, Catherine Sheldrick, Lynn (E. F.) McKechnie, and Paulette M. Rothbauer. *Reading Matters: What the Research Reveals about Reading, Libraries, and Community*. Westport, Conn: Libraries Unlimited, 2005.

Rubin, Rhea Joyce. *Using Bibliotherapy: A Guide to Theory and Practice*. Phoenix, Ariz.: Oryx Press, 1978.

Runco, Mark A., and Steven R. Pritzker, eds. *Encyclopedia of Creativity*. 2 vols. San Diego: Academic Press, 1999.

Russell, David L. *Literature for Children: A Short Introduction*. 5th ed. Boston: Allyn & Bacon, 2004.

Saettler, Paul. *The Evolution of American Educational Technology*. 3rd ed. Mahwah, N.J.: Lawrence Erlbaum Associates, 2005.

Salem, Linda C., ed. *Children's Literature Remembered: Issues, Trends, and Favorite Books*. Westport, Conn.: Libraries Unlimited, 2003.

———. *Children's Literature Studies: Cases and Discussions*. Westport, Conn.: Libraries Unlimited, 2005.

Sampson, Henry T. *Swingin' on the Ether Waves*. Lanham, Md.: Scarecrow Press, 2005. [A Chronological History of African Americans in Radio and Television Programming, 1925–1955].

Samuel, Raphael, and Paul Thompson, eds. *The Myths We Live By*. London: Routledge, 1990.

Schneirov, Matthew. *The Dream of a New Social Order: Popular Magazines in America, 1893–1914*. New York: Columbia University Press, 1994.

Schultheis, Constance. "A Study of the Relationships between Gender and Reader Preferences in Adolescents." Master's of Library Science research paper, Kent State University, 1990. ERIC document no. ED 367 376.

Siler, Carl R. *Oral History in the Teaching of U.S. History*. Bloomington, Ind.: ERIC Clearinghouse for Social Studies/Social Science Education, 1996. ERIC document no. ED 393 781.

Silvey, Anita, ed. *The Essential Guide to Children's Books and Their Creators*. Boston: Houghton Mifflin, 2002

Slater, Alan, Ian Hocking, and Jon Loose. "Theories and Issues in Child Development." In *Introduction to Developmental Psychology*, ed. Alan Slater and J. Gavin Bremner, 34–63. Malden, Mass.: Blackwell, 2003.

Snellman, Leena M. "Sixth Grade Reading Interests: A Survey." Research report, University of Virginia, 1993. ERIC document no. ED 358 415.

Stan, Susan, ed. *The World through Children's Books*. Lanham, Md.: Scarecrow Press, 2002.

Stanley, Liz. *The Auto-Biographical I: The Theory and Practice of the Feminist Auto-Biography*. Manchester, UK: Manchester University Press, 1992.

Stevens, Jen. *The Undergraduate's Companion to Children's Writers and Their Web Sites*. Westport, Conn.: Libraries Unlimited, 2004.

Stielow, Frederick. *Building Digital Archives, Descriptions, & Displays: A How-To-Do-It Manual for Archivists & Librarians*. New York: Neal-Schuman, 2003.

Storey, John. *An Introductory Guide to Cultural Theory and Popular Culture*. 2nd ed. Athens: University of Georgia Press, 1998.

Stott, Jon C. *Gerald McDermott and You*. Westport, Conn.: Libraries Unlimited, 2004.

Straley, Dona S. *The Undergraduate's Companion to Arab Writers and Their Web Sites*. Westport, Conn.: Libraries Unlimited, 2004.

Strinati, Dominic. *An Introduction to Theories of Popular Culture*. 2nd ed. New York: Routledge, 2004.

Stryker, Sheldon, Timothy J. Owens, and Robert W. White, eds. *Self, Identity, and Social Movements*. Minneapolis: University of Minnesota Press, 2000.

Sturken, Marita. "Personal Stories and National Meanings: Memory, Reenactment, and the Image." In *The Seductions of Biography*, ed. Mary Rhiel and David Suchoff, 31–41. New York: Routledge; 1996.

Sturm, Brian W. "Dogs and Dinosaurs, Hobbies and Horses: Age-Related Changes in Children's Information and Reading Preferences." *Children and Libraries* 1 (Winter 2003): 39–51.

Sullivan, Michael. *Connecting Boys with Books: What Libraries Can Do*. Chicago: American Library Association, 2003.

Sutherland, Zena. *Children and Books*. 9th ed. New York: Allyn & Bacon, 1997.

"Teenage Boys and Reading Theme Issue." *Teacher Librarian* 30 (Feb. 2003): 9–31.

Thomson, Rachel, Robert Bell, Janet Holland, Sheila Henderson, Sheena McGrellis, and Sue Sharpe. "Critical Moments: Choice, Chance and Opportunity in Young People's Narratives of Transition." *Sociology* 36 (May 2002): 335–54.

Tilley, Lisa Michele. "Reading Experiences and the Making of Self: A Case Study Investigating the Construction of Subjectivity by Adolescent Girls." Dissertation, University of Georgia, 2000. Abstracted in *Dissertation Abstracts International* 61-A (Feb. 2001): 3092.

Tobin, Elayne L. "Fearing for Our Lives: Biography and Middlebrow Culture in Late Twentieth-Century America." Dissertation, University of Pittsburgh, 2001. Abstracted in *Dissertation Abstracts International* 62-A (May 2002): 3089.

Tompkins, Jane P., ed. *Reader-Response Criticism: From Formulism to Post-Structuralism*. Baltimore, Md.: Johns Hopkins University Press, 1980.

Tough Guise: Violence, Media & the Crisis in Masculinity (VHS, DVD). Written by Jackson Katz and Jeremy Earp. Northampton, Mass.: Media Education Foundation, 1999.

Tyson, Lois. *Critical Theory Today: A User-Friendly Guide*. New York: Garland, 1999.

Veccia, Susan H. *Uncovering Our History: Teaching with Primary Sources*. Chicago: American Library Association, 2004.

Weinberg, Steve. *Telling the Untold Story: How Investigative Reporters Are Changing the Craft of Biography*. Columbia: University of Missouri Press, 1992.

Weisblat, Tinky. "Will the Real George and Gracie and Ozzie and Harriet and Desi and Lucy Please Stand Up? The Functions of Popular Biography in 1950s Television." Dissertation, University of Texas at Austin, 1991. Abstracted in *Dissertation Abstracts International* 52-A (Oct. 1991): 1402.

White, Lawrence J. *The Public Library in the 1980s: The Problems of Choice*. Lexington, Mass.: Lexington Books, 1983.

White, Robert W. *The Enterprise of Living: A View of Personal Growth*. 2nd ed. New York: Holt, Rinehart and Winston, 1976.

Wills, Garry. *John Wayne's America: The Politics of Celebrity*. New York: Simon & Schuster, 1997.

Wong, Frieda. "Experiences of Successful Second-Generation Chinese American Women with Cultural Stereotypes and Parental Expectation." Dissertation, University of Massachusetts, Amherst, 2003. Abstracted in *Dissertation Abstracts International* 64-B (April 2004): 5243.

Woolls, Blanche, and David V. Loertscher, eds. *Whole School Library Handbook*. Chicago: American Library Association, 2005.

Young, Katherine A. *Constructing Buildings, Bridges, and Minds: Building an Integrated Curriculum through Social Studies*. Portsmouth, N.H.: Heinemann, 1994.

Zarnowski, Frank. *All-Around Men: Heroes of a Forgotten Sport*. Lanham, Md.: Scarecrow Press, 2005.

Zarnowski, Myra. *Learning about Biographies: A Reading-and-Writing Approach for Children*. Urbana, Ill.: National Council of Teachers of English, 1990.

Zipes, Jack David. *Happily Ever After: Fairy Tales, Children, and the Culture Industry*. New York: Routledge, 1997.

———. *Sticks and Stones: The Troublesome Success of Children's Literature from Slovenly Peter to Harry Potter*. New York: Routledge, 2001.

Zornado, Joseph L. *Inventing the Child: Culture, Ideology, and the Story of Childhood*. New York: Garland, 2001.

INDEX

About the Author

W. BERNARD LUKENBILL is Professor, School of Information, University of Texas, Austin. He has written several other books for Libraries Unlimited.